FUNDAMENTALISM AND LITERATURE

FUNDAMENTALISM AND LITERATURE

Edited by

Catherine Pesso-Miquel and Klaus Stierstorfer

FUNDAMENTALISM AND LITERATURE

First published in 2007 by
PALGRAVE MACMILLAN™
175 Fifth Avenue, New York, N.Y. 10010 and
Houndmills, Basingstoke, Hampshire, England RG21 6XS.
Companies and representatives throughout the world.

PALGRAVE MACMILLAN is the global academic imprint of the Palgrave Macmillan division of St. Martin's Press, LLC and of Palgrave Macmillan Ltd. Macmillan® is a registered trademark in the United States, United Kingdom and other countries. Palgrave is a registered trademark in the European Union and other countries.

ISBN-10: 1-4039-7491-8
ISBN-13: 978-1-4039-7491-4

Library of Congress Cataloging-in-Publication Data is available from the Library of Congress.

A catalogue record for this book is available from the British Library.

Design by Macmillan India Ltd.

First edition: January 2007

10 9 8 7 6 5 4 3 2 1

Printed in the United States of America.

Contents

CHAPTER 1

INTRODUCTION: FUNDAMENTALISM AND LITERATURE

CATHERINE PESSO-MIQUEL AND KLAUS STIERSTORFER

Ever since September 11, 2001, and the so-called war on terror subsequently declared by the U.S. government, fundamentalism has probably been one of the most used words and most discussed phenomena in the media worldwide. The continuing unrest in Afghanistan and Iraq, the Madrid train bombing of 2004, and the London bombings of 2005 have all contributed to keep an enormous pressure on this discussion. The dazzling limelight of this media attention has also cast into bold relief other instances of fundamentalist activities in recent history, from earlier bombings in the United States to the most incisive instances of fundamentalist political activity, starting with Khomeini's cataclysmic takeover of Iran (1979), events in Sudan (1993) and in Afghanistan and Turkey (1996), mass violence unleashed on Muslims by Hindu nationalists in the Indian state of Gujarat (March 2002), as well as the ongoing battle in Palestine. Also, journalistic comments, cultural analyses, and historical works on these earlier developments have not only been reprinted and reread with renewed and heightened interest, but appeared to be confirmed as quasi-prophetic statements through the events of 9/11 and its aftermath. Samuel P. Huntington's catchphrase of the "clash of civilizations" has received new currency, and the 1990s Fundamentalism Project of the American Academy of Arts and Sciences, which resulted in seventy-five case studies and comparative essays published in five monumental volumes between 1991 and 1995,[1] is consulted by students worldwide. As many readers, awakened to the new realities by the pictures of the tumbling twin towers in New York, have noticed with surprise, a pattern has begun to emerge: fundamentalism is a force that is here to stay and one that is to be reckoned with in any account of, in the title phrase of Anthony Trollope's Victorian novel, "*the way we live now.*"

For people concerned with literature, be they authors, publishers, or literary and cultural critics, the urgency of these developments had certainly been driven home long before by the "Rushdie affair" of 1989 when Khomeini pronounced the death penalty against the author of *The Satanic Verses* for the book's supposed blasphemy against Islam. As a particularly drastic example, the *fatwa* against Rushdie has not only left a lasting impression on the vulnerability of the arts in the face of grim fundamentalist coercion; the very fact that fundamentalists such as Khomeini and his ilk bother with writers of fiction and their works also shows how much, to put it simply, literature matters in this context and how strong an intervention authors apparently can be seen to pose for any fundamentalist agenda.

This is why further investigation into the strategies and wider engagements of literary negotiations with fundamentalism in recent years seems such a particularly promising field of study: It is not only that new light may be shed on our understanding of fundamentalism as a phenomenon specific to our own time, but also that new perspectives may conversely be opened on literature as a discourse and a function within a cultural context characterized by postmodernist concerns with art as well as by attempts to question and transcend positions vaguely summarized as "postmodern" in the widest sense.

What this volume presents in the following contributions, then, has two major trajectories. First, readers are presented with a wide view of the complexities of various fundamentalisms in their diverse historical, cultural, political, and religious contexts, as cast into relief and refracted in their literary negotiations. Black-and-white dichotomies, generally seen as typical of fundamentalist discourses, are to be broken up into negotiable units and understood in their various contingencies. Second, the contributors to this volume provide in-depth studies of various literary negotiations of fundamentalism, which appear especially powerful and revealing and can be understood as representative of particular patterns or contexts. In order to structure the work of individual contributors and suggest coordinates for the reader's orientation, the volume has been subdivided into three major parts. Needless to add that comprehensiveness is impossible in a study of this kind and scope, but every effort has been made by its editors and contributors to open its range as far as possible and to provide as representative and illustrative samples in the individual contributions as it was possible to achieve within the limits of this project.

Part I, titled "The Many Guises of Fundamentalism: Expanding Visions," is specifically designed to enhance the understanding of fundamentalism in various historical, geopolitical, and cultural dimensions. A widening of horizons is the major objective pursued by the contributors assembled here. Thus, the discussion is opened by Gordon Campbell, who establishes a wide historical link from John Milton's *Samson Agonistes* to the attack of the U.S. Navy on Tripoli (1801) under conditions that Campbell projects as striking historical parallels to the events of 9/11 and the ensuing war on terror. Whereas Campbell had Milton as his starting point, Anne Barbeau Gardiner moves the focus to eighteenth-century Britain and to Jonathan Swift. Gardiner identifies a concept of Christian fundamentalism that informs Swift's thought and can be traced in his writings, both fictional and nonfictional. Returning to our own time, Axel Stähler explores approaches to fundamentalism in recent Jewish fiction in English, presenting his readings of major, representative novels in that highly specialized and stimulating field.

"Beyond the Binary: Literary Interventions in Polarization" delineates the program of the second part of the volume. Here, contributors concentrate on investigating literary interventions against fundamentalist tendencies toward dyadic patterns, notably black-and-white dichotomies and other instances of "tunnel visions" of the world. Three outstanding writers are scrutinized for this purpose. Wendy O'Shea-Meddour approaches Hanif Kureishi's contribution to the subject through his novel *The Black Album;* Catherine Pesso-Miquel focuses on Rohinton Mistry's *Family Matters;* and Susanne Peters zooms in on Arundhati Roy's conflicting roles as novelist and political critic.

In part III, finally, the discussions of part II are continued, but now move from an emphasis on binaries and dichotomies to postmodernist contexts. Klaus Stierstorfer takes Tariq Ali's *Islam Quintet* as his point of reference and compares it to works by Flannery O'Connor, Salman Rushdie, and others. Helga Ramsey-Kurz returns to Kureishi's seminal *The Black Album* and foregrounds its variations on the sacredness of the text and literature. Kevin Cope rounds up this volume by taking a close look at the phenomenally successful *Left Behind* novels by LaHaye and Jenkins as apocalyptic fiction and their reverberations of fundamentalist ideologies.

The parts of this volume mark the trajectories of a field study that clearly shows not only the astonishing variety of fundamentalisms and the wide range of the phenomena involved, but also the richness in literary responses to and the multifaceted engagements with fundamentalist agendas and movements writers have felt stimulated to undertake.

The writers in this volume have taken an open approach. They do not see themselves as politicians but as literary and cultural critics, so that their critique and investigations are aimed at literary negotiations with and in fundamentalism; they do not see it as their main objective to pass judgment on ideas and religious convictions of any kind, much less on the people who hold them. They all share the hope that the contributions in this volume may stimulate further discussion and study of fundamentalist positions in an atmosphere of tolerance and openness, and they also share the conviction that literature, past and present, has a role to play in this undertaking.

As always, the enterprise of this volume itself would not have been possible without the help and encouragement of many persons who cannot all be named here. The editors wish to express their particular thanks to Amanda Johnson, senior editor at Palgrave Macmillan, for seeing this project through its many stages into print; to Dr. Axel Stähler, now project coordinator of an ongoing project on fundamentalism at the University of Münster, for also coordinating the editorial process of this book; and to Ludwig Perick, cand. phil., for his assistance in producing an acceptable typescript.

NOTE

1. Martin E. Marty, ed., *The Fundamentalism Project,* 5 vols. (Chicago: University of Chicago Press, 1991–95), I: Fundamentalisms Observed (1991), II: Fundamentalisms and Society (1993), III: Fundamentalisms and the State (1993), IV: Accounting for Fundamentalism (1994), V: Fundamentalisms Comprehended (1995).

PART I

THE MANY GUISES OF FUNDAMENTALISM: EXPANDING VISIONS

CHAPTER 2

"To the Shore of Tripoli": Milton, Islam, and the Attacks on America and Spain

Gordon Campbell

Our history is characterized by silences. Literary historians of the early modern period in England have, in recent decades, become aware of the silence of women and the silence of the underclass, and have started to dig for evidence; there has been some success with women, because there is a documentary record, but little with the underclass, who for the most part eluded officialdom. In the case of Islam, we have until recently been completely silent, despite a documentary record in official archives and an imaginative record in the drama of the period. The issue of Islam in England received its first serious treatment in 1998, when Cambridge University Press published Nabil Matar's study *Islam in Britain, 1558–1685;* one reviewer commented that the most amazing aspect of the book was its title, which begged the question: Was there any Islam in Britain during this period? We have been encouraged to think of women as the only obscured other, but at least there is a general awareness that women existed. The same cannot be said of Muslims, who have been written out of much history. In our world of literary study, one of the most interesting recent books is Daniel Vitkus's *Turning Turk,* published in 2003, which examines the representation of conversion to Islam on the English stage. On the specific subject of Milton and Islam, there was a pioneering work called *John Milton and Arab-Islamic Culture,* published in 1987 by Eid Dahiyat, who is now president of a university in

Jordan. The topic is still alive, in part, because of the ending of Milton's *Samson Agonistes,* about which I will say more below.

I come to the subject with two interests that I should like to declare. For the past thirty years I have been writing about Milton, but in the course of these three decades I have also been traveling in the Islamic world, to which I have made an uncounted number of journeys that must run well into three figures, and ranges geographically from Indonesia in the east to Morocco in the west. I do not, I should make clear, propose to make a distinction between "true Islam" or "true Christianity" and the religious beliefs of those who commit acts of terror. Although subscribers to both religions are on the whole peaceful, I see nothing to justify constructing a sentimental notion of any religion as "true" simply because it is peaceful. In the case of Christianity, its founder declared that he came not to bring peace but a sword, and the sword has been similarly important in the history of Islam. It follows that I am not willing to ignore the link between religion and violence. Believers are for the most part eager to deny any such link, but that is another way of saying that they are in denial. Muslims who insist that 9/11 was such a dreadful crime that it could not have been committed by Muslims and must instead have been the work of the Mossad are guilty of the same evasion as Christians who deny that the Holocaust was a crime committed by Christians; in my view, 9/11 was only a Muslim crime in the same sense that the Holocaust was a Christian crime. In both cases it is true in the limited sense that the perpetrators were members of those religious groups and acted from motives that were rooted in religious bigotry (the Christian charge of deicide and the Muslim hatred of the hegemonic infidel in the West); in both cases it is untrue in the larger sense that most Muslims and most Christians deplore those crimes unequivocally. It is also worth remembering that not all terrorists with religious affiliations are religious: some IRA terrorists were secular nationalists, and two of the 9/11 hijackers went to a lap-dancing club on the evening of September 10.

I should like to consider a narrative set in the first year of a new century. A group of Muslim terrorists armed with knives has attacked America in a campaign financed by a wealthy enemy of America; American citizens have been hijacked and murdered by bandits who have no respect for human life. The president of the United States, faced with a national cry for vengeance and a need to ensure that such incidents never happen again, bombs the miscreants and sends in American ground troops backed by troops from America's allies. The enemy is destroyed.

The new century that I have in mind is the nineteenth, of which the first year was 1801. The president was Thomas Jefferson, that most

Miltonic of presidents, the president who extracted many passages from *Samson Agonistes* in his commonplace book. The wealthy Muslim who bankrolled the attack was Yusuf Karamanli, Pasha of Tripoli, then one of the Barbary states of North Africa, the one of which the successor state is Libya. The tradition of Barbary piracy was centuries old; when Edward King, Milton's *Lycidas,* made his will just before setting out for Ireland, he did so in the knowledge that five years earlier a ship sailing on the same route had been captured by Barbary pirates, and its crew and 150 passengers sold into slavery in North Africa. After America broke away from Britain, Britain made it clear to the pirates of North Africa that American shipping was fair game and that it would not intervene to protect attacks on American ships.

At the time Jefferson became president, some 2 million dollars a year, which was one-fifth of the tax revenue of the United States, was being paid to ransom American citizens who had been captured by Barbary pirates. Pasha Yusuf thought that his share of this amount was insufficient, and demanded a lump sum of $250,000 and an annual payment of $25,000. The American press, which presumably reflected popular opinion, adopted the slogan "millions for defense, not one cent for tribute." On May 16, 1801, Jefferson ordered the U.S. Navy to attack Tripoli. The memory of this assault has faded, but it is enshrined in the opening line of the U.S. Marine Corps Hymn; I wonder how many Americans could now identify the halls of Montezuma or the shore of Tripoli. Despite a successful commando raid by Lieutenant Stephen Decatur (after whom ten towns in America are named), America came close to losing the war, and might have done so had William Eaton, the distinctly unwholesome American consul in Tunis, not decided to overthrow the pasha. The USS *Constitution* ("Old Ironsides") shelled Tripoli, and Eaton invaded with his international force of sixteen U.S. marines (hence the hymn), Greek and Italian soldiers, Arab cavalry, and 190 camels of unknown nationality. This was the first time that America's troops had been used to defend American interests abroad, and when Eaton's force stormed Derna and raised the American flag (the first time an American flag had been raised on a captured outpost), the pasha, fearing that they would do the same in Tripoli, surrendered. In the peace treaty that followed, the American captives were released, the pirates promised not to attack American shipping, and the pasha was paid $60,000 and allowed to keep his job. I shall not go on with the story, save to note that the United States continued to pay tribute to Barbary pirates until 1815 and to note Decatur's words the following year: "Our country, in her intercourse with foreign nations, may she always be in the right, but [she is] our country, right or wrong."

I raise this historical precedent among fellow academics, because I think that academics have a role to play at times of national crisis. Academics can offer specialist expertise in politics, religion, geography, and even structural engineering. Universities are places in which balanced discussions can take place, and academics in the humanities, who always take the long view, can resist the rush to judgment and the demonizing of what our theoretical colleagues call the "other." As it happens, I receive half my salary as a Milton specialist and half as a Middle East specialist, but it is not simply the latter interest that has been engaged by the events of 2001, the subsequent wars in Afghanistan and Iraq, and the attacks on Madrid and London. To put it another way, the teaching of literature is not just a job; the literature that we study and teach intersects with the values by which we live. This raises the question: How should we respond to literature that seems to endorse terrorism?

For a Miltonist, the obvious locus for such questions, as has been clear from debates on both sides of the Atlantic and in a series of conference sessions on "Milton and Terrorism," is Samson's suicide attack on Philistine civilians. Samson believes that he has been instructed by his god to pull down the theater, killing thousands of Philistines and in the process killing himself. In the moral perspective of the play, killing civilian Philistines is unproblematical, but killing oneself in the process raises questions about the legitimacy of suicide for a noble cause. Milton's answer seems to be that God is not subject to his own rules (he "made our laws to bind us, not himself," 309), and so "hath full right to exempt / Whom so it pleases him" (310–11): Jesus was allowed voluntarily to give his life, and so was Samson. Milton's account of the massacre differs from the equally barbaric biblical account in Judg. 16 in one significant detail, which is Milton's insistence that "the vulgar only 'scaped who stood without" (1659); in Milton's poem, the victims are the "choice nobility and flower" of Philistian society, not the ordinary people.

I do not wish to linger for long on this episode, as others have done so at length, but would like briefly to consider the perspective of the Philistines; in doing so I remind you that just as modern Israelis claim descent from ancient Israelites, so modern Palestinians claim descent from ancient Philistines; in most European languages, though not in English, the word for Palestinian is also the word for Philistine. I would not presume to comment on the truthfulness of either of those claims, but that is not my point: I am simply arguing that there is more than one perspective implied by the action of the play. From the Philistine perspective, Samson is a suicidal fundamentalist member of the ascetic Nazarite sect. He is prompted by the rousing motions of a god in whom the Philistines do not believe to commit mass murder in the name of that god and at the cost of his own life, which he sacrifices in the foolish belief that the act will earn him a place in paradise.

Clearly one man's terrorist is another man's freedom fighter. In our own time, we might think of Menachim Begin, Nelson Mandela, Gerry Adams, and Yasser Arafat, all of whom have been accused of using terrorism to achieve political ends and all of whom have been excused because of the legitimacy of those ends. Think how difficult it was for Israelis to watch Bill Clinton shaking hands with Yasser Arafat; think how difficult it was for Britons to watch Bill Clinton shaking hands with Gerry Adams. To many of us their handshake seemed to be a symbol of America's willingness to harbor and finance IRA terrorists. Britain, in turn, harbors a great many people intent on committing terrorist acts in other countries—think of all those organizations in South London representing the democratic front for the liberation of any number of third-world countries, and of our collection of radical mullahs. And so it is with Samson. Indeed, I can assure you that in Libyan historiography the Tripolitan war of 1801–05 is viewed rather differently.

I do not subscribe to Samuel Huntington's "clash of civilizations" hypothesis, but I do see some continuity between the events of 2001 and the events of 1801. The origins of that antagonism can be traced back to late antiquity, when Islam expanded into the political space vacated by the collapse of the Roman empire. I propose to ignore the first millennium of Islam for the purposes of this chapter, and instead to construct a sketch of Islam in seventeenth-century England, a background against which we might consider Milton. The caliphate was not yet centered in Turkey (that claim did not arise until the late eighteenth century), but the Ottomans ruled the eastern and southern flanks of what we call Europe and contemporaries called Christendom, and to Christians, Ottomans represented Islam. The lines between those territories were and are disputed: Islamic scholars distinguish the "territory of Islam" (*dar al-Islam*) from the "territory of war" (*dar al-harb*). A country is deemed to be *dar al-harb* if it has been conquered by infidels, and the list (as articulated, for example, by Abdallah Azzam, the Palestinian academic and terrorist) includes Eritrea, the Philippines, Spain, and Uzbekistan, all of which have suffered Islamist violence arising from this doctrine.

The mention of Islamist violence leads me to mention one last distinction before turning to the seventeenth century. The piracy of seventeenth-century Muslims was primarily driven by the profit motive rather than religious conviction, and those involved were not markedly religious. Fundamentalist Islam came later: the Wahhabi movement emerged from the sands of Arabia in the mid-eighteenth century. Fundamentalist religion is not necessarily militant (there are millions of peaceful fundamentalists of varying religious persuasions), and the mutation that produced a militant fundamentalist movement appeared in Sudan with the rise of Muhammad Ahmad, who claimed to be the Madhi. The Madhists were slaughtered by Kitchener in 1898, but the movement lived on, and in 1989 its inheritors (who included the Madhi's great-grandson) organized the Islamist coup in Sudan. It was this government, through the political Islamist Hassan al-Turabi, that sheltered Osama bin Laden and fostered al-Qaeda. The relevance of this potted history to my argument is that we must beware of reading backward from our present perceptions. For centuries Islam was tolerationist, famously giving shelter to Jews expelled by Christians, whereas Christianity was intolerant, burning those deemed to be heretical. In the twenty-first century the positions are in some measure reversed, because Christianity is largely tolerationist, but some strands of Islam are not: there are no churches in Saudi Arabia.

Milton knew none of this, but Islam nonetheless impinged on his world, and he was certainly aware of the conflict. I have already mentioned the pirate raid of 1632, the one mentioned in Milton's collection of elegies *Justa Eduardo King* (1638). We should, I think, acknowledge the scale of such raids, of which Matar has assembled a daunting list. In the first eight years of Milton's life, 466 English ships were captured and their crews and passengers enslaved. In June 1624, when Milton was a pupil at St. Paul's School, there was a national appeal for funds to ransom 1,500 English captives being held in North Africa. In the following summer, August 1625, there was a Sunday morning raid on a church on the Cornish coast, and sixty worshippers were captured. By May 1626, when Milton was finishing his first year at Cambridge, there were 1,500 British captives in Sali and 3,000 in Algiers. In 1640, the families of 3,000 English captives in Algiers petitioned the king for assistance. Throughout the early 1640s, a series of ordinances attempted to regulate the payment of ransoms. In addition to this considerable corpus of legislative material, the state papers are filled with appeals from the families of kidnap victims: to give but one example, when sixty sailors from Dartmouth were captured off Lizard Point in September 1635, the mayor appealed to the Privy Council for assistance in looking after the wives and children. Why, I wonder, is this material so unfamiliar? Have we perhaps occluded our historical memory of Muslims in early modern England even more successfully than we have of women?

What happened to all these captives? Many were released and returned to England on payment of a ransom; others died in captivity or embraced Islam and assimilated. Some, of course, embraced Islam and returned to England. The spirit of the conversions is hard to judge. Some may have been faked to secure early release or the chance of escape, but that pretence was less likely at a time when apostasy was a capital offence and religion was something more than a childish toy. It seems more likely that a considerable proportion of conversions was genuine. The difficulty for converts who returned to England was that English Christianity was intolerant. The penalty for apostasy was death, and the only god one could worship was the Protestant one. The very existence of English Muslims is an inference, because they could not confess their faith publicly.

This narrative of the Tripolitan war is one of many that I could have chosen. I picked this one not only because of the 9/11 parallel, but also because it points to an important feature of the West's relationship with the Islamic world. In the case of European contacts with native Americans or sub-Saharan Africans, the narratives are of conquest; in the nineteenth and twentieth centuries it is possible under the umbrella of orientalism to construct similar narratives of exploitation. In the early modern period with which we are concerned, however, the orientalist model does not work, because Christendom did not self-evidently have the upper hand. Indeed, just as Columbus captured native Americans to present to his king, so did Barbary pirates capture native Europeans for financial gain and in some cases for presentation to their rulers. Said's orientalism hypothesis only works from the point at which he started his analysis, the mid-eighteenth century. Before that the Islamic world was not a place that the West conquered, but one that threatened to conquer the West. Vienna, you will recall, was besieged by Ottoman forces in 1529 and 1532, and attacked again in 1683. In North Africa, piracy continued to be a threat until 1830, when France conquered Algiers. Many of the pirates were Muslims, but it is worth pausing to note that some were Christians (e.g., the Oxford-educated Sir Francis Verney, who was based in Algiers) and some were apostates, bad angels who had once been good angels: the pirate responsible for the infamous raid of 1631 on the Irish town of Baltimore, whose inhabitants were sold into slavery, was Murad Reis, a Flemish convert to Islam who was quartermaster of the Algiers fleet. His commanding officer, the admiral of the pirate fleet, was also a Flemish renegado.

In considering Miltonic references to the Islamic world, we should jettison Said and orientalism and think in terms of fear and apostasy. As a preliminary to that, we should attend to geography, because what we think of as the Islamic world is not what Milton thought it was. Britain now has 1.6 million Muslims, Germany has 3 million, and France has almost 6 million; I live in a city with a large Muslim community, and indeed sit on the advisory board of our local Islamic foundation. Europe, in some measure, is now part of the Islamic world. When we look back to the early modern period, we imagine a Europe that is Christian, with a Jewish minority, and a non-European world that in the Middle East and North Africa is Islamic. That overly simplistic view sometimes leads us to misread Milton. I propose to illustrate the point with four examples: Arabia, Ormus, Almansor, and the Ottomans.

First, Arabia. If you were to ask an educated modern Westerner where Islam is centered, the reply would be Saudi Arabia, the land of the two holy mosques at Mecca and Medina. If you were to say "Arabia" to someone of Milton's class and generation, the association would not be with Mecca and Medina or even the haj port of Jeddah, where Eve is buried, but with Arabia Felix and Arabia Deserta. Arabia Felix, which was centered in what is now Yemen, was associated with frankincense and balsam, the smell of which was deemed to drift out to sea. That idea is articulated in Herodotus and Diodorus Siculus, and appears in book 4 of *Paradise Lost;* the only additional fact that you need to know is that the Sabeans were one of the four tribes in that part of the peninsula, and that it is better known as Sheba, whose queen married Solomon and founded the royal house of Ethiopia. As Satan approaches Eden, which was traditionally placed in Arabia Felix, he can smell the odors of the garden:

> As when to them who sail
> Beyond the Cape of Hope, and now are past
> Mozambique, off at sea north-east winds blow,
> Sabean odours from the spicy shore
> Of Araby the Blest, with such delay
> Well pleased they slack their course, and many a league
> Cheered with the grateful smell old Ocean smiles. (4.159–65)

This is not Saudi Arabia the birthplace of Osama bin Laden, but Araby the Blest, the Arabia Felix that constituted a blurred pagan adumbration of the Judeo-Christian Garden of Eden. Milton's lines are of course a commonplace: think of Fletcher (in *The Bloody Brother*) talking about "the sweetness of Arabian wind" or Massinger's comparison of a lady's breath to the "smooth gales that glide o'er happy Araby" (in *The Great Duke of Florence*) or, elsewhere in Milton, "of gentlest gale Arabian odours fanned" (*Paradise Regained* 2) and the phoenix, which Milton associates in *Samson Agonistes* with "the Arabian woods."

In addition to Arabia Felix, there are the Arabias of the north, which were controlled in antiquity by the Romans in the West (Petraea) and the Persians in the East. These areas were known as Arabia Deserta. Here the associations are hostile, but they are again not Islamic. In early

Milton one thinks of the "remote wastes and rough desert of Arabia" in
Elegy 4; in late Milton the story is the same: think of the Jesus of
Paradise Regained looking south toward "the Persian Bay / And inaccessible
th'Arabian drought" (3.273–74). This is not the Empty Quarter
(*Rub'al Khali*) beloved of British explorers (and me), but rather large
tracts of the Middle East, which Milton and his contemporaries thought
to be one big desert. Arabia, we may conclude, was not associated by
Milton's generation with Islam.

The next example on which I should like to pause is Ormus, which
is too often given the orientalist treatment. It is, like the odors of Arabia
the Blest, a commonplace. Think of Marvell's "jewels more rich than
Ormus shows" (Bermudas) or Ben Jonson's ship coming from Ormus
laden with drugs (*Alchemist* 1.3.59); there was even a play set in Ormus,
Fulke Greville's *Alaham*. At the beginning of book 2 of *Paradise Lost,*
Milton associates Ormus with Satan's throne in hell ("High on a throne
of royal state, which far outshone the wealth of Ormus or of Ind"), and
so echoes a passage in the final scene of Greville's play in which the
usurper cries: "Is this Ormus? Or is Ormus my hell,/ Where only furies
and not men doe dwell?"[1]

Where, I hear you ask, is Ormus? If you look on a map, you will
find it spelled Hormuz, and it is an island in the Strait of Hormuz,
which is the narrowest part of the Persian Gulf; I last flew over it in
February to inspect it. The key fact about Hormuz now is that it is a
desert island that belongs to Iran. The key fact about it at the time of
Jonson and Greville and Marvell and Milton is that it was neither
Arabian nor Iranian, but European. It was captured by Albuquerque in
1507, and he wrote the name in Portuguese, which is why it was spelt
in English, including Milton's English, without an aitch, despite the fact
that the "o" was breathed. In the course of the next century, Hormuz
evolved from being a strategic link on the Portuguese sea route to Asia
into a jewel and spice market through which goods from the East were
traded. Shah Abbas, the ruler who built the world's finest square in
Isfahan, resented the Portuguese occupation of his island, and in 1621
his agents entered into an agreement with the English East India
Company. On February 18, 1622, the English besieged Hormuz, which
fell on May 1; you recall that this was the period during which Portugal
was annexed by Spain, with whom England enjoyed a fragile peace that
was strained by this episode. Whatever the political cost, there was a
financial gain. Both King James and the Duke of Buckingham required
sweeteners, and they received £10,000 each. You will by now see my
point. The association of the throne of Milton's Satan with the wealth
of Ormus has nothing to do with orientalist myths about fabled wealth

and ruthless warriors and hubble-bubbles and belly dancers, but is rather an allusion to the Catholic Portuguese and the corrupt English monarchy. It has nothing to do with Islam.

Thus Arabia and Ormus, neither of which is in Milton's eyes Islamic. Almansor, however, qualifies. At the end of *Paradise Lost* Adam is led by Michael to a hilltop from which he can see

> . . . Atlas Mount,
> The kingdoms of Almansor, Fez and Sus,
> Morocco, and Algiers and Tremisen. (11.402–04)

Atlas Mount is Mount Toubkal, in the High Atlas, and in March 2005 I hired a mule to explore it. The difficulty with Almansor is that it is not a name or a place, but a title (meaning "the victorious") borne by any number of Arab conquerors. Let me help you with the names of the five kingdoms. Fez, which some readers will know through *The Spider's House* by the American novelist Paul Bowles, was the imperial capital until the French shifted it to Rabat; the Kairaouine University in Fes was founded in A.D. 857, which makes it the world's oldest university, and it was through this university that much Islamic learning passed to the West. Sus, with apologies to the editors of the Oxford World's Classics Milton, who get the passage entirely wrong, is not Tunis, which has never been known as Sus, nor is it the holiday resort in Tunisia known in English and French as Sousse and in Arabic as Susah, but is rather a province of southern Morocco that was until the twentieth century an independent sultanate. "Morocco" is Marrakesh, a sultanate in what is now Morocco; Algiers had been freed from the Ottoman yoke by Barbarossa and had fended off Spanish attacks, and in Milton's time was the principal port of the Barbary pirates. Tremisen, now Tlemcen in western Algeria, was an Arab sultanate from 1282 to 1553, when the Ottomans conquered it. And who was Almansor? The Victorian scholar David Masson said that it was the eighth-century Abbasid caliph Abu Jafer bin Mohammad, the man who founded Baghdad and never went anywhere near the places that Milton mentions. Alastair Fowler comes up with a tenth-century amir of Cordova, who never ruled the places that Milton lists; indeed, he was a chief minister, not a caliph, so he did not rule anything. In the Oxford Milton, Orgel and Goldberg follow obediently behind, making up a few facts to support this improbable assertion. In fact the only al-Mansur described in the accounts of North Africa that could have been known to Milton (all of which derive from Leo Africanus) was a twelfth-century ruler, the Almohad emir Abu-Yusuf Ya'qub al-Mansur. I make the point in order to suggest that one of the barriers to an understanding of the interface between England and the Muslim world of the seventeenth century is our ignorance of Islamic history. In the same passage, editors routinely fail to note that Mombasa, Quiloa (now Kilwa Kisiwani), and Malind(i) were all Islamic colonies. Milton knew much more about the Islamic world than do we, though the only point at which he is known to have been in direct contact with that world occurred in April 1656, when he drafted on behalf of the English government two letters to Pasha Ahmed VI, the dey of Algiers. He was clearly unable to convert the Islamic date, because he thanks the Pasha for his letter "dated on the third day of the second moon of Rabia in the year 1066 according to your account"; the date is in fact January 30, 1656.

My fourth and final example concerns the Ottomans. The Ottoman administration was far more tolerant than any Christian administration, but Milton, in common with his contemporaries, saw it as a tyranny. In *Eikonoklastes,* he draws a parallel between the English under the yoke of Charles I and the Turks under the Sultan. The rule of Charles is described as a "Turkish tyranny," a phrase that Milton was to use again in the *Articles of Peace* and in the *Commonplace Book,* on both occasions with reference to Charles IX of France. Ottoman imagery also pervades the scenes in hell in *Paradise Lost.* In Book 10, Satan returns to hell, and

Forth rushed in haste the great consulting peers,
Raised from their dark divan. (10.456–57)

The literal meaning of Turkish *divan* and Arabic *diwan* is "meeting place," but Milton's use of the term invites the common sense of an imperial court. The Ottomans are, in Milton's view, the rulers of an evil empire. As a young man at Cambridge Milton took an unusual line on why the Ottomans were so barbaric, and in so doing contrasted the Ottoman Turks with the Saracens, that being the seventeenth-century term for Arabs. Speaking in Latin, he explained that

the Saracens, to whom the Turks are indebted almost for their existence, enlarged their empire as much by their study of liberal culture as by force of arms.[2]

This passage hints at an awareness of the centrality of learning and literature to the Arab culture of the medieval and early modern periods. The disappearance of such an acknowledgment is now an important grievance in the minds of Islamist radicals. The argument runs that for a millennium the Islamic world enjoyed a cultural and scientific hegemony that laid the foundations for the culture, science, and technology of the modern world. That superiority was destroyed by the nation-states created by the colonial powers, who subdivided and so enervated the global Islamic nation (the *umma*). The intellectuals of Milton's generation were the last to acknowledge the importance of this civilization. Even now, textbooks on subjects such as computing begin in the Islamic world with prefaces excoriating the West for its failure to acknowledge, for example, that without the invention of zero by Arabic mathematicians, there would be no computing.

There are misunderstandings on both sides, and one might think of them in terms of orientalism and occidentalism. In the context of early modern literature, including the work of Milton, it is the inappropriate use of the imperialist model that skews our perceptions. In the world of early modern literary studies one of the most influential figures is Stephen Greenblatt, who inaugurated the practice of reading Renaissance drama (especially Marlowe and Shakespeare) as the cultural products of imperialist expansion that was focused on America. This crude attempt to relocate early modern English literature in America may satisfy a need to keep America at the center of the map, but it will not stand up to scholarly scrutiny: there was no English empire in America or anywhere else; that came much later. The characters of *The Tempest*, for example, are not, with the exception of Gonzalo, concerned with colonization; they rather use the island as a remote base from which to recover political power in Milan, to which they want to return. It is absurd to think of this as colonialism.

The application of an imperialist model to Renaissance literature creates many distortions, chief of which is the creation of the "other." Britain did not begin to colonize the Islamic world until the eighteenth century; indeed, it was the other way round. In the representation of Muslims on the English stage, what we do *not* have is the creation of what in theory-speak is described as the creation of a space for subject peoples through the production of knowledge of colonizer and colonized. There was no such binary opposition. Far from being the other, separated by an absolute barrier, Muslims were people that Christians could become; good angels, as in *Paradise Lost,* could fall into apostasy and become bad angels, just as Christian captives could become Muslims. This was phrased not in terms of "embracing Islam," as it would be now, but rather in terms of "turning Turk." The phrase is telling, because it defers not to religious authority but to the dominant political power. Christians converted because Islam was stronger. It is such conversions that lie at the center of English anxieties. Think of Othello:

Are we turned Turks, and to ourselves do that
Which heaven hath forbid the Ottomites?[3]

Such conversions could be real, but there are also emblematic conversions: in Ben Jonson's *Masque of Blackness,* for example, Queen Anne and her ladies were blacked up as noble moors; they became Muslims for the evening. Vitkus's important book supplies many examples of conversions, such as those in Robert Daborne's *A Christian Turned Turk* and Massinger's *The Renegado.* In Milton's England the official line was that one converted from the sinful state of Islam to the redeemed state of Christianity, but the hard fact was that conversions were overwhelmingly in the other direction. It is this anxiety that underlies so much English Renaissance literature; in Milton's case his epic focuses on the horror of angels and our first parents converting from innocence to guilt, in effect enacting the spiritual equivalent of turning Turk.

I should like to conclude with an example of Miltonic occidentalism. Milton was on occasion able to admire the rigor of other religions. In *Of Reformation,* for example, he praises "the Turkish and Jewish rigour against whoring and drinking." There are echoes of this kind of thinking in modern Arabic writing on Milton, of which Eid Dahiyat gives an excellent account. The Egyptian Ahmed Khaki, for example, admires the tension between reason and desire in Milton's poetry, commenting that "Milton was a sexual maniac restrained by religious and ethical standards; this inner struggle is transformed into a struggle between the forces of good and evil in his poetry." Luwis Awad, who taught English in Cairo in the 1960s, undertook an extraordinary act of cultural appropriation. Milton's beliefs, he explains, are wholly consistent with the teachings of Islam: Milton was monotheistic and anti-Trinitarian, he rejected the prelates and their pretended mediation between God and his creatures, he loved earthly life, he hated the rituals of the church, he hated icons, and he considered men superior to women. Awad therefore concluded that Milton was not a Christian, but rather a pious Muslim. This assertion of Milton's Islamic credentials is a mirror image of the assertion that Muslims are good people and so could not have been responsible for 9/11. Occidentalism distorts almost as much as orientalism.

NOTES

1. *Poems and Dramas of Fulke Greville,* ed. G. Bullough, vol. 2 (London: Oliver and Boyd, 1939), 210, ll. 41–42.
2. *The Complete Prose Works of John Milton,* ed. Don M. Wolfe, vol. 1 (New Haven: Yale UP, 1953), 299, ll. 1624–42.
3. William Shakespeare, *Othello,* Arden Edition, ed. E. A. J. Honigmann (London: Thomas Nelson, 1997), 2.3.172–73.

JONATHAN SWIFT AND THE IDEA OF THE FUNDAMENTAL CHURCH

ANNE BARBEAU GARDINER

Jonathan Swift's religious writings and *Gulliver's Travels* have been thought to be irreconcilable, but as one scholar has noted, "religion" keeps "entering the story" of Gulliver.[1] Curiously, Swift told a kinsman that he had "laid the design of Gulliver eighteen years before it was printed,"[2] that is, around 1708, the same period in which he wrote some of his major essays on religion. I will give evidence, first, that Swift was a fundamentalist in his religious writings, and second, that this outlook shapes the hidden design of *Gulliver's Travels*.

The word *fundamental* is related to the foundation of a building. In his writings on the church, Swift uses the terms *foundation* and *fundamental* to refer to apostolic Christianity as the groundwork on which the church edifice of his day has to stand, if it means to survive. He says, with caustic irony, that to try to restore a "*real* Christianity," such as existed in "primitive Times" and influenced "Mens Belief and Actions," would be "to dig up Foundations." But since a *real* faith is "inconsistent with our present Schemes of Wealth and Power," those foundations have been abandoned.[3] He calls *fundamental* the doctrines that "have been held inviolable almost in all Ages by every Sect that pretends to be Christian," and he includes here the Trinity, the divinity of Christ, and the soul's immortality.[4]

Swift is a fundamentalist in that he regards conscience, the Christian mysteries, biblical miracles, and church authority as based on objective criteria. He explains that conscience judges actions "by comparing them with the Law of God" and advises one who objects to the rites of his church to examine "thoroughly" all such points by "Scripture, and the Practice of the ancient Church," and only then will his conscience have enough knowledge to determine "whether those Points are blameable or no." For Swift, then, conscience is not a feeling, but a "Judge" controlled by evidence from sacred texts and church history. An objective rule is necessary because conscience is corrupted and fails to take "Cognizance" of our sins because of hard-heartedness, self-interest, ignorance, or neglect.[5]

Swift sees the Christian mysteries and biblical miracles as *facts*. Regarding the Trinity, he says, "God himself hath pronounced the Fact, but wholly concealed the Manner," and on the same page repeats the word *fact* to say that God commands us "by our Dependence upon his Truth, and his holy Word, to believe a Fact [the Trinity] that we do not understand." To deny such mysteries as the resurrection of the dead is to go against "the whole Tenor of the New Testament."[6] When he remarks that ancient philosophers were ignorant of "Matters of Fact" that happened long after them, he includes under this rubric of *fact* the birth, miracles, death, resurrection, and ascension of Jesus Christ.[7] Biblical miracles are also facts, for though they are as "contrary to common Reason" as the Trinity, they are also "positively affirmed in the Gospel." Again, he offers the same either/or choice—"believe, or give up our Holy Religion to Atheists and Infidels." Warning that our reason is corrupted by self-interest, passions, and vices, he tells us to beware of judging "every Thing impossible" that our reason cannot conceive, or of setting our reason up "blasphemously" to "controul the Commands of the Almighty." Calling it "an old and true Distinction, that Things may be above our Reason, without being contrary to it," Swift affirms that Christianity is grounded on the rock of facts.[8]

The spiritual authority of the church, as independent of the state's authority, is another plain fact for Swift. This is why he is hostile to bishops "of the Whig Species" who are willing to reduce his religion to an arm of the British state. He insists that it can be "directly proved" or "deduced" from "the words of our Saviour and his Apostles" that there were priests and bishops in the primitive church, that none but priests prayed, preached, and administered the Lord's Supper, and that "all Questions, relating either to Discipline or Doctrine, were determined in Ecclesiastical Conventions." The nations that received that church of the "purest and earliest ages" are bound to her "Divine Law," which can no more be altered than the "common Laws of Nature." When secular men usurp church authority, they are Lilliputians: "Put the Case, that walking on the slack Rope were the only Talent required by Act of Parliament for making a Man a Bishop," Swift says, yet despite that law, the man would no more be a bishop than my watch would be a "Turnip" by my calling it so. Thus, Swift sees a church that truckles to the state as *unreal.* And yet, Swift wants the state to uphold the church: "We are sure Christianity is the only true religion, and therefore it should be the Magistrate's chief Care to propagate it."[9] As for the pretended Saxon origin of the British state, Swift dismisses it as a myth and says this form of government is not older than the Norman king Henry I.[10]

The view that human nature is corrupted by original sin is still another feature of Swift's fundamentalism. This doctrine is also at the "Foundation," since without Adam's Fall, there would be no need for a Redeemer.[11] Swift's conviction that human nature is prone to degeneracy detaches him from the optimism of the early Enlightenment. What does it matter that Europeans are making strides in science, since they "degenerate" every day by their vices and "Inhumanity"?[12] Even in Brobdingnag, the most religious and virtuous nation that Gulliver visits, original sin is present: "In the Course of many Ages they have been troubled with the same Disease, to which the whole Race of Mankind is Subject."[13] Not only does fallen human nature cause every institution to decay, but it also undermines attempts at reform. By the sixteenth century, the church had declined so far from its first perfection that it needed to be reformed "to preserve Christianity itself," but the endeavors of those "who intended well" were undermined by passions and vices so as "to pervert and confound" that work. In every country, the Reformation was "carried on in the most impious and scandalous manner that can possibly be conceived. To which unhappy proceedings we owe all the just reproaches that Roman Catholics have cast upon us ever since."[14] This passage shows that Swift sees all Christians as sharing equally in the legacy of original sin.

Swift, however, is not a Calvinist type of fundamentalist. First, he rejects the Calvinist belief in supralapsarian predestination—the conviction that from eternity God has willed the salvation of only some chosen individuals—and teaches instead that God has placed "all Men upon an equal Foot" in their capacity for "Salvation."[15] Second, he rejects the view that worldly rewards are a sign of God's favor and teaches instead that material advantages are "almost engrossed" by bad men.[16] And third, he does not identify the Roman Catholic Church with the Whore of Babylon or the pope with the Antichrist; while he thinks the pope usurped more authority than was his, he regards a global Catholic Church as a "Necessity" to preserve Christianity, and he hopes that national churches will join in a "general Council," as colleges do in a university, to "preserve Fundamentals." There is nothing "improper in this Notion of the

Catholick Church," he insists, for Christianity has been "corrupted" for lack of "such a Communion."[17] Charles Lesley had proposed a union between the Anglican and Gallican Churches,[18] and Swift (arguing against Burnet) defends him, saying there is nothing "Evil in proposing an Union between any two Churches in *Christendom*."[19] Alluding to the Christ's pledge that his church will stand firm against "the gates of hell" (Matt. 16:18), Swift directs this promise to the global church, declaring that the fundamentals "have been ever maintained by the universal Body of true Believers from the Days of the Apostles, and will be so to the Resurrection; neither will the Gates of Hell prevail against them."[20]

Still another feature of Swift's fundamentalism is the antithesis of temporal and eternal. He considers the hope of heaven to be necessary to keep what is "earthly" from competing with the "Danger of offending his Creator, or the Happiness of pleasing him."[21] He speaks of hell, too, as when he observes that some divert their attention during sermons for fear of having "their Sins laid open in true Colours" and finding "eternal Misery the Reward of them."[22] The antithesis of temporal and eternal helps Swift face personal suffering—as when his beloved Stella is dying and he finds comfort in pondering how God afflicts his children "for their own Good," either to make them repent or to "punish them in the present Life, in order to reward them in a better."[23] Perhaps recalling that he and his friends in Queen Anne's ministry were maligned for their part in the Treaty of Utrecht, he calls it a comfort for one accused by "evil mercenary Tongues" to know that in a few years he can appeal to "an all-seeing Judge."[24]

Surely the most important ingredient in Swift's fundamentalism, however, is his claim that atheists are *not* virtuous. Pierre Bayle's work *Continuation des pensées diverses* (1704) was in Swift's library, so he knew who was the originator of the idea that atheists are paragons of virtue. Bayle had praised Spinoza, the first systematic atheist, as a supreme model of virtue, and envisioned a society of virtuous atheists that would put Christian societies to shame. This unprecedented exaltation of atheists was spread in Britain by Matthew Tindall and Anthony Collins. Swift's sarcastic abridgment of Collins's "Atheology" contains this maxim: that "a perfect moral Man must be a perfect Atheist; every inch of Religion he gets loses him an inch of Morality." This is Bayle in a nutshell.[25] Collins also boasts, like Bayle, that the "most virtuous People in all Ages" were atheists.[26]

In many of his writings, both religious and satirical, Swift keeps answering Bayle, because he sees the idea of the virtuous atheist as sapping the foundations of Christianity. In his reply to Tindall, he argues that atheists must surely prefer vice to virtue, because only such a preference can explain why they give their faith to colossally absurd systems: "The Faith of Christians is not as a Grain of Mustard Seed in Comparison with theirs [atheists'], which can remove such Mountains of Absurdities, and submit with so entire a Resignation to such Apostles [i.e., Spinoza and Bayle]." Atheists would not be "confirmed in such Doctrines" unless they were already "confirmed in their Vices."[27] He tells a young man just ordained that "Men always grow vicious before they become Unbelievers," and that "Infidelity" becomes rampant only where there is already a "universal Corruption of Morals."[28] Atheists want to "overthrow all Religion," he insists, so they can "gratify their Vices" without reproach from conscience. When they look for a weak side in Christianity, it is because "they wish it were not true, and those Wishes can proceed from nothing but an evil Conscience."[29] The words *always* and *nothing but* indicate that these points are fundamental with him.

Swift believes that vice not only precedes atheism, but is also bound to follow it, because atheists will obey "Nature" (i.e., fallen nature) whenever they see no danger to their self-interest. Their pride, lust, avarice, or ambition will thus "certainly break" through every tie—here the word *certainly* indicates again that this point is fundamental with him. He even calls it "impossible" for an atheist in public office to give "any reasonable Security that he will not be false, and cruel, and corrupt, whenever a Temptation offers, which he valueth more than he does the Power wherewith he was trusted." No oath of office can bind him, because oaths are appeals to God and he does not believe in God.[30] As a result of this outlook, Swift sees a real danger in a government run by Whigs, for he affirms that ninety-nine out of a hundred "professed *Atheists, Deists,* and *Socinians*" (author's emphasis) are Whigs.[31]

Gulliver's Travels can be read as a twofold apocalypse, personal and public. It traces the implosion of both an individual and a nation. By a series of parables, Swift ponders the origin, progress, and culmination of the spiritual desolation he sees around him. In Lilliput, he ponders degeneracy; in Brobdingnag, the glory that was; in Laputa, apostasy; and in Houyhnhnmland, the final stage—Bayle's society of virtuous atheists. Swift assumes a vatic role, as the names *Lilliput* and *Laputa* suggest, for this is the tale of the Whore (*Puta*) of the Apocalypse. He had access to some interpretations of the book of Revelation,[32] and he knew from his upbringing that nearly all his Protestant contemporaries identified the Whore of Revelation 17 with the Church of Rome, yet he follows Christian antiquity in seeing the signs of the end-times in his own milieu. For St. Paul laments that "the mystery of iniquity doth already work" (2 Thess. 2:7), and St. John that "even now are there many antichrists" (1 John 2:18). It is telling that Swift encouraged Pope to write *The Dunciad,* which is another satirical apocalypse like *Gulliver's Travels.*

LILLIPUT, OR DEGENERACY

Lilliput, the Little Whore, is the first stage of Gulliver's and Britain's apocalypse. The size of Lilliputians represents their low spiritual stature, caused by worldly pride and abandonment of religion. If Gulliver is large by comparison, it is that he grew up in humble circumstances— "a Stranger to Courts, for which I was unqualified by the Meanness of my Condition." Yet he is already a materialist at the start of the *Travels,* since the Lilliputians mistake his watch for "the God that he worships" (53).

Just as Swift, in his religious writings, defends the independent authority of the church, so in Lilliput he does the same indirectly, using the royal councillor Reldresal to tell the story of how this island's religion came to be altered by a king and finally abandoned. In chapter 4, Reldresal explains that Lilliput and Blefuscu have been engaged in a religious war for a long time: Blefuscu accuses Lilliput of "making a Schism in Religion, by offending against a fundamental Doctrine of our great Prophet *Lustrog*"—the name *Lustrog,* derived from *lustre,* glances at St. John's Gospel, where Christ is "the Light" (64–5). In turn, Lilliput accuses Blefuscu of "Heresy," as we see in Article 2 of Gulliver's impeachment (79).

Reldresal admits that the present king's grandfather changed the religion of Lilliput for his private reasons. He also admits that everyone agrees "the primitive way of breaking Eggs before we eat them, was upon the larger End," but that the former king "published an Edict, commanding all his Subjects, upon great Penalties" to follow the new practice. The key point here is that the *primitive* and *ancient* practice was Big-Endianism. In his religious writings, Swift always uses the word *primitive* for the Apostolic Church of the first three centuries, whose doctrine and practice must be embraced without demur. Reldresal explains that the royal edict caused "six Rebellions," in which "one Emperor lost his Life, and another his Crown" (alluding to the execution of Charles I in 1649 and the exclusion of James II in 1688). Also, "eleven Thousand Persons have, at several Times, suffered Death, rather than submit to break their Eggs at the smaller end" (64). Oddly enough, the only ones Reldresal mentions as being persecuted in Lilliput are the Big-Endians. By the time Gulliver arrives in Lilliput in 1699, the Big-Endians are "incapable by Law of holding Employments"—an allusion to the Test Acts of 1673 and 1678 that made an oath against transubstantiation a requirement for public employment. This allusion to the Test Acts provides a key to the rest: "Big-Endianism" is a belief in transubstantiation, in a real presence both on the altar and in the communicant.

Despite the havoc wrought by the former king's edict in religion, Reldresal defends the change on three grounds: scripture, conscience, and the authority of the state. He cites a verse from chapter 54 of their scripture (alluding to John 6:54, the much controverted verse that was interpreted figuratively by Calvinists),[33] as directing "true Believers" to "break their Eggs at the convenient End." He insists that this passage leaves the matter "to every Man's Conscience, or at least in the Power of the chief Magistrate to determine" (65). Thus, Reldresal sees the *primitive* and *ancient* practice of the church as irrelevant and is content to let private conscience and the state decide, without consent of the church. This was the Calvinist view, but the exact opposite of what Swift urges in his religious writings, for he insists there that in religious questions, Christians should be guided "by Scripture, and the Practice of the ancient Church."[34]

The result of the Little-Endian innovation is that the temple where Gulliver is chained has been desecrated and abandoned. Only the "Vulgar" still follow the custom of burying the dead with their heads down in preparation for the resurrection. Commenting on this passage, Swift's kinsman says it defends the belief in "a state hereafter, (although connected with some vanities and absurdities, which are the effects of superstition)" as the "ground-work of all religion." The word *ground-work* implies that the resurrection was a fundamental point with Swift, whom this kinsman calls "truly orthodox."[35]

The climax of the first voyage comes when Gulliver captures the enemy fleet and is ordered to persecute: in the articles of impeachment, the king says he "commanded" Gulliver to go "put to death not only all the *Big-Endian* Exiles, but likewise all the People of that Empire, who would not immediately forsake the *Big-Endian* Heresy," but Gulliver refused "upon Pretence of Unwillingness to force the Consciences, or destroy the Liberties and Lives of an innocent People" (79). In a covert way, Swift accuses the British state here of having waged an endless war with France out of an anti-Catholic bias. For making peace with Blefuscu, Gulliver is accused of being "a *Big-Endian* in your Heart" (81), just as Swift and his friends were called "Popish" for bringing about the Treaty of Utrecht.

Swift highlights the link between corruption in religion and corruption in morals and politics: in Lilliput, the rope-dancing, which is now the test for public office, was introduced arbitrarily by the very same king who brought in the Little-Endian worship by edict. In the original constitution the test for office had been belief in "Divine Providence." Gulliver reports this, but he himself does not believe in divine providence, for at the start of this voyage he says that "Fortune" disposed of him, and at the end, that "Fortune" sent him a boat (42, 85). In the second voyage, he attributes all that happens to him to "Chance" and

"Fortune." There is a glimmer of hope, though, for on leaving Lilliput, he resolves "never more to put any Confidence in Princes" (86). This line echoes Psalm 118, but tellingly, Gulliver leaves out the first half: "It is better to trust in the Lord than to put confidence in princes." The reason he will not keep his resolve is given in one of Swift's sermons: "He who hath no Faith, cannot, by the Strength of his own Reason or Endeavours, so easily resist Temptations, as the other who depends upon God's Assistance in the overcoming his Frailties, and is sure to be rewarded for ever in Heaven for his Victory over them."[36]

BROBDINGNAG, OR THE GLORY THAT ONCE WAS

In the second voyage, Gulliver contemplates a Britain that is glorious, though still imperfect. This nation is invulnerable to outside foes because it is surrounded by a range of mountains "thirty Miles high" (114), an allusion to Psalm 125:2, where God is compared to a circle of mountains around those who believe in him: "As the mountains are round about Jerusalem, so the Lord is round about his people." In Brobdingnag, size again represents a measure of virtue, for just as the Lilliputian king was petty and vicious compared to Gulliver, so now Gulliver is petty and vicious compared to the giant king.

The religion of the giants is alive, since the farmer's family and the king's household both observe the "Sabbath." Glumdalclitch teaches Gulliver the language out of a book containing "a short Account of their Religion," but typically, he tells us only the size of that book, not its content (104–05, 110). By now he is a Lilliputian who sees only material surfaces close up, as when he speaks of a giant breast, a huge louse on a beggar, and the great height to which blood spouts at an execution, while ignoring the persons to whom these things are connected. He also reduces religion to the material and measurable: comparing the royal oven in Brobdingnag to the cupola of St. Paul's, numbering each religious sect in Britain without saying what they believe, and calculating the pinnacle of the temple in Brobdingnag to be shorter, proportionately, than Salisbury Steeple. Even so, Gulliver still gives us an important clue to the religion of Brobdingnag when he describes the exterior of their chief temple. He says it is "adorned on all Sides with Statues of Gods and Emperors cut in marble larger than the Life, placed in their several Niches" (116). Evidently, this is a church that cherishes its past. The statues reflect a sacred history, for the word *gods* here stands for saints—as in John 10:34, "I have said, ye are gods"—and the word *emperors* for Christian monarchs. Swift did not believe that the Mosaic Law forbade all statues, and he complained bitterly that iconoclasts had destroyed many "statues of saints," as well as those of "ancient prelates" and "kings."[37]

When he offers gunpowder to the giant king to "ingratiate" himself into royal favor, Gulliver shows how far he has fallen since the first voyage. In Lilliput, he resisted a tyrant king; now he tempts a good king to become a tyrant by offering him what will enable him to "batter down the Walls of the strongest Town in his Dominions in a few Hours," should it resist his "absolute Commands." This offer only confirms the king's opinion of Gulliver as subhuman: "He was amazed how so impotent and groveling an Insect as I (these were his Expressions) could entertain such inhuman Ideas" (133). Swift implies that a certain level of virtue is needed to qualify as belonging to the human species. And such virtue is not attainable by someone who lacks the hope of immortality. Francis Gastrell, later bishop of Chester, expresses the underlying lesson of this whole voyage in this passage: "*Human Nature,* if there be no future State, is the silliest, most irregular, most fantastical Nature in the Universe." Without belief in the hereafter, he says, even the "Use of *Reason,* is ridiculous."[38]

Gulliver remarks that no modern king in "*Europe*" would have refused his offer and faults the wise giant for "Narrowness of Thinking," a "confined Education," and "short Views," as well as for not having "reduced *Politicks* into a *Science,* as the more acute Wits of *Europe* have done" (133–34). The implication here is that Europeans are as self-deluded as Gulliver in thinking that they surpass their virtuous ancestors by enlightened thinking and Machiavellian politics. There are numerous references to *Europe* in the second voyage, of which these are a few: Gulliver's boat can hold "eight *Europeans,*" the beggars are the most horrible thin "that ever an *European* Eye beheld," the blood at the execution rises higher than the "*Jet d'Eau* at *Versailles,*" and the giant king is incapable of grasping the new philosophies of Europe, with their "Ideas, Entities, Abstractions and Transcendentals" (115, 121, 135). Evidently, Swift wants this voyage to have a very wide application.

Among the giants, too, it is the "Women and the Vulgar" who have the most regard for tradition. They value an old treatise that recounts how the human being has degenerated into a "diminutive, contemptible, and helpless Animal" compared to "ancient Times." Gulliver cannot believe that people in past *times* could have had greater stature, but can accept that people in another *place* might: "Who knows but that even this prodigious Race of Mortals might be equally overmatched in some distant part of the World, whereof we have yet no Discovery?" (136–37). The "old" author may be right, for though the giants vastly outmatch an eighteenth-century European, they are bound to be outmatched by primitive Christians, whom Swift puts at the apex of spiritual grandeur.

In this voyage, Gulliver deludes himself repeatedly by saying that he has proven his humanity to someone, but the facts always belie him. When he displays his courtly manners and shows his money to the field giants, he announces that "The Farmer by this time was convinced I must be a rational Creature" (95). But the farmer exploits him as a performing monkey. Then he says that his nine-year-old "nurse" regards him as having modesty and honor. But she dresses and undresses him like a doll and compares him to a lamb her parents "pretended" to give her the previous year, but later sold to a butcher (102). The giant king at first mistakes Gulliver for an animal and then "a piece of Clock-work." Will he finally recognize his humanity after hearing him speak at length about the recent history of Britain? On the contrary, for that history is purely materialistic. It leads the king to conclude that the "Bulk" of Gulliver's countrymen must be "the most pernicious Race of little odious Vermin that Nature ever suffered to crawl upon the Surface of the Earth" (132). This is Swift's rebuke to his enlightened contemporaries. They, too, he implies, would find it impossible to prove their humanity to their ancestors and would pass for animals. Gulliver deludes himself when he says he designed his box like a London room (109), for he admits later it was a *cage* and a *dungeon*. By the end of this voyage, the giant king is so sure Gulliver is subhuman that he wants to "propagate the Breed" to keep it in "Cages like tame Canary Birds" (138).

A spiritual implosion results from Gulliver's failure to prove his humanity: he sinks into self-contempt and compensates for it with a giant pride. First, he can no longer "endure" to see himself in a mirror because it gives him too "despicable a Conceit" of himself. So he compensates by looking down on others his own size, saying that if he had then "beheld a Company of *English* Lords and Ladies . . . Strutting, and Bowing and Prating," he would have been "tempted to laugh as much at them" as the giants did at him. When he returns home, he looks down on everyone "as if they had been Pigmies" (142, 145–46). No wonder the Captain who rescues him compares him to Phaeton, who perished for his overweening pride. Yet there is a curious echo of scripture at the end of this voyage, a hint that providence is active in Gulliver's life, if he would only take notice. A great "Eagle" delivers him, an allusion to God's rescues in Exod. 19:4 and Rev. 12:14, and he is saved from a "Dungeon" like Jeremiah (Lam. 3:55).

LAPUTA, GLUBBDUBDRIB, AND LUGGNAGG, OR THE APOSTASY

In the first two voyages, Swift shows that his contemporaries have reduced themselves to something artificial and inhuman. In the third, he draws from the prophecies of the end-times to depict the growing apostasy—the same apostasy that he bemoans in his religious writings—the "falling away" that is to precede, St. Paul says, the coming of the Antichrist (2 Thess. 2:3).

In the opening scene, some Japanese pirates, among whom is a Dutchman of "some Authority," capture Gulliver and his crew. This is the only time in the entire book that Gulliver calls himself a *Christian.* He begs the Dutchman, "in Consideration of our being Christians and Protestants, of neighboring Countries, in strict Alliance," to intercede with the Japanese pirates. But the name *Christian* enrages the Dutchman, who turns and speaks to the Japanese captain with vehemence, "often using the word *Christianos*" (150). Since Japanese law forbade Christians to come near Japan on pain of death, the Dutchman—who evidently passes himself off as a non-Christian for the sake of trade—is asking that the English captives get the death penalty. When the Japanese captain decides to spare the lives of the English captives, Gulliver gently rebukes the Dutchman, saying he is "sorry to find more Mercy in a Heathen, than in a Brother Christian" (151). The name *Christian* once again enrages the Dutchman, who now prevails on the Japanese captain to set Gulliver adrift alone in a canoe.

Thus, at the start of the third voyage, Gulliver is persecuted for the name of *Christian,* but he reaches safety and sleeps "under the Shelter of a Rock"—an echo of Psalm 61:2–3 and another hint of providence. Later in the same voyage, however, Gulliver will call himself a "*Hollander;* because my Intentions were for *Japan,* and I knew the *Dutch* were the only *Europeans* permitted to enter into that Kingdom." He has seen that the Dutch in Japan pass themselves off as non-Christians, so by calling himself a "*Hollander,*" he implicitly denies the name of *Christian.* This is his first denial. Then, when he asks the Japanese emperor to excuse him from the test "imposed on my Countrymen of *trampling upon the Crucifix,*" and the emperor wonders aloud if he is "a real *Hollander*" and not "a CHRISTIAN," Gulliver remains silent. This is his second denial. Finally, while he is traveling home on the Dutch ship *Amboyna*—a name that represents the massacre of English merchants by Dutch rivals in the spice trade in the 1620s—he is "often asked by some of the Crew" if he has trampled the crucifix. He answers equivocally, saying that he has "satisfied the Emperor and the Court in all Particulars." Thus he leads them to think he has performed a ritual that the Japanese (not knowing about European iconoclasm) regard as an abjuration of Christianity itself. This is his third denial. Swift had studied St. Cyprian in the 1690s,[39] so he knew that in the treatise on the "Lapsed," Cyprian said that Christians who bought certificates saying they had already sacrificed to idols were "not free from crime," even if they had not engaged in the act of apostasy. Gulliver is like those equivocating Christians when he lets the Dutch believe that he has renounced his religion.

The two encounters with apostate Dutchmen on each end of the third voyage provide a frame for Gulliver's visits to Laputa, the Academy of Lagado, Glubbdubdrib, and Luggnagg. All these places have a connection with apostasy. The king of Laputa is a figure of the Antichrist in being able to "raise the Island above the Region of Clouds and Vapours," an echo of a prophecy applied to the Antichrist: "I will ascend above the heights of the clouds: I will be like the Most High" (Isa. 14:14). By preventing the sun and rain from falling on rebellious towns, this king punishes his subjects with famine and pestilence, two biblical judgments reserved for God. Laputa is the modern state as the Whore of Babylon— a flying island detached from the church, which is the "ground of truth" in scripture (1 Tim. 3:15). In the illustration Swift provides, there are Christian churches on the ground below Laputa, as shown by steeples with small crosses dotting the continent of Balnibarbi. We learn that the flying island could "fall to the Ground" if it descended abruptly on towns with "high Spires or Pillars of Stone" (i.e., Christian churches), for these can crack the "Bottom or under Surface of the Island" (164). The phrase *under surface,* which is a mordant substitute for *foundation,* refers to the Settlement of 1689, the basis of the eighteenth-century government.

The apostasy of Laputa has resulted in a sense of looming natural disaster. The educated people on the island fear that the sun will soon "give no more light" and that a comet will set the earth on fire in thirty-one years—*Gulliver's Travels* was published in 1726, and Halley had predicted a comet would return in 1758. The Laputans cannot sleep for fear, or enjoy life (158–59). Gulliver reports this in a scientific tone and coolly gives the size of the comet's tail that will set the earth on fire. But Swift surely expects his readers to recall these biblical passages—that the Whore (*La Puta*) "shall be utterly burned with fire" (Rev. 18:8), that the sun shall be "darkened" and stars "fall from heaven" (Matt. 24:29–30), and that "men's hearts" shall fail them "for fear, and for looking after those things which are coming on the earth" (Luke 21:26). The Laputans mirror these scriptures perfectly: they foresee a dying sun, a comet falling from heaven, and a fiery doom for them, so that their hearts fail them for fear.

One result of apostasy is to fall into absurd beliefs. For all their science, the Laputans place "great Faith in judicial Astrology," only "they are ashamed to own it publickly." Again, this echoes a biblical prophecy applied long before to the City of Antichrist: "Let now the astrologers, the stargazers, the monthly prognosticators, stand up, and save thee from *these things* that shall come upon thee. Behold, they shall be as stubble; the fire shall burn them" (Isa. 47:13). In a treatise on the Antichrist, the primitive church father Hippolytus applied this verse from Isaiah to the Whore, the City of Antichrist (211).

Gulliver leaves the island after two months and visits the Academy of Lagado, a place founded forty years earlier after some men spent a few months on the flying island and came back eager to revolutionize "all Arts, Sciences, Languages, and Mechanicks" (169). In scripture, the Whore makes "the inhabitants of the earth drunk" (Rev. 17:2). The projectors always meet with failure, but they never doubt that they will succeed, provided they have enough money and time. In the first two voyages, Gulliver attributes everything to Chance. Now in the third voyage, he sees projects that rely on Chance: a sundial put on a weathervane so the motions of earth and sun can be reconciled with the chance motions of wind; a "raffle for Employments" so senators can blame Chance for their disappointments; a machine made for writing books by chance arrangement of words; and a blind person mixing colors randomly for painters (172, 174, 180). In Lagado, the Laws of Nature are resolved into Chance.

In the school of languages, there is a project that bodes ill for religion and virtue (beyond the utilitarian)—it is a plan to get rid of all words on the ground that "Words are only Names for *Things*." In one swoop, all faith in the supernatural could be wiped out. Tellingly, "many of the most Learned" in that land already follow the "new Scheme," while "the Women in Conjunction with the Vulgar and Illiterate" threaten to rebel if not allowed to speak "after the Manner of their Forefathers" (175–76). Again, the common people are the last bastion of humanity, but Gulliver condemns them as the "Enemies to Science." Also related to religion is the project in which a certain proposition is written on "a thin Wafer, with Ink composed of a Cephalick Tincture," and students are forced to swallow it on a "fasting Stomach" so the proposition will mount to their brains (176–77). Swift wants us to observe in this materialist version of transubstantiation that those who reject the sacrament of the High Church will embrace a sacrament like this one.

After Lagado, Gulliver visits Glubbdubdrib, where a sorcerer pretends to raise "the Dead" for twenty-four hours. At his bidding, the ancient and modern dead appear, answer his commands, and disappear "with a Turn of his Finger" (183). Gulliver soon follows his example and raises the dead. Now the primitive father Tertullian speaks of such "sorcerers" as creating a "lying wonder" in the manner of Antichrist, because "all souls are kept in Hades until the resurrection."[40] Victorinus, another primitive father, warns that Antichrist will create delusions and make "even the dead appear to rise again."[41] Swift alludes to both Tertullian and Victorinus in his writings.[42] When he calls up Brutus and grows rapturous at the sight of this ancient hero, we see how self-deluded Gulliver is: only a little while ago he was tempting the giant king to tyranny by offering him gunpowder, and soon he will be licking the dust before the tyrant of Luggnagg, yet here he is, pretending he cherishes liberty. Of course, he admires a virtue here that costs him nothing.

That Gulliver has no hope of a resurrection is confirmed in the next episode of the Struldbruggs. As soon as he hears of people who never die, he falls into raptures and declares that he has already worked out a scheme of how he would spend the first two centuries. He speaks of the "natural Desire of endless Life and sublunary Happiness" (196), but Richard Fiddes, a clergyman whom Swift knew and approved, had written that the desire of not dying was no longer natural after the Fall, for now, to seek for life and immortality on earth was "to seek the Living among the Dead."[43] The episode of the Struldbruggs is truly apocalyptic. It is one of the last steps in the descent to end-times, for St. John writes, "In those days shall men seek death, and shall not find it; and shall desire to die, and death shall flee from them" (Rev. 9:6). The Struldbruggs indeed envy those who can die and find rest. Gulliver's fantasy of an earthbound immortality ends with his accepting death without any hope of immortality. He says he would like to bring home two Struldbruggs "to arm our People against the Fear of Death" (199), implying that these ghastly creatures are needed to help his countrymen face their personal extinction.

After the king of Laputa and the sorcerer, the third figure of Antichrist in this voyage is the king of Luggnagg. When Gulliver comes before him, he crawls on his belly and "licks the dust" before the king. It had been prophesied that foreigners would prostrate themselves to the Messiah with "their face toward the earth" and would "lick up the dust" (Isa. 49:23, Ps. 72:9, Mic. 7:17), but now a tyrant demands this supreme homage. He is far from being a messiah, for he kills his subjects without warning and perverts justice by not punishing murder. Gulliver "cannot altogether approve" his doings, and yet he becomes the tyrant's favorite during a three-month stay. For unmentioned (unmentionable?) services, he receives 444 large pieces of gold and a diamond worth £1,100 on his departure to England. The king also makes him "very honourable offers," though he chooses to go back to his wife.

Luggnagg's king has an image that speaks for him (alluding to Rev. 14) and shows him as "*A King lifting up a lame Beggar from the Earth*" (200). These words—*lifting, lame,* and *beggar*—are all found in Acts 3:1–7, where St. Peter, in the name of Christ, heals a lame beggar. In this image, the king lays claim to miraculous powers bequeathed to the Apostles (Matt. 10:8). In the first London edition (1726), this section has only two phrases in italics, and on facing pages—"*A King lifting up a lame Beggar from the Earth,*" and "*trampling upon the Crucifix.*" Swift invites us to compare the two images—a tyrant exalted to the sky, and a God humbled to the dust. At the end of the voyage, Gulliver carries for his deliverance the seal of the king of Luggnagg on a letter to the emperor of Japan and lets everyone think he has trampled the crucifix, the Christian seal of deliverance.

HOUYNHNMLAND, OR THE SOCIETY OF VIRTUOUS ATHEISTS[44]

In the fourth voyage, Gulliver travels to the future and visits Britain again, only now it is a society where Horses rule. Psalm 32:9 warns: "Be ye not as the horse, or as the mule, which have no understanding." St. Augustine explains that the horse in this verse represents philosophers who refuse to worship God or acknowledge his providence.[45] In addition, John Donne devotes an entire sermon to Psalm 32:9, identifying the horse with modern philosophers who pursue virtue without "a Church and Sacraments" and end up with "the Horses pride."[46] The High Churchman Lancelot Andrewes also speaks of the atheist as an "untamed horse" to be "held with bit and bridle."[47] So the Horse can be a symbol of the atheist. But where scripture warns, "Be ye *not* as the horse," Gulliver is so deluded that he exhorts us throughout this voyage to "be as the horse." St. Paul prophesies that after the "falling away" of apostasy will come a "strong delusion" and the belief in "a lie" (2 Thess. 2:1–12). This lie is Houyhnhnmland.

The key to this voyage comes at the end, when Swift alludes to the Trojan Horse. He does it at the point where Gulliver declares that his "Maxim" for the rest of his life will be to imitate the Horses and "strictly adhere to Truth." Just then, Swift exposes him. For Gulliver confirms his "Maxim" right away by quoting in Latin the words of the most colossal liar known in Western literature—the perjured Sinon, from Book II of the *Aeneid:* "Nor if cruel fortune has made Sinon miserable, shall she also make him false and deceitful" (262). In this passage Swift drops his mask entirely. For if Gulliver's truth is comparable to Sinon's, then everything he has said is a lie, and especially about the Horse. For Sinon, by his treacherous tale and avowals of sincerity, persuaded his listeners to take the Trojan Horse into their city and bring about their own destruction. Swift's concluding message is loud and clear: Gulliver is *gulling* you into accepting a Trojan Horse. Do not believe Bayle and Tindall when they say that the atheist is the supreme model of virtue and that a society of virtuous atheists is best of all.

In his answer to Tindall in 1708, around the time he told his kinsman he had designed *Gulliver's Travels,* Swift used certain animals to symbolize the chief atheists of the past century. He wrote that "Socinus, Hobbes, and Spinosa" are "the Bull, the Elephant, the Horse, and the Bear."[48] Plainly, Swift saw the Horse as symbolizing one branch of modern atheism, and by placing Spinoza and the Horse in third place, he invited the reader to connect them. It is known that Swift regarded Spinoza as the chief source of atheism in his day and that he owned not only the *Tractatus,* where Spinoza had launched an unprecedented attack on the Bible (Swift's annotated copy survives in Ireland), but also the *Ethics,* where Spinoza had questioned the superiority of man to animals—a major theme in the fourth voyage.[49] Tindall also depicted the modern atheist as a Horse trying to throw off his "old Rider," the clergy. Tindall cited another atheist who lamented that the clergy still "bridle us, they saddle us, they harness us, they spur us."[50] And so, the Horse was a symbol of atheism even for the atheists themselves. It is telling that Gulliver's project at the end of the *Travels* is the same as Tindall's: to keep Horses as "Strangers to Bridle or Saddle" (261).

After Spinoza died in 1678, his disciples proposed him as a pattern of moral perfection.[51] So when Gulliver says that "The Word *Houyhnhnm* in their Tongue, signifies a *Horse;* and in its Etymology, the *Perfection of Nature,*" Swift glances at this new idea of the atheist as the ultimate model of virtue. Gulliver uses the term *imitation* pointedly in chapter 10, when he says he will spend the rest of his life proposing the "Virtues" of the Horse for "the Imitation of Mankind" (253). The *Imitatio Christi* of Thomas à Kempis was popular and had appeared in Swift's lifetime in several editions. Now Swift, in his religious writings, declares that a virtuous atheist is an impossibility, for without grace or hope of heaven, an atheist cannot rise above utilitarianism, which is only self-interest writ large. We see this in Gulliver, who does whatever cruel thing is useful to him in the fourth voyage—as when he kills adult Yahoos to use their skins as a covering for his canoe, and then kills infant Yahoos to stitch their skins together for his sail. Self-preservation is the measure of virtue for him, and the more cruel he is, the more he vaunts his virtue. In Lilliput he was against persecution, but now he is for it.

For who are the Yahoos? During most of the voyage, Gulliver tricks us into seeing them as mere animals with human shapes. But near the end, he lets us know, as if it were minor information, that their ancestors were shipwrecked Europeans. But the question is, How did Europeans come to live like animals without a language? Gulliver informs us in chapter 9 that after the Yahoos came to the island, they began to multiply. The Horses resented their growing numbers—for they themselves are careful never to have more than two offspring—and so they suddenly attacked the Yahoos without warning, in what they called their great "Hunting." In that revolution they killed all the Yahoos who could speak and left only infants to be raised as slaves. So when Gulliver arrives, the Horses have had Yahoo slaves for many years. Swift may have found a hint for the Horses' great Hunting in the primitive church father Commodianus, who wrote that the "obscene horses" of Antichrist would slaughter Christians with "kicking heel."[52] Likewise, in Rev. 13, the "Beast" makes "war with the Saints" and wins a temporary victory.

The island Yahoos are a vision of Europe's future. This is the coming "tribulation" of which scripture warns: "Then shall be a great tribulation, such as was not from the beginning of the world to this time, no, nor ever shall be" (Matt. 24:24). The martyrs of the primitive church were called evil, too, and dressed in animal skins to make their deaths in the Coliseum look ridiculous. But the Yahoos are in an even worse state— they are reduced to living, not just dying, like animals. Even so, the Horses hate them so much that the only topic ever debated in their Great Assembly is, "Whether the *Yahoos* should be exterminated from the Face of the Earth" (245).

By the start of chapter 5, Gulliver applies the name *Yahoo* explicitly to *Christendom,* as when he says that "the greatest Powers of *Christendom*" were engaged in a war that killed about a "Million of *Yahoos*" (224). This is the only time in the *Travels* that he uses the word *Christendom,* and he does it pointedly to equate European Christians with the hated Yahoos. After he leaves the island, he will reserve the name *Yahoo* for Europeans, for when he sails to "New Holland," he calls the inhabitants there *natives* and *savages,* not *Yahoos,* but as soon as the Portuguese sailors arrive, he calls them *Yahoos.* The word *Yahoo* derives from Yahweh,[53] as in the name of the Israeli politician Netanyahu. The letters YH, meaning I Am, are the first half of the Tetragrammaton and are found in the name of Christ, *Yehoshua,* which means, Yahu saves. In Rev. 13:6, we read that Antichrist will open "his mouth in blasphemy against God, to blaspheme His Name." This is what happens in Houyhnhnmland—the name *Yahoo* is equated with evil and constantly combined with other words to describe everything bad (249).

With this in mind, we should consider that perhaps much of what the Master Horse and Gulliver say about Yahoos is atheist ideology. For these dialogues hold a mirror up to the writings of Bayle, who presented European history as a tale of unrelieved and monstrous evil and divided Europeans into two groups—the enlightened few (Houyhnhnms) and a multitude of "groveling Wretches" (Christians) with "only the Shape of Men."[54] Of course, Swift has it both ways: he lashes the vices of Europeans through the mouths of Gulliver and the Horse, and at the same time warns Europeans of the tribulation in store if their apostasy continues and atheists come to rule over them. Yet he knows that Christian virtue survives somewhere, so he introduces the saintly Portuguese Captain Pedro de Mendez as a pattern of true virtue, in contrast to the Houyhnhnms, who are talking animals with no hope of eternal life, and consequently only a utilitarian type of virtue.

While in Houyhnhnmland, Gulliver comes to believe that humans were once quadrupeds who became deformed by walking upright. The primitive church taught, on the contrary, that God designed human beings to walk upright so they would fix their eyes on heaven.[55] Gulliver starts to loathe his "own Form" and to recall his absent family and friends with revulsion, because they are "*Yahoos* in Shape and Disposition" (251). In this passage, Swift hints that Gulliver has become the disciple of Spinoza, a pantheist who denied that God ever granted Adam dominion over the animals. Indeed, Spinoza taught that the idea of such a dominion is the source of all "prejudices concerning good and evil, merit and sin, praise and blame, order and disorder, beauty and deformity."[56] He saw that traditional religion and morality rested on this foundation, and he shook the foundation by calling the human race only a modification of Nature, like the other animal species, a variation on a single, infinite substance. At the start of the last voyage, Gulliver thinks the Horses might be sorcerers who have changed their shapes, but by the end he believes that there is no substantial difference between a Man and a Horse.

When Swift lets down his mask at the end and identifies Gulliver with the perjurer Sinon, he reveals that *Gulliver's Travels* is about a new Trojan Horse—the exaltation of the atheist in the place of Christ as the supreme model of virtue. The whole design of the *Travels*—which is all of a piece with Swift's religious writings—is an apocalyptic descent toward this idolatry of Antichrist. The degeneracy of Lilliput leads to the apostasy of Laputa (a sign of the end-times in Luke 18:8—"When the Son of Man cometh, shall he find faith on the earth?") Then the apostasy of the third voyage leads to the rule of the Beast, who comes with a "strong delusion, that they should believe a lie" (2 Thess. 2:11). Gulliver is seduced, and he witnesses the "great tribulation" without a trace of pity, even joining in on the persecution. What Swift's kinsman writes about the *Project to Advance Religion* could be said about *Gulliver's Travels,* which was designed around that same year: "Dr Swift appears in the character of a great inspired prophet" and "rebuketh all ranks of men for their depravities and corruptions, their profaneness, their blasphemy and irreligion" in an attempt to give "remedies against that torrent of iniquity."[57]

NOTES

1. Irvin Ehrenpreis, *Swift: The Man, His Works, and the Age,* 3 vols. (Cambridge, MA: Harvard University Press, 1983), 3:459.
2. Deane Swift, *An Essay upon the Life, Writings and Character of Dr Jonathan Swift* (New York, London: Garland, 1974; repr., London: Charles Bathurst, 1755), 280.
3. *Argument against Abolishing Christianity,* in *The Prose Works of Jonathan Swift,* ed. Herbert Davis (Oxford: Basil Blackwell, 1957), 2:27. Hereafter this edition will be cited as *PW.*
4. *A Project for Advancement of Religion, PW,* 2:60.
5. *On the Testimony of Conscience, PW,* 9:150–51.
6. *On the Trinity, PW,* 9:167–68, 162.
7. *Letter to a Young Gentleman, PW,* 9:73.
8. *On the Trinity, PW,* 9:164–66.
9. *Remarks upon a Book, PW,* 2:89.
10. *Remarks upon a Book intituled "The Rights of the Christian Church," PW,* 2:75–82. Swift echoes the Tory historian Robert Brady in making this point, as well as when he adds that what Whigs call their immemorial "rights" are to be traced no farther back than the concessions of the Norman conqueror.
11. *Mr. C[olli]ns's Discourse of Free-Thinking, PW,* 4:34.
12. *Further Thoughts, PW,* 9:264.
13. Jonathan Swift, *Gulliver's Travels,* ed. Christopher Fox (Boston, New York: Bedford Books of St. Martin's Press, 1995), 137. Pages to this edition will be given in the text.
14. *Concerning that Universal Hatred, which Prevails against the Clergy, PW,* 13:125.
15. *The Poor Man's Contentment, PW,* 9:190.
16. *On Mutual Subjection, PW,* 9:144.
17. *Remarks upon a Book, PW,* 2:105.
18. *The True Notion of the Catholick Church, in a Letter to the late Bishop of Meaux, written by the reverend Mr. Charles Lesley* (September 26, 1703), in *Several Letters* (London: Richard Sare, 1705), 313–20. On p. 319 Lesley makes the same point as Swift about colleges.
19. *A Preface to the B[isho]p of S[a]r[u]m's Introduction to the Third Volume of the History of the Reformation of the Church of England, by Gregory Misosarum, PW,* 4:79.

20. *On the Trinity, PW,* 9:163.

21. *On the Testimony of Conscience, PW,* 9:154.

22. *On Sleeping in Church, PW,* 9:215.

23. *Three Prayers Used by the Dean for Mrs Johnson, in her last sickness, 1727, PW,* 9:254.

24. *On False Witness, PW,* 9:185.

25. Pierre Rétat, *Le Dictionnaire de Bayle et la lutte philosophique au XVIIIe siècle* (Paris: Audin, 1971), 37, 200. The virtuous atheist was the incarnate negation of the necessity for natural religion. Like Swift, Cardinal de Bernis, in *La Religion Vengée* (1737), created an imaginary isle of atheists à la Bayle.

26. *Mr. Collins's Discourse, PW,* 4:41.

27. *Remarks upon a Book, PW,* 2:73.

28. *Letter to a Young Gentleman, PW,* 9:79.

29. *On the Trinity, PW,* 9:165–66.

30. *On the Testimony of Conscience, PW,* 9:153, 157–58.

31. *Preface to the Bishop of Sarum, PW,* 4:63.

32. In his own library, Swift had Henry More's interpretation. See Dirk F. Passmann and Heinz J. Vienken, eds. *The Library and Reading of Jonathan Swift. Part I: Swift's Library in Four Volumes* (Frankfurt, etc: Lang H/M., 2003), 2:1283. He had access to Brightman's in his friend Thomas Sheridan's library.

33. "Whoso eateth my flesh, and drinketh my blood, hath eternal life; and I will raise him up at the last day." Calvinists applied this text to the word of Christ, not the Sacrament.

34. *On the Testimony of Conscience, PW,* 9:151.

35. Deane Swift, *An Essay upon the Life,* 181, 116, 372.

36. *On the Trinity, PW,* 9:164.

37. *On the Martyrdom of King Charles I, PW,* 9:225.

38. [Francis Gastrell], *The Principles of Deism Truly Represented* (1708), 2nd ed. (London: W. and J. Innys, 1722), 63. This is spoken by a sceptic in a dialogue with a Deist.

39. Camille Looten, *La Pensée religieuse de Swift et ses antinomies* (Lille, Paris: Desclée, 1935), 40.

40. Tertullian, *A Treatise on the Soul* (chap. 57), trans. Peter Holmes, in *Ante-Nicene Fathers,* 10 vols., Alexander Roberts and James Donaldson, eds. (Peabody, MA: Hendrickson, 1995; repr., 1886), 3:234.

41. Victorinus, *Commentary on the Apocalypse* (chap. 13), trans. Robert Ernest Wallis, in *Ante-Nicene Fathers,* 7:356.

42. Looten, *Pensée religieuse,* 43. While he recognizes Swift's allusions to these fathers, Looten is not convinced that Swift actually studied them. But Patrick Delany, who was close by, says that Swift renewed his Greek and Latin and studied "the early fathers" between 1714 and 1721. See *Observations upon Lord Orrery's Remarks on the Life and Writings of Dr Jonathan Swift* (London: W. Reeve and A. Linde, 1754), 100–01.

43. *The Doctrine of a Future State . . . in a Second Letter to a Free-Thinker* (London: J. Pemberton, 1721), 59–60.

44. This is adapted from my essay "'Be ye as the horse!'—Swift, Spinoza, and the Society of Virtuous Atheists," *SP* XCVII (Spring 2000), 229–53.

45. "Sermon 76" in *Sermons on Selected Lessons of the New Testament,* trans. R. G. MacMillen, in *Nicene and Post-Nicene Fathers,* 1st ser., 14 vols., ed. Philip Schaff (Peabody, MA: Hendrickson, 1995; repr., Oxford 1886), 6:482.

46. *The Sermons of John Donne,* Evelyn M. Simpson and George R. Potter, eds., 10 vols. (Berkeley, Los Angeles: University of California Press, 1958), 9:379.

47. *The Works of Lancelot Andrewes,* 11 vols. (New York: AMS Press, 1967; repr., Oxford 1841), 2:9.

48. *Remarks upon a Book, PW,* 2:72.

49. *Spinoza's Ethic, Demonstrated in Geometrical Order,* W. Hale White and Amelia Hutchinson Stirling, eds., 4th ed. (London: Humphrey Milford and Oxford University Press, 1937), 1st pt., app., 38–41.

50. *The Rights of the Christian Church Asserted,* 4th ed. (London, 1709), 221, 257.

51. Pierre Bayle, in the 1683 ed. of *Pensées diverses,* and Jean Maximilien Lucas, in *The Life of the Late Mr. De Spinosa,* in *The Oldest Biography of Spinoza,* ed. A. Wolf (London: Allen and Unwin [1927]).

52. *The Instructions of Commodianus* (chap. 42), trans. Robert Ernest Wallis, in *Ante-Nicene Fathers,* 4:211.

53. See Herbert Zirker's essay, "Horse Sense and Sensibility: Some Issues Concerning Utopian Understanding in *Gulliver's Travels,*" *Swift Studies* 12 (1997): 85–98.

54. William Law, *Remarks upon a Late Book* (London, 1724), 105, 18, 53.

55. Lactantius, *The Divine Institutes* (bk. 7, chap. 5), in *Ante-Nicene Fathers,* 7:201. Lactantius deduces from this that immortality "is not the consequence of nature, but the reward and recompense of virtue."

56. *Spinoza's Ethic,* 1st pt., app., 38–41; 3rd pt., 104.

57. Swift, *An Essay upon the Life,* 141.

CHAPTER 4

The "Aesthetics" of Fundamentalism in Recent Jewish Fiction in English

Axel Stähler

In the minds of many Westerners, Muslim fundamentalism has replaced communism as perhaps the greatest single "threat" to the existing world order. From this perspective the Palestinian intifada becomes just another episode in a "clash of civilizations." For them, there is an intrinsic link between Palestinian "terrorism" and, say, the al-Qaeda bombing of an American warship off Yemen. Almost totally absent from such arguments is any inclination to examine Jewish fundamentalism, or so much as to ask whether it, too, might be a factor in the conflict over Palestine, one of the reasons why it seems so insoluble.

There is, in fact, a great ignorance of, or indifference to, this whole subject in the outside world, and not least in the United States. This is due at least in part to that general reluctance of the mainstream American media to subject Israel to the same searching scrutiny to which it would other states and societies, and especially when the issue in question is as sensitive, as emotionally charged, as this one is. But, in the view of the late Israel Shahak, it reflects particularly badly on an American Jewry which, with its ingrained, institutionalized aversion to finding fault with Israel, turns a blind eye to what Israelis like himself viewed with disgust and alarm, and unceasingly said so.

American Jews, especially Orthodox ones, are generous financiers of the shock troops of fundamentalism, the religious settlers; indeed a good 10 percent of these, and among the most extreme, violent, and sometimes patently deranged, are actually immigrants from America.[1]

David Hirst's observations, published in the American newsweekly *The Nation* in 2004 and extracted from the latest edition of his *The Gun and the Olive Branch: The Roots of Violence in the Middle East* (1977; 3rd rev. ed. 2003), were strongly disapproved of by some representatives of American Jewry. Abraham H. Foxman, national director of the Anti-Defamation League, maintained in a letter to the editor that "David Hirst's absurd thesis of so-called 'Jewish fundamentalism' as a threat to the world order and the leading factor in the Israeli-Palestinian conflict has nothing to do with the reality of the Israeli political structure" and, after emphasizing the commitment of the State of Israel to its democratic values, Foxman in conclusion reiterated "the threat posed by the religious fundamentalists in countries such as Saudi Arabia and Iran" instead.[2]

However, the phenomenon of "so-called" Jewish fundamentalism is a concern not at all exclusive to Hirst. Published one and a half decades earlier and one of the first book-length studies on Jewish fundamentalism in Israel in English was Ian S. Lustick's *For the Land and the Lord: Jewish Fundamentalism in Israel*[3] in which the political scientist had already argued that "[d]espite divisions on the Arab side, and the intransigence of many Palestinians, it is the Jewish fundamentalist movement that has emerged as the greatest obstacle to meaningful negotiations toward a comprehensive Arab-Israeli peace settlement."[4] Lustick's study, significantly, "originated in a research paper written under contract for the Defense Academic Research Support Program of the United States Department of Defense."[5] Since then, occasioned no doubt by the resurgence of fundamentalisms and their proximity to terrorism, a flood of publications not only on Islamic and Christian fundamentalisms but also on Jewish fundamentalism (some of them comparative) has appeared in print, most notable among them in the Jewish context, perhaps, *Jewish Fundamentalism in Israel* (1999) by Norton Mezvinsky and Israel Shahak, to whom Hirst refers as well.[6]

Little, or no attention is given in these studies to the interrelations between fundamentalisms and fiction. And yet, even before academic interest in the rather recent phenomenon of modern Jewish fundamentalism in Israel noticeably manifested itself in the English-speaking world, anglophone Jewish writers acknowledged its topicality and its attraction for the relatively small number of American Jewish immigrants to Israel. Indeed, fundamentalism, particularly Jewish fundamentalism, seems to have become a salient topic in Jewish fiction in English in recent years. Especially since the Lebanon War in 1982, a number of Jewish authors writing in English and engaging themselves in debates about the moral integrity of the State of Israel and about Jewish identities have addressed the rise of Jewish fundamentalism in Israel. In this chapter, I propose to discuss this emerging pattern (as opposed to the more familiar topic of Jewish Orthodoxy) with reference to novels by Philip Roth, Tova Reich, Melvin Jules Bukiet, and (in several ways the odd one out) Simon Louvish. I argue that each of the novels under consideration here is based on the assumption that fundamentalism, however misguided, is in some way part and parcel of the "Jewish condition," or even of the *condition humaine,* and—although this dilemma cannot be resolved—needs to be confronted as such.

As anticipated by Alvin H. Rosenfeld as early as 1973,[7] during the last three decades the confrontation with Judaism has gained more and more prominence in anglophone, particularly American, Jewish literature. Writing in 1991, Miriyam Glazer confirmed Rosenfeld's suggestion that there was emerging a new Jewish "literature of the theological imagination,"[8] and in the intervening years this trend seems to have lost nothing of its momentum.[9] Prominent among those writers who have recently engaged in their fiction with Judaism (most of them, quite intriguingly, women writers) are, for instance, Tova Reich, Pearl Abraham, Allegra Goodman, Tova Mirvis, Aryeh Lev Stollman, and, with uncharacteristic success for an anglophone writer from Israel, Naomi Ragen, whose best-selling novels—in which the author (who emigrated to Israel from the United States in 1971) explores the world of ultra-Orthodox Jewry—are hugely popular in the United States.

While fundamentalism in many respects appears to be a trait particular to the religious, it is important to keep in mind that, as Lustick argues, it is not exclusively so but "is conceived as a style of political participation characterized by unusually close and direct links between one's fundamental beliefs and political behavior designed to effect radical change."[10] Accordingly, in the further discussion of the subject I will adopt as a working definition of fundamentalism that suggested by Lustick, who, for the purposes of his own study, defines a "belief system" as fundamentalist "*insofar as its adherents regard its tenets as uncompromisable and direct transcendental imperatives to political action oriented toward the rapid and comprehensive reconstruction of society.*"[11] [author's italics]

Jewish fundamentalism in Israel appears to manifest itself predominantly in two distinct and irreconcilable varieties: nationalist-religious and ultra-Orthodox. The "operational objective" of Jewish nationalist-religious fundamentalists in Israel, as summed up by Lustick, is

> to accelerate the pace at which the Jewish people fulfills its destiny. This includes, for most of these activists, establishment of Jewish sovereignty over the entire, biblically described, Land of Israel, substitution of "authentically

Jewish" forms of governance for Western-style liberal democracy, and rebuilding the Temple in Jerusalem, thereby implementing the divinely ordained, albeit long-delayed, messianic redemption.[12]

It is quite important to note that while the fulfillment of all these objectives is considered essential for the advancement of redemption, Jewish (and that does not necessarily mean Israeli) sovereignty over the whole of the Land of Israel (*Eretz Yisrael hashelema*) is the necessary prerequisite for all the others. Hence, the territorial gains of the Six Day War of 1967, which "restored" to Israel not only the Gaza Strip and the Golan Heights but also, more importantly, the biblical lands of Judea and Samaria (more commonly known as the West Bank) and the Eastern part of Jerusalem, were interpreted by fundamentalists—both Jewish and Christian—as a sign of the beginning of redemption (*at'halta d'geulah*). This explains why Jewish fundamentalism in Israel began to emerge as a recognizable force only in the aftermath of this war, although its antecedents reach much further back into history.[13] The shock of the Yom Kippur War just a few years later, in 1973, which despite Israel's eventual, and dearly bought, victory exposed the nation's vulnerability and the (alleged) incompetence of the ruling Labour Alignment, precipitated the formation of an organized fundamentalist movement and prepared the ground for the political ascendance of Menachem Begin and the Revisionist Zionism of the right-wing Likud coalition in 1977.

Best known among the various fundamentalist groups in Israel and arguably for a long time politically the most influential is, perhaps, the Gush Emunim (the Bloc of the Faithful), which was established in 1974 and which (more or less in collusion with successive Likud governments and other nationalist-religious parties since 1977) promotes Jewish settlement in the occupied territories. This movement receives its theological inspiration largely from the teachings of Rabbi Abraham Isaac Kook (1865–1935; a.k.a. Rav Kook), the first Ashkenazi Chief Rabbi of Palestine, and, more particularly, his son Rabbi Tzvi Yehuda Kook (1891–1982; a.k.a. Rav Tzvi Yehuda), who elaborated on his father's ideas and, by virtue of his charisma, assumed a leading role in the movement. It was especially Rav Tzvi Yehuda who, by "linking specific political events (the Six Day War and the Yom Kippur War) and concrete political programs (Jewish settlement and annexation of the occupied territories) to the divine plan for the final redemption,"[14] provided authoritative imperatives of what has been called the "Zionism of Redemption" (Hanan Porat).[15]

When in 1982 the Israeli town of Yamit in the Sinai was dismantled prior to the peninsula being returned to Egypt in accordance with the

Camp David Accords of 1978/1979, Gush Emunim's futile intervention only weeks after Rav Tzvi Yehuda's death precipitated a severe crisis for the movement. The question of how to advance their cause more effectively proved to be a divisive issue. While some of its adherents were in favor of gaining broad support from the Israeli public with a campaign of "political and cultural outreach,"[16] others urged direct and decisive action to promote redemption against all opposition—if need be, violent action.[17]

Also very much opposed to the promotion of redemption is Haredi fundamentalism in Israel, largely ignored by Lustick in his study.[18] The term, which means "God-Fearer," refers to a "variety of groups making up the ultra-Orthodox wing of Judaism."[19] Although also messianic in outlook, Haredi doctrine differs from nationalist-religious fundamentalist ideology as embodied by the Gush Emunim most substantially in the related questions of the beginning of redemption and of human agency. Haredim strictly refuse to acknowledge the alleged beginning of redemption (the victory of the Six Day War is of no significance to them in this context) and strongly oppose to Zionism, because, in their view, redemption cannot be promoted otherwise than by an observant life. For this reason, they are even prepared to cede territory to save Jewish lives. These seemingly moderate views, however, as Shahak and Mezvinsky have pointed out, are situated within an ideological superstructure that is no less inflexible and intransigent than that of nationalist-religious Jews.[20] The Haredi operational objective is the establishment of a theocracy and the strict enforcement of the *Halacha* (the Jewish law) in Israel.[21]

When Glazer confirmed Rosenfeld's suggestion that there was emerging a new Jewish "literature of the theological imagination,"[22] she referred to Anne Roiphe's *Lovingkindness* (1987) as "the most problematic and controversial" of its kind, an assessment accounted for by the critical reception the novel received in the American press.[23] In this novel, Roiphe explores in great detail the transitional state of the "returnee," to the Jewish faith and to Israel. Through her story, the reader witnesses the metamorphosis of the narrator's daughter from an insecure American dropout girl into an Orthodox Jewish woman living in a women's yeshiva in Jerusalem and, finally, into another returnee's wife. Confronted with the emerging "other" in her daughter, and against her innermost resistance, the narrator (who, to some degree, appears to be an alter ego of the author)[24] finally comes not only to accept her daughter's decision but also, having relearned "cultural relativism" and having been made aware of her own spiritual dearth by recurrent dreams of Rabbi Nachman of Bratslav, finds herself compelled to reconsider her own existence as a secular and feminist Jewish–American intellectual.[25]

"I am different from when you last saw me,"[26] Annie's daughter tells her on the phone, calling unexpectedly from Israel. A difficult child, Andrea suffered from eating disorder, indulged in self-mutilation, and had three abortions. "Please call me Sarai," she now writes in a letter to her mother, "I have changed my name to one in keeping with my new life" (7). Her choice of name denotes a new beginning that envisions perpetual growth and redemption in fulfillment of the covenant, the transformation from barren Andrea, in both spiritual and physical senses of the word, into Sarah, who after her initial barrenness became "the mother of us all" (67).

Suzy Durruty argues that Roiphe's novel is organized around the dichotomy of catastrophe and redemption and suggests that the territories of the United States and of Israel, respectively, embody that very dichotomy. She interprets America as an "espace du péché" and Israel as an "espace possible de la rédemption" and as a mirror highlighting the vices of American society.[27] It certainly is true that Annie is very self-critical and that she acknowledges the hollowness of the American way of life and even of her own feminism. Yet, in Israel to see her daughter, she feels "a stranger among strangers in an alien land" (260) and finally returns—not to the faith, at least not yet[28]—but to her own native United States.

Roiphe's novel is of interest in the present context not because of its portrayal of fundamentalists in Israel for, indeed, there is none: the religious men and women she describes are Orthodox, not fundamentalist, Jews—although the borderlines, to some extent, may be considered to be fluid.[29] *Lovingkindness* is relevant here rather because it addresses, in much detail, the lack of orientation among the younger generation of American Jews in the 1980s[30] and the political disappointment and spiritual dearth of their parents' generation. It thus serves to explain, to some extent, the phenomenon of the spiritual "return," which provides the motive to emigrate to Israel for a disproportionally high number of the altogether relatively few American Jews having made *aliyah* (Jewish immigration to the Land of Israel, literally "ascent" or "going up").

Arguably, in Tova Reich's *Master of the Return* (1988), the line between Orthodoxy and fundamentalism has been crossed.[31] The novel is set among the followers of a Hasidic sect in Israel whose objective is the restitution of the Temple Mount to the Jews and the erection of the Third Temple. With these pretensions, according to Lustick's definition, they appear to be fundamentalist rather than "merely" Orthodox. Reich explores with her description of this fundamentalist "groupuscule"[32]—latter-day followers of the very Rabbi Nachman of Bratslav (1772–1811) who also invades Annie's dreams—the phenomenon of the return both to the Land of Israel and to the Jewish faith, the *teshuva.*

Whoever accomplishes the *teshuva* is a *ba'al teshuva,* a "master of the return"—hence the novel's title. Yet, although the fundamentalist community she describes comprises Jews of various Ashkenazi backgrounds as well as Oriental Jews and descendants of those Jews who settled in Palestine prior to the Zionist immigration waves, Reich's particular focus is on *ba'alim teshuva* from the American diaspora. The significance of the concept of the *teshuva* for the negotiation of contemporary American Jewish identities that Reich projects in this as well as in her next novel, *The Jewish War* (1995), is confirmed by the fact that she received for her *Master of the Return* the prestigious Edward Lewis Wallant Award, established to honor outstanding works of fiction that have significance for the American Jew.

The journal of Shmuel Himmelhoch, addressed to his newborn son Akiva and presented in excerpts in the first part of the novel, records his various attempts, both spiritual and physical, at reaching the small Ukrainian town of Uman. Rabbi Nachman is interred in Uman and to his latter-day followers in Israel it has become a symbol of the purity to which they aspire. Shmuel, whose journal is therefore a record also of his attempts at "expunging every remnant of the defilement" that was in him before going about the task of creating his "new self"[33] (13), never quite reaches Uman. Instead, the corpse of the former hippie and light designer for "the most notorious rock groups" (4) is discovered close to the tomb of a revered rabbi some time after his journal has been found.

Rich in absurd detail, Reich's narrative subsequently describes the conveyance of the body by members, both male and female, of his sect to the cemetery in Safad. Shmuel's own obsession with purity, augmented by what appears to be a "fundamentalist" misogyny resting on the certainty of female impurity and the danger of women distracting the men from their thoughts of purity, is echoed in the conversations among the members of the cortege. A particularly bizarre instance is the debate over whether his crippled widow, Ivriyah, should be allowed to talk to the men about Shmuel. After a lengthy discussion, she is finally allowed to say a few words, provided that she cross the little stream and the men turn their backs toward her and do not gaze upon her (79). Yet after she has finished, it emerges that none of the men actually heard what she said, because, to be on the safe side, they stuffed their fingers into their ears, while the corpse was being carried away by an even more zealous yeshiva student who would not "permit" either himself or the deceased to listen to the voice of a woman (80).

The role of women, subject to the patriarchal mode adopted by the fundamentalist sect, is further explored in the following chapters, in which a wedding and a pilgrimage to Mount Sinai are narrated. There, the little boy Akiva and the Haredi Abba Nissim, apparently searching for him, go missing. The loss of the child is used by Reich to construe a reworking of the biblical narrative of the sacrifice of Isaac (the *akedah*), which she invokes as an archetype of both fundamentalist single-mindedness and the gender relations in fundamentalist communities. As the Bible has it, Sarah, when she learned that she was going to be pregnant, though well stricken in age, laughed within herself.[34] Sarah's laughter, Reich suggests, "was not from intellectual arrogance or common skepticism," but that,

> riding the keen edge of prophecy, she had seen that the child she would bear would not be hers at all; no, as soon as this child was weaned, the moment she released the child, he would be claimed by his father, by his faith-driven father, Abraham (239).

The attempted sacrifice of Isaac is the ultimate proof of Abraham's blind faith in his God and the final confirmation of the covenant that promises Abraham not only the multiplication of his seed but also "the land wherein thou art a stranger, all the land of Canaan, for an everlasting possession."[35]

In *Master of the Return* the *akedah* is literally reenacted. Abba Nissim, the Haredi abductor of Ivriyah's son Akiva, leads the boy secretly in the dawn of the second day of the Jewish calendar to Mount Moriah, where he prepares to perform the sacrifice. He is already wielding the blank steel when Israeli soldiers capture him. "God sees!" he cries ecstatically, referring to the name given to the site of the attempted sacrifice by Abraham,[36] and: "Now I see that God sees!" (237). For Abba Nissim the once more rejected sacrifice signifies the renewal of the covenant, and when shofar blasts pierce the morning air he believes redemption to be at hand. It is typical of Reich's satirical stance that those shofar blasts are produced by another rapturous soul seeing the commotion around Abba Nissim and Akiva and that the religious import of the whole episode is thus revealed to be ambivalent, to say the least.

In *Lovingkindness*, the sincerity of the transformation of Andrea into Sarai is questioned by her mother in various ways.[37] In *Master of the Return*, the returnees' way of life is more severely denounced as a mere pose by an emphatically secular character in the novel:

> You people aspire to becoming tragic figures, and you're even willing to incur the most hideous suffering to earn the right to assume that pose.

Or ecstatic figures, or mystic figures—whatever the role, it's nothing more than aesthetics. What does it have to do with faith? Not that you wouldn't like to believe. You wish for it ardently, you long for it, you strain for it, but for the most part you just don't have it in you. So you settle for the counterfeit of faith, for the style, the externals, the costume, which appeal to you so much aesthetically. And what aesthetics boils down to in the end . . . is nothing less than *avodah zarah*, idol worship. (226)

While this criticism does not, I believe, reflect the overall bias of the novel, the point it makes seems valid enough and, if it were true, would indeed present a serious challenge to the "fundamentals" of this particular brand of self-styled fundamentalists. For idol worship is, of course, not only a violation of the first and second commandments but also the most prominent among the reasons for the expulsion from the Promised Land; it is the ultimate breach of the covenant. Indeed, in the novel, the sect's hopes of the rebuilding of the Temple are dashed when their own headquarters in the Muslim quarter of Jerusalem adjacent to the Temple Mount is razed to the ground by the Israeli authorities and redemption is once more deferred.

In her next novel, *The Jewish War,* Reich returned to the subject of Jewish fundamentalism in Israel and, indeed, it is probably the most comprehensive and the most pertinent literary contribution to the discussion of Jewish fundamentalism to date. It chronicles the rise and fall of a fictitious group of secessionist Jewish settlers who, at the end of the twentieth century, create the Kingdom of Judea and Samaria with a view to promoting redemption. Weaving together in her narrative the opposing doctrines of ultranationalist-religious (fundamentalist) settlers, ultra-Orthodox Haredi anti-Zionists, pragmatic Zionists, and evangelical fundamentalists, Reich in *The Jewish War* once again deeply probes the dimensions of fundamentalisms, Jewish identities, and the meaning of the "Land of Israel."

In the center of the novel is the process of transcending the "caterpillar stages"[38] of the American diaspora existence of the main protagonists. In its course, all of them metamorphose into full-blown nationalist-religious fundamentalists who, by acting out their beliefs, pose a serious threat from within to Israeli security. The novel's main protagonist is Yehudi HaGoel—Jerry Goldberg as was. His chosen second name means "The Redeemer," and it supposedly indicates that the "butterfly stage" is really his true and essential nature, for

The true Goldberg was the emerging Yehudi HaGoel, . . . a self-created entity who would soon tear himself from the roots that anchored and constrained him, would shed his sullied, middle-class skin, and would appear for all the world to see, complete and fully formed. (31)

The allusion to Yehudi's metamorphosis is taken up again later. For, traveling, as it were, "by coffin" to Israel during the war of 1967 to circumvent the official traveling prohibition, Yehudi, enclosed in his narrow box, was "in a holding stage, as in a cocoon"; in fact, it was "as if he had died in America and would be resurrected in Israel . . . It was resonant with metaphor and symbol" (52). In Hebron, his destiny is, some thirty years later, to become the "anointed" king of the Kingdom of Judea and Samaria and then to lead his followers, including his three wives and his children, to their sacrificial suicides in the Cave of Machpelah.

From early on, Yehudi is accompanied by Hoshea HaLevi, formerly known for his baseball skills as Herbie "Hubba-Hubba" Levy (8). As adolescents they meet at a Zionist summer camp, financed by Yehudi's father, where they are immersed in Zionist doctrine, preparing for "the radiant day when they would cast everything aside and make the ultimate ascent to the Zion of their dreams" (13). Unlike many of their fellow "campers," they never lose sight of their purpose, and throughout their time at Yeshiva College they anticipate "the transforming, climactic moment of *aliyah*" (14). Yet the ground where Yehudi and Hoshea first prove themselves is Kugel's Hotel and Country Club in the Catskill Mountains ("acknowledged Jewish territory" [35]). Hoshea has a summer job there as a waiter, but he also stands in as master of the ceremonies in the casino and shows considerable oratorical talent:

> And then he would seize and wring their hearts like dishrags, purge the dross from their souls with an account of the modern-day State of Israel—draining the swamps, reclaiming the deserts, campfires and accordions and *horas,* stunning dark-skinned girl soldiers in thight khaki uniforms, boy soldiers with knitted yarmulkes clipped to their hair leaning on submachine guns, an open Talmud spread out in front of them across the back of a tank. Ah, Jerusalem, Jerusalem, her cupolas golden in the sunset, bins of golden oranges and grapefruits, the novelty, the glorious novelty, of healthy Jews with muscles and good teeth, nerve and sass. (18)

The images Hoshea conjures up are a clever blend of romanticizing Orientalist and Zionist stereotypes and, surprisingly, at this early stage, are entirely lacking any religious profundities but rather invoke something of the American pioneer spirit of the frontier. The description of his success among the affluent elderly American Jews vacationing at

Kugel's not only proves the power of his words but also anticipates the novel's catastrophe (in both senses of the word) and reflects on a particular aspect of diaspora–Israel relations:

> "For the *aliyah* fund," they whispered conspiratorially, patting him on the back and on the bottom, squeezing his biceps, and, in general, sizing him up and checking him out as if they were considering buying him, as if they were claiming him in the way they might claim the live chicken they twirled around their heads on the eve of Yom Kippur, the bird that would expiate their sins, that would serve as their ransom and their substitute, the poultry that would be dispatched to the slaughter in their stead and would allow them, thus absolved, to remain comfortably at Kugel's or wherever to carry on with the good life—a good, long, and peaceful life; meanwhile, he, Hoshea, a consenting adult and to all appearances sane, would be willingly sent in their name, like the fowl of atonement, to make this *aliyah* he craved so passionately—to that land teeming, by his own admission, with fetid swamps to be drained, barren deserts to be reclaimed, and doomed boys and girls battling to survive every blessed sacrificial minute. (18–19)

To the American Jewish establishment, Israel does not appear to be the "safe haven" as it has been promoted through the Zionist narrative but rather as its very opposite and, indeed, as a kind of sacrificial offering for the "good life" in the American diaspora. At the same time it is implied that, from the point of view of Kugel's clientèle, all those wanting to make *aliyah,* sacrificing the good life, and most probably also themselves, are gullible fools. On another level, the lack of idealism and the general indifference of those American Jews, subject to the base instinct of feeding themselves and preoccupied with their bowel movements (17), as well as their own blatant gullibility, are the targets of Reich's satire. Yet there is still another level of meaning to this passage. For at the end of the novel, there will indeed be a "sacrificial" (self-)slaughter on another Day of Atonement, not, however, for the "good life" but to further the process of redemption—and, paradoxically, this very sacrifice will constitute a major threat from within to the security of the secular State of Israel.

Like Hoshea, and perhaps even more, Yehudi possesses the power of the word, which, compounded with his personal charisma, he uses to astounding effect—and, again, it is remarkable that the religious dimension is as yet absent from his magniloquent triumphs:

> His presence turned into vapor the question "Who does he think he is?" as it was emerging from between the skeptic's lips; without being able to define his effect exactly, it was undeniable that Yehudi HaGoel was

somebody. His power over the crowd was to mold it into a single organism that reflected, exactly, his mood. When he was up, crying, "Israel is home! Israel is life! Israel is ours! Israel Is!" the crowd soared with him, ready to drop on the spot everything that ever used to be important and to make the ascent at once. When he was down, wailing, "Remember the camps! Remember the gas! Remember the ovens!" the men and the women in the throng understood him completely, understood the danger they were in, yes, even here, even here in the Land of the Free, understood the historical imperative, understood why Israel was absolutely necessary, necessary without qualification or compromise, understood the morality of why not only their own lives, but also the lives of all humankind on the planet would be irrelevant, no longer worth sustaining or preserving should Israel be annihilated. (33)

Paradoxically, it is precisely the almost disappointing lack of "proper" anti-Semitic discrimination that, in the early 1960s, riles Yehudi, or Jerry Goldberg, as he then still was:

Despite its reputation as the land of equal opportunity, never was Yehudi really given a fair chance in America to pull out all of his Jewish guns and show what he could do. And he deeply resented this deprivation. At rallies in protest against any threat to the State of Israel, Yehudi in those days would declare himself a disciple of Martin Luther King, Jr.: "Martin Luther King is my *rebbe*," Yehudi would cry. He would cross lines, chain himself to fences, trespass on property, go limp like a noodle, be carted off in a paddy wagon, undergo routine processing at a police station, and despite his vehement objections, to his utter chagrin, be released back onto the streets. It was neither pleasant nor fitting for Yehudi to be dismissed as harmless; such treatment hurt him deeply. (34)

Although she never overtly psychologizes and eschews facile explanations, Reich manages to convey a certain sense of the inevitability, or at least of the consistent linearity, and of the plausibility of the development of her main characters toward their fundamentalist stance. In Yehudi's case it is a formidable single-mindedness that lets him focus exclusively on the path of his redemptive project and his self-fashioned identity as "The Redeemer." In Hoshea's case, his singularity of purpose is rooted in a "revelation" he experienced at Camp Ziona. When Yehudi's team "miraculously" defeated Hoshea's in a color war, although the actual scores suggested the very opposite,

Hoshea completely comprehended, absorbed in his molecules, the concept of divine personal supervision. In Judaism, this is a central tenet, one of the essential principles of faith without which one cannot be said to believe truly. Real faith came at last to Hoshea HaLevi after the toilet paper race at the truce ceremony at the end of the color war in Camp Ziona; it struck him with the force of revelation. Moreover, Hoshea resolved then and there to link his destiny with Yehudi, who, thanks to the concept of divine personal supervision, could never be defeated, would never lose. (13)

It is a resolve to which Hoshea remains true, even unto the end. But before that, acting the role of high priest of the Kingdom of Judea and Samaria, he will be the one to anoint Yehudi.

The power of the word is attested to in Reich's novel not only by the passionate and well-wrought sentences of Hoshea and Yehudi but also, for instance, by the intertextual reference to Leon Uris's world bestseller *Exodus* (1958):

> Ben-Canaan was a compact, muscular, intense man, from Galveston, Texas, originally, Eddie Cohen he had been called in those days, whose life had been changed irrevocably when he picked up the novel *Exodus* in an airport lounge before boarding his flight from Houston to Los Angeles, where he was journeying in the hope of launching a career as a movie stunt man. Within a month, he was on his way across the American continent corrupted by its cowboys and its commercials, across the ocean polluted by its sunken luxury liners and pirate ships, across the decadence and gas chambers of Europe to Israel. Almost immediately, Elkanah Ben-Canaan was drawn into the settlement movement, which seemed to him to embody the spirit, the idealism, the adventure, the rejection of materialism, the heroism of the original Zionist pioneers. (113)

Once again, the fundamentalist stance is suggested to be a pose, which, in this case, is generated and sustained by the impact of literary fiction on the impressionable Eddie Cohen. For him, Uris's novel provides the narrative of an ideal state of purity to whose reconstruction (see Lustick's definition of fundamentalism) he aspires to contribute.

Quite intriguingly, Israel as a redemptive project of the fundamentalist settler movement appears to embody the very same pioneer spirit that "made" America but which America, long since "corrupted by its cowboys," seems to have lost. A possible inference—relayed through the internal focalizer (Eddie/Elkanah)—is that Israel, as a "space of redemption," achieves significance as a model for the "universal" process of redemption. The affinity between the pioneer spirit of the Zionists and of the settlers in America observed here by Reich has also been remarked upon by Ella Shohat, who perceives it to be one of the reasons for the

American bias toward Israel to which Hirst referred in the text prefixed to this chapter:

> The classical images of sabra pioneers as settlers on the Middle Eastern frontiers, fighting Indian-like Arabs, along with the reverberations of the early American biblical discourse encapsulated in such notions as "Adam," "(New) Canaan," and "Promised Land," have all facilitated the feeling of Israel as an extention [sic] of "us"—the U.S.[39]

Reich's novel itself is, in many ways, a counter narrative to Uris's strongly ideologically informed myth-making bestseller. Myth-making is, of course, a corollary of narrative, and in her novel, Reich subtly engages in the metafictional and metahistoriographic debate initiated by Hayden White's well-known and much-debated challenge to "fact"-writing historiography.[40] In *The Jewish War*, the narrative construal of myths and their potential for propagandist exploitation is repeatedly remarked upon. Early on in the novel, Yehudi's encounters with instances of anti-Semitism, regrettably lacking in menace, are described as "common skirmishes of no consequence and no mythic resonance" (34). Mythic resonance is, however, what he aspires to, although until he made *aliyah*, "there really was only one occasion when Yehudi had the opportunity to confront the enemy—the prototypical, classical Jew-hater—in something that resembled full-scale battle, and to prove himself" (34). Yet this event,

> generally unheralded in its time and sung of by only a small number who knew the words, later became a critical element in the emerging Yehudi HaGoel legend, the ordeal that, in retrospect, in some measure defined and authenticated him, launched him into the position of a fighting leader, cast him as a hero who might be prepared, when necessary, to abjure even the nonviolent teachings of the exemplary Rabbi King [i.e., Martin Luther King]. (34–35)

Any myth, it is implied, is a narrative construction. Yet at the same time, myth is also seen to influence subsequent events. However, the poietic function of narrative emphasized here and almost a commonplace in the wake of New Historicist theories not only reflects on Yehudi's acumen in manipulating his "legend" but also constitutes simultaneously an indirect metafictional and, indeed, a "metafundamentalist" comment. For fundamentalisms, it is suggested, are also narrative constructions that contribute toward the formation of a "fundamentalist imaginary," as do fictional narrative constructions of fundamentalisms, like Reich's—or, for that matter, of the other authors discussed in this chapter 4.

After his initial enthusiasm, boosted by the victory of the Six Day War, Yehudi feels a growing enmity toward the secular State of Israel, which originates in his disapproval of what he deems to be its reconciliatory policy (e.g., the Camp David Accords).[41] To him and his followers, this appears to be a sin that excites the wrath of the Lord and forestalls redemption. Protesting against the alleged inability of the Israeli Defence Force (IDF) to protect Jewish settlers from Arab terrorists, Yehudi presents his argument picketing an army camp immediately after the Israeli pullout from Lebanon in 1982:

> The miracle of the Six-Day War heralded the beginning of redemption and ushered in the messianic age wherein all reality is sanctified, political reality no less than religious reality; everything is holy, even the secular is consecrated, holiness embraces all things; the land itself, which has been wrested from the forces of evil through the miracle of the war, is imbued with holiness, with the Divine Presence, the *Shechinah;* to cede even a minuscule portion of this holy soil would be a fatal capitulation to the evil powers; the era of tolerance has passed, a new, benevolent totalitarianism has taken its place, the totalitarianism of holiness; sanctity has been bestowed on the individual and on society, on commerce and on politics, on the land and all that it contains; the duty to settle, to wage war, to conquer, to intervene actively to further the redemption and bring about the fullness of the messianic era is the loftiest, the most sublime, the most exalted, the holiest form of worship. (138–39)

This "theology of holiness" and the concomitant bid for a "totalitarianism of holiness" quite clearly derive from the writings of Rav Kook and encapsulate the position of the Gush Emunim. Yehudi's firm belief in the beginning of redemption, which he undertakes to further not only with peaceful actions (hunger strikes and pickets) but also with terrorist acts against his Arab neighbors, is manifest as well in the name he gives his daughter: At'halta D'Geula literally means "the beginning of redemption" (101). That his daughter is later abducted by Haredim is surely another instance of an event "resonant with metaphor and symbol" (52): the "Messiah-Waiters," as they are called in the novel (63), obviously carry the day—redemption, as in *Master of the Return,* once more is deferred.

Yehudi's "official" antagonist is General Uri Lapidot of the IDF, who, time and again, during the various stages of his military career, is entrusted with enforcing the claims of the state against the messianic-Zionist sect. In the novel, he represents a pragmatic and liberal Zionism. Equally repelled by the "barbaric intolerance" (136) of the Haredim, by their rejection of the secular state and its organs, and by Yehudi's religious nationalism, Lapidot perceives his own and any other enlightened Israeli–Jewish identity to be threatened by the contending varieties of Jewish fundamentalism (134–36). As the commanding officer of the siege of Yehudi's kingdom, which by now quite literally exists in the "underground" (in the Cave of Machpelah), he reflects:

> And today, down there in Hebron, the city of *his* forefathers, too, there was this other aberration holding down the fort, this breed of religious Jews who, unlike the black-hatted ultra-Orthodox, did not disdain the army—far from it, they enlisted willingly, trained diligently, fought enthusiastically, they knew all the tricks—a lethal mixture, as Lapidot saw it, of messianic religious zeal and rabid nationalism. And where did all of this lead? To this sickly mutation, this rotting fossil, the so-called Kingdom of Judea and Samaria. (136–37)

The foundation of this very kingdom crowns Yehudi's travails to advance redemption and the coming of the Messiah. With its foundation the novel commences and, after narrating the events that lead to its inception, it ends with its destruction—the collective suicide of Yehudi and his followers as the last and most effective resort in the struggle for their beliefs. While the deathly drug administered to nigh on a thousand men, women, and children, is having its effect, Lapidot, observing the besieged compound from his commanding post, after having finished reading a valuable antiquarian copy of Flavius Josephus's *The Jewish War,* muses about the "authenticity" of the historical account:

> In the opinion of General Uri Lapidot, *The Jewish War* was a novel, despite Josephus's protestations that what he had aimed for in his so-called historical account was the truth from beginning to end. Masada, certainly, was real; there was abundant archaeological evidence of its existence, and if Lapidot believed in anything at all, he believed in stones. But as for the mass suicide that took place there, all that remains of significance is Josephus's report, and, as a historian, Josephus was not reliable. As far as Lapidot was concerned, Josephus was a notorious opportunist and self-server, a writer of fiction. (270)

The simultaneity of Lapidot's skeptical reading of Josephus's "history" and of the collective suicide in the Cave of Machpelah at the very end of the novel once again emphasizes the insoluble intertwining of fact and fiction in narrative representations. While in the fictional world of the novel the analogy prompts an affirmative reading of the historical precedent recounted in Josephus's *The Jewish War,* the reader of Reich's eponymous novel has, of course, been made aware of its fictional character, and then the analogy may work, in turn, further to discredit Josephus. All the same, the events narrated in the novel are associated not only with the "historical" fate of Masada,[42] but also with more recent historical precedents, for example, with the collective suicide of the followers of James Warren Jones in Jonestown, Guyana (1978), repeatedly alluded to in the text,[43] or with the storming of the "Branch Davidian" compound in Waco, Texas (1993), by agents of the Bureau of Alcohol, Tobacco, and Firearms (ATF). These references emphasize the resilience, and the contingency, of fundamentalisms and, again, lend credibility (or at least verisimilitude) to the events described in Josephus's *The Jewish War* as well as in Reich's.

Like Eleazar ben Jair, the leader of the Jews in Masada, Yehudi, in an address to his followers, calls for their collective suicide. But where Eleazar, according to Josephus, admits that the rebellion may have been misguided,[44] Yehudi insists on the exalted purpose of this ultimate expedient in furthering redemption:

> After all, Yehudi cried, what do we, what does the Kingdom of Judea and Samaria signify except the embodiment of a principle? That principle is our unnegotiable right to possess and dwell in the heart and soul of the ancient biblical homeland promised to us alone by the God of our fathers. And that principle can prevail even if we, the people of the Kingdom of Judea and Samaria, do not survive; indeed, even if, to assure the perpetuation of that principle, it is absolutely necessary that we die. . . . it is the most bitter blow that we can inflict upon the State of Israel, a shock from which it can never recover when it enters our underground halls in its customary pride and arrogance to be struck with amazement by our death and by our courage, to discover dreadful silence, to find us at peace, our bodies still bedecked in the pure penitential garments of this Yom Kippur . . . the State of Israel will be chastened and humbled once and for all. Never again will it dare to risk acceding to the surrender of even a millimeter of this holy land that is the province of God alone to give and to take. In the struggle between the State of Israel and the Kingdom of Judea and Samaria, the Kingdom will perish, but it will be the State that will be defeated. That will be the miracle and the wonder. (265–66)

After the collective suicide, in the dark sky above the Cave of Machpelah a ghostly procession seems to pass:

> A tall, slender, bridelike figure in a white robe at its head, trailed by a long column of smaller, nearly transparent figures, like children, also

clothed in white. It was as if they were all dancing toward some heavenly being, yet never quite reaching him. (269)

The allusion is to the *Shechinah,* in the Kabbalah the bride of God and His feminine principle. According to different traditions in the Talmud and Midrash, the *Shechinah* either withdrew from earth after the destruction of the First Temple to return in the time of redemption or went into exile with Israel to return to the Land with the Chosen People.[45] The reunion of the male and female aspects of divinity—the final metamorphosis, aspired to but not yet achieved—betokens the beginning of redemption.[46] Yet Yehudi, "The Redeemer," does not achieve redemption as the ascending *Shechinah*-like figure, leaving the earth, never quite reaches God.

The only character in the novel to harbor any doubts about the chosen path of Yehudi and his followers is Hoshea's wife, Emunah. Ironically, her Hebrew name translates into Faith—indeed, formerly she was known as Faith Fleischman from Flatbush. Divided in her innermost self, Faith, although she feels the ardent desire to make *aliyah,* attempts, at least temporarily, to escape her externally prescribed and predestined role as a "Jewish woman" (44–45) by joining the Peace Corps for two years. Later, as Emunah, it is she alone—among all the other women in the "Kingdom" who, quite willingly, submit to the patriarchal mode imposed upon them by Yehudi's fundamentalist views—who experiences serious doubts about the course of events. In anguish, she writes to a friend who witnessed the tragedy of Jonestown and who, in her correspondence, had described the horrible sight to her:

> "Felicity," Emunah wrote, "the day we hand the children over to their fathers, on that day we become accomplices. Felicity, when they came to Jonestown, those poor souls, do you suppose they were coming to die or to live? For centuries my people have come to the Holy Land to die and be buried. The novelty of Zionism was the idea of coming here to live. What hubris must have possessed us when we subscribed to the notion that we of all Jews past and to come could change things? Felicity, I am buried alive." (247)

Her misgivings are reminiscent of the premonitions attributed to the biblical Sarah in *Master of the Return* (239). In the end, however, Emunah, like the archetypal Sarah, and like all the other women in the "Kingdom," acquiesces in the fate prescribed to her and her children by the faith-driven male.

Yet Reich does not target only Jewish fundamentalisms in her novel. That her criticism is leveled at any kind of fundamentalism becomes clear in her satirical characterization of a Christian fundamentalist preacher who joins Yehudi's picket. The Reverend Chuck Buck combines his religious zeal profitably with commercial adroitness and, in contrast to Yehudi, although he too stage-manages his actions with a view to their propagandistic value, the Reverend's credibility is severely compromised by his show-biz mentality. In Jerusalem, he organizes a congress of anti-Semitic "self-accusation," whose climax is his own confession that culminates in his declaration to have himself circumcised:

> And yes, Reverend Buck confessed, yes, to his everlasting shame, he had not once, no, never in those days had he questioned the truth of the iniquity of the Jews . . . And, in truth, the proof of the horrendous guilt of the Jewish people had, in those days, seemed to him implicit in the centuries of punishment they endured, beginning with the destruction of their Temple and their exile from the Holy Land less than twoscore years after the crucifixion of our Lord, Jesus Christ, and then their suffering, the horrendous suffering over the nearly two millennia of diaspora that ensued . . . this suffering was so extreme, so unremitting, that it could not have been accidental or arbitrary, it could not have been interpreted as anything other than the will of God, or so Reverend Buck had reasoned before he saw the light . . . Indeed, to indulge in pity for them would have meant to question God's judgment . . . (167–68)

As for Yehudi, thus also for the Reverend, the "miracle" of the Six Day War proved to be decisive:

> And then, one day, he was suddenly struck down by the crisis that ripped his assumptions apart, and changed, yes, changed his life. That crisis was the stunning miracle of the Six-Day War and the sinking in of the reality of the return of the Jewish people to Zion, the establishment of the State of Israel, the beginning of the end of the diaspora, the restoration of Jewish sovereignty over the holy city of Jerusalem and the biblical homeland. . . . From that day forth he devoted himself heart and soul to the Jewish State, for its destiny and the destiny of its people, he now understood, were inextricably bound up with his own, and the survival of Israel was laden with the promise of the end of days and the ultimate unconditional acceptance by the Jewish people of the glory of Jesus Christ. (168–69)

The appropriation of the eschatological significance of the Jewish possession of the Land of Israel by the fundamentalist preacher, whose latent anti-Semitism is only thinly veiled by his jovial humor (146 and 150), is an immediate reminder of the dark chapter of the Christian "mission" among the Jews, itself, arguably, a manifestation of an age-old Christian fundamentalism.

In her novel, Reich analyzes the problems that the association of the embattled Land of Israel with a fundamentalist eschatological vision— both Jewish and Christian—creates for both the present and the noneschatological future of the Middle East. Despite its satirical acuity and sparkling humor, *The Jewish War* is a profoundly tragic novel[47] that, although it pillories rabid religious and nationalist zeal and the fundamentalisms sustained by it, reminds us of their origins in our common humanity.

Like *Master of the Return*—but significantly, I think, unlike Roiphe's *Lovingkindness*—Reich's *The Jewish War* is written in the satirical mode. It may, of course, simply be Reich's particular gift to excel, as she does, in political and religious satire. But this does not seem to be a satisfactory explanation of the fact that hers are not the only works of fiction dealing with Jewish fundamentalism (as opposed to Orthodoxy) that resort to the satirical mode. Indeed, it seems to me, that the satirical is the preferred mode of Jewish authors engaging with Jewish fundamentalism. Certainly, all the texts I discuss here conform to this pattern.

To my knowledge, the first anglophone novel to address the phenomenon of Jewish fundamentalism in Israel is Philip Roth's *The Counterlife*. When the novel was first published, in 1986, the phenomenon itself, although by then in evidence for more than a decade, had not yet made much of an impact on English-language academic work. Largely a novel about the negotiation of Jewish identities between the parameters of diaspora and Israel, in its convoluted structure various "counterlives," alternative (fictional) constructions of reality ("one's own antimyth"),[48] are explored by Roth's alter ego and narrator Nathan Zuckerman. Faced with his brother Henry's choice of counterlife, to become an "authentic Jew" (74) in a Jewish settlement in the West Bank, Nathan visits Israel with the intention of reclaiming his brother. Yet the confrontation with the fundamentalist settlers whom Henry (now calling himself Hanoch) has joined leaves the professional writer almost "speechless" and he confesses himself to be "outclassed" (130). In his narrative he reflects on the intense atmosphere:

> If I had nothing to say to Henry right off it was because, following Lippman's seminar, language didn't really seem my domain any longer. I wasn't exactly a stranger to disputation, but never in my life had I felt so enclosed by a world so contentious, where the argument is so enormous and constant and everything turns out to be pro or con, positions taken, positions argued, and everything italicized by indignation and rage. (130)

In Roth's novel, the fundamentalists are not predominantly religiously inspired. They are rather of the ultranationalist variety and their arguments have a certain persuasive, if fantastic, potential. They are less motivated by the religious imperative to conquer and settle the land, but rather by the notion of the perils of the diaspora and the image of Israel as a safe haven—a Zionist stereotype provokingly inverted in Roth's later novel *Operation Shylock* (1993). In America, one settler's argument in *The Counterlife* runs, assimilation and intermarriage

> are bringing about a second Holocaust—truly, a spiritual Holocaust is taking place there, and it is as deadly as any threat posed by the Arabs to the State of Israel. What Hitler couldn't achieve with Auschwitz, American Jews are doing to themselves in the bedroom . . . First there was the hard extermination, now there is the soft extermination. And this is why young people are learning Hebrew at Agor—to escape the Jewish oblivion, the extinction of Jews that is coming in America, to escape those communities in your country where Jews are committing spiritual suicide. (103)

The American Jewish influx to the Land of Israel, extolled here as a countermeasure to the impending Jewish oblivion, is assessed by another, liberal Israeli voice in the novel as unsettling:

> Who comes to this country now to settle and live? The intellectual Jew? The humane Jew? The beautiful Jew? No, not the Jew from Buenos Aires, or Rio, or Manhattan. The ones who come from America are either religious or crazy or both. This place has become the American Jewish Australia. Now who we get is the Oriental Jew and the Russian Jew and the social misfits like your brother, roughnecks in yarmulkes from Brooklyn. (77)

As in Roiphe's *Lovingkindness*[49] and, to some extent, also in Reich's novels, Israel, in *The Counterlife,* appears to be a hotbed of American Jewish zealots. Yet, concerned mainly with the negotiation of Jewish identities between diaspora and *Eretz Yisrael* in the personal sphere, the representation of fundamentalism in Roth's *The Counterlife* does impart only a very oblique sense of menace. A heightened sense of the potential dangers emanating from the Jewish fundamentalist movement in Israel is increasingly perceptible in the novels of Tova Reich and, particularly, in Melvin Jules Bukiet's *Strange Fire* (2001).

Bukiet's text is an intricate political satire told by Nathan Kazakov, the blind and homosexual Russian émigré speechwriter to the hawkish prime minister of Israel in the novel. When Nathan is shot by a fundamentalist settler, whose real target he presumes to have been his employer, his investigation of the matter enmeshes him more and more in a web of conspiracies climaxing in an attempt at blowing up the Temple Mount involving settlers, Arab terrorists, the Israeli secret service, and his former colleagues. In the course of his investigation, Nathan encounters nationalist-religious fundamentalists in their settlement of Beis Machpelah near Hebron with which the group, from which the would-be assassin also originated, stakes the Jewish claim to the Promised Land: "God gave us this country thousands of years ago, complete with milk and honey," Nathan is told, to which he adds dryly: "And mud."[50] For the settlers' livelihood ironically depends on their selling the very soil of the God-given land (sediments of the Red Sea) by the bagful as a "natural cosmetic." (155)

Like other members of the group, its leader (now known as Der Alter) is Brooklyn-born, and Nathan, in a very few sentences, sketches the rabbi's profile:

> Born as Moshe Zuckerman, my host changed his name to Moshe X as a youthful member of the JDL back in America in the late 1960s. This act of willful social provocation occurred before he discovered God and Israel in the 1970s and swapped his signature beret for a yarmulke. Yet even when the ordained and Aliyahed Rabbi X's beard reached his *pupik* and he became the venerable Der Alter in the 1980s, the fire in his belly still burned. (154)

This profile appears to be paradigmatic of the type of American Jewish immigrant to Israel with strong fundamentalist pretensions portrayed in all the novels under consideration here. Mordecai Lippman in Roth's *The Counterlife* and the protagonists in Reich's novels have a similar pedigree and so had, in real life, the notorious Rabbi Meir Kahane who founded the Jewish Defense League (JDL) in the United States in 1968 prior to his emigration to Israel, where he then established the ultranationalist and religious *Kach* party, since banned in Israel; so also had Baruch Goldstein, a fundamentalist settler from Kiryat Arba who killed twenty-nine Muslims in the prayer hall of the Patriarchs' Cave in Hebron in 1994.[51]

Another central issue targeted by Bukiet's political satire is the potentially close association between fundamentalist groups and the elected government of Israel. While cynically exploiting fundamentalist ideas for his own ends, Simon Levy, the Israeli prime minister in the novel, obviously succumbs to his own rhetoric, forming foolish ideas of kingship and messianic redemption. He is supported in his schemes by the inner circle of his advisers. Their plan is to blow up the Muslim shrines on the Temple Mount and thus to provoke a major conflagration:

> Only if the war to come entails pain will it produce the desired results. Another six-day wonder would secure the region temporarily, but there would be even more refugees, which would re-create the scenario that has proved so debilitating for the last half century. Only a truly devastating war, one which they almost win, one with casualties, will secure the future. Only if our backs are to the sea can we use the weapons we have. (324)

The reference is, of course, to Israel's nuclear arsenal and Bukiet's text seems to echo here the concern expressed by Shahak and Mezvinsky in their study that Jewish fundamentalism could "substantially affect Israeli nuclear policies."[52] Furthermore, Bukiet's text seems to suggest that religious fundamentalism, if translated into political terms, evolves an uncomfortable proximity to fascism:

> But for us, it's Israel's last chance for a truly, ultimately, eternally unified Holy Land, not under elections. Democracy is a frail system that allows people like Weiner to mess up the works. No, we need to return to the days of glory. We need to return to the Bible, whose ways we have abandoned. (325)

Again, like in Reich's *The Jewish War,* no "closure" is provided and it is left to the reader's imagination to probe the potential effects of this (pseudo-)fundamentalist action. Yet, while in *The Jewish War* the threat is mainly to the internal equilibrium of Israel, in *Strange Fire* the explosion in the tunnel system penetrating the Temple Mount, and killing the pretender to the Davidic Throne as well as his henchmen and women, poses an international threat and may well launch Armageddon. The only hope is that Nathan and a few others who escaped from the tunnels just in time may avert the impending doom by explaining what happened.

There seems to be, among anglophone Jewish writers, a mounting sense of the urgency of engaging with the phenomenon of Jewish fundamentalism and with the growing threat it poses not only to the fragile "balance" of the Middle East and the precarious peace process but also to the internal equilibrium of the State of Israel and its commitment to democracy. For, if viewed in chronological sequence, the novels address its potential wider ramifications with increasing seriousness.

In *The Counterlife,* ultranationalist fundamentalist attitudes to some extent appear to be the articulation of a kind of paranoia that, however fantastic it may seem, is partially vindicated by subsequent events in the novel when Nathan Zuckerman experiences British anti-Semitism. Still, the exploration of the fundamentalist as one of several possible, and eventually discarded, "counterlives" is primarily part of a personal identity quest and although a certain menacing aspect seems to adhere to the actions and to the ideology of the fundamentalist settlers, this is not really the issue in Roth's novel.

Both of Reich's novels are focused exclusively on different manifestations of Jewish fundamentalism in Israel. In *Master of the Return*, a minor, and in some of its aspects perhaps even "quaint" and endearing, "aberration" is portrayed—eventually dealt with confidently, and effectively, by the Israeli authorities. In this novel, Reich's interest is centered largely on "crazy" individuals and the dynamics within the group, which are determined by gender tensions and the religious-ideological strife between Haredim (Abba Nissim, 118, 134, and 201) and religious nationalists (Reb Lev Lurie, 119).

In Reich's later novel, *The Jewish War*, the impact of what appears to be not merely a random group or "groupuscule" but a rigidly organized movement reminiscent of the Gush Emunim, and very well able to upset the internal Israeli consensus, emerges in her narrative as a serious threat from the inside to Israeli security. However, it is neither the continuous activism of Yehudi and his followers against Israeli Arabs or their fellow Jews (modeled on "historical" Gush Emunim schemes) that proves to be most explosive, nor yet the unilateral establishment of the secessionist Kingdom of Judea and Samaria (so far without historical precedent), but rather its fatal (and fatalistic) end. Indeed, the dimensions of the blow Yehudi and his followers deal the State of Israel with their sacrificial suicide may not readily be recognized by the non-Jew and perhaps not even by the non-Israeli Jew. Not only the historical reference to the mass suicide of Masada, a central "myth" of Zionist ideology, is significant in this context but, less obviously, though perhaps even more decisively, also the loss of Jewish lives occasioned by the conciliatory and therefore "traitorous" and "faithless" policies of the State of Israel (e.g., the Camp David Accords). In Jewish fundamentalist thought, strongly influenced by the Lurianic Kabbalah, "Jewish blood," as Shahak and Mezvinsky have pointed out, is considered superior to "the blood of non-Jews," which, for religious Jews, "has no intrinsic value."[53] According to Shahak and Mezvinsky, this tenet is well-known, although not generally endorsed, in Israel, and they see it also as underlying certain Israeli policy decisions.[54] In the light of this notion, the loss of almost a thousand Jewish lives on the holiest day of the year, the Day of Atonement, is indeed to be considered a terrible calamity for the State of Israel, internally and potentially also externally.

In Bukiet's novel, finally, the fundamentalist voice once again is given much less scope than in Reich's novels. Yet fundamentalist doctrines are shown to have penetrated deeply into political culture in Israel and the potential political effects of messianic fundamentalism are envisaged as a cataclysm of apocalyptic proportions.

Earlier, I suggested that Jewish fundamentalism appears to be a salient topic in Jewish fiction in English. However, none of the texts I discuss here was published after 9/11.[55] This was not a deliberate choice on my part, but, indeed, I am not aware of any anglophone Jewish writing published after the destruction of the World Trade Center that in a comparable way engages with Jewish fundamentalism in Israel. This may not mean anything. After all, 9/11 was only a few years ago and this may simply be too short a period to draw any conclusions. Yet, if not merely a token of my ignorance, it may mean something after all: Is Jewish fundamentalism, once again and even in the literary imagination, eclipsed by a "spectacular" act of outrage connected to Islamist fundamentalism? Or, perhaps also by the "fundamentalist" war on terrorism waged by the United States and her (mostly less dedicated) allies? Is, in the most recent "clash of fundamentalisms," the Jewish variety in Israel merely an also ran?

A similar constellation of opposing fundamentalisms, if without the added horrors of 9/11, was explored almost a decade earlier by Simon Louvish in his *The Days of Miracles and Wonders: An Epic of the New World Disorder,* first published in 1997—fully five years after its completion. In this novel, Jewish fundamentalism is mentioned only in passing as one of many[56] and is encompassed in an "apocalyptic" vision that takes issue with fundamentalism not in its various manifestations but as a constituent of the *condition humaine.*[57] The historical backdrop to the novel is the Gulf War of 1991 and the period immediately prior to it. But to this level are added many layers, among them the resurrection in the flesh (if without the heart and entrails) of Richard *Coeur de Lion,* the reflections on humanity and history of the undead early Christian saint Simon the Stylite, and disturbing descriptions of the shell-shocked life in the Palestinian refugee camps in Lebanon during the early 1980s. Any attempt at condensing the multiple layers and voices of Louvish's novel—which include the sad and resigned musings of a "smart" bomb seconds prior to its impact, the bland outlook on life of a sandworm on the Lothian shore, and authentic newspaper clips—must of necessity come to naught. But from its orchestration of voices it emerges that Louvish's highly satirical and deeply unsettling novel is very much about the "clash of fundamentalisms," long before Tariq Ali coined the phrase in reference to Samuel P. Huntington's *The Clash of Civilizations and the*

Remaking of World Order (1996)[58]—indeed, Louvish quite uncannily seems to have "anticipated" even the latter half of Huntington's title with the subtitle of his novel.[59]

With reference to an earlier novel of Louvish's, *City of Blok* (1988), also featuring his (anti-)hero Avram Blok who makes his reappearance in *The Days of Miracles and Wonders*,[60] Bryan Cheyette wrote in a review that Louvish "has probably anticipated—better than anyone outside Israel—further madness to come."[61] If anything, *The Days of Miracles and Wonders* is a rendering of this further madness. A madness, however, that is increasingly perceived in its global context and not centered on Israel even though Louvish's focus remains the Middle East.

Another reincarnation in Louvish's novel is that of the tenth-century founder of the Druze religion, the Caliph Abu Ali Mansur al-Hakim, whom the author conflates with the apocalyptic "Hidden Imam" expected by Shi'ites to return at the End of Time from his occultation.[62] In a dream, the Caliph is thrown by the Stylite, whose column has grown out of all proportion, into the abyss, his descent reminiscent of Gibreel Farishta's fall no less than Satan's. In the light of this analogy and its subject matter it may be no surprise that Louvish did not at first find a publisher for his novel. Indeed, Louvish himself, as quoted in a review by Teddy Jamieson, attributed this reluctance to the effects of the fatwa pronounced on Salman Rushdie in 1989: "I think that in the wake of the Rushdie affair, people didn't want to touch something which dealt with the Middle East and its conflicts. Anything to do with an Islamic theme was immediately verboten."[63] Yet, as pointed out before, *The Days of Miracles and Wonders* is not a novel about any particular fundamentalism and in addition to Islamic, Jewish, and Christian[64] fundamentalisms another, and no less threatening or frightening, brand of fundamentalist belief is exposed in the self-righteous and single-minded commitment of U.S. "state-fundamentalism"[65] to the "remaking of world order" according to its pseudo-transcendental principles.

When, after his fall, the Caliph finds himself stunned on a hillock of sand in the Arabian desert, he is apprehended by U.S. soldiers. Yet the force of his charisma is so great that he later "converts" not only his captors, black Muslim soldiers, but also an entire unit of the U.S. Air Force, "three hundred young men of all races,"[66] to whom he announces the End of Time. They, along with some journalists, follow him on a long march through the burning desert toward the holy city of Mecca. Although his progress is entirely peaceful, he and his followers are blasted to smithereens by an overkill of all the firepower the U.S. Air Force can muster. Louvish's description—evoking painful images of the media coverage of the destruction of Iraqi columns during the Gulf War—is an enactment of the clash of civilizations and of fundamentalisms in an apocalyptic vision of the time when "everyone can hear the beat of the drums and the thunder of the chariots of war, and the clash of infidel against infidel, transgressor against transgressor, false *jihad* against false *jihad*" (311–12).

Gazing into the "intellectual confusion, moral vacuity and delusional fugues" (238) of the mind of a Maronite warlord, which may be paradigmatic of this age of fundamentalisms, this is what Simon the Stylite sees, before he withdraws in disgust:

> The end justifies the means and the end is nigh. He has noted all the usual signs and portents. Ingathering of the Jews. Collapse of the communist Antichrist. Resurgence of the Caesaropapist hordes. Collapse of all morals, disintegration of the family, the loss of faith in reason. The iron needs of dog eat dog. Now, our rival eschatologies face each other naked on an open battlefield. Good versus evil. Gog and Magog, the only question being, which is which? (237–38)

The question, so easily settled according to the various fundamentalist truths, remains, quite deliberately I think, unresolved in Louvish's text. Yet the ending of the novel may, perhaps, be read as a sort of answer:

> And it came to pass, in the six hundredth and first year, in the first month, the first day of the month, the waters were dried up from off the earth, and Noah removed the covering of the Ark, and looked, and behold, the face of the ground was dry . . . And the Lord said in his heart: I will not again curse the ground any more for man's sake, for the imagination of man's heart is evil from his youth, neither will I again smite any more every thing living, as I have done. While the earth remaineth, seedtime and harvest, and cold and heat, and summer and winter, and day and night shall not cease. (415)[67]

This answer to the question of good and evil, if answer it is, bodes no good. The evil inclination of humankind seems to be allowed to run free, its playing ground the Armageddon for which the unconcerned and innocent world provides the stage.

Some measure of relief is, however, projected in the novel by characters like the Greek-American "terrorist" doctor "Angel" (Petros Angelopoulos), who performs his own kind of medical miracles in the Palestinian refugee camps in Beirut. Yet Angel himself is painfully aware of the inadequacy of the merely "physical." As the inescapable quandary of our times he diagnoses that

People have to redefine themselves. That's the horrific challenge. How to find the magic equilibrium. To be true to your origins, your culture, your roots, but also to a non-conformist reality. The mind and the heart. How to connect them. The nerves, the arteries, the veins. I've done the physical route, cutting and repairing. Like reasphalting the roads. But beyond that? (81)

"It's a job for poets and writers," he answers himself, only to continue: "[B]ut who has any time for them?" For

There are also powerful people who hear Voices, and then hire enforcers to make sure those Voices don't fade away. They mold and sculpt the Voices into convenient forms, ironing away the ragged edges, leaving an efficient tool. It's the abuse of the creative urge, that's all. The superego gone wrong. (81)

The direct competition of literature and fundamentalisms in providing orientation to a humanity that has lost its bearings, it is suggested by Angel's reflections, rests on their common, yet irreconcilable nature: on the basis of the "creative urge," both in effect appear to be narrative practices, which, since the "narrative" or "discursive turn," are understood to "provide fundamental devices that give form and meaning to our experience."[68] To distinguish between literature and fundamentalisms as aids to human orientation, Angel introduces a moral dimension, of good and evil, when he suggests that fundamentalisms are the product of abuse.

Perhaps it is Angel's peace-seeking Israeli girlfriend Naomi, who, in a letter to the "terrorist" doctor, comes closest to the solution of the dilemma, by reducing the "superego" to its common humanity:

Of course, we no longer believe in opposites, since Freud everything is in the same pot. So keep on in your contradictions, Petros. The world does not need saints, just human beings, stop. Not Beyond Good and Evil, but realizing our capacity to be both. This is getting too heavy. But we'll have to let trauma pass into memory before we can try a lighter note. Keep up the good work! KEEP THOSE MIRACLES COMING! Love from all, angel, in friendship. (404)

In the review of Louvish's *City of Blok* mentioned above, Bryan Cheyette suggested that the author's "commitment to a saner world is clear but his fiction is in danger of becoming an unmediated reflection of the irrationality it condemns."[69] I understand Cheyette's criticism to point to the fine balance between the mere aesthetization of irrationality, fundamentalisms in the case of the novels discussed here, which may come perilously close to a tacit condonement, and the literary engagement with the issue.

With regard to the perception of Jewish fundamentalism, Shahak and Mezvinsky claim that the great majority of academic studies in English "falsify their subject matter,"[70] mostly by omission. To ask whether fictional texts are complicit in this "falsification" may be off the mark. After all, the criteria for inclusion or exclusion in fictional texts are not only different but it is the (in contemporary Western discourse usually) undisputed prerogative of the authors of fictional texts to select and (re-)arrange their material. Yet certainly, the "translation" of fundamentalist doctrine into fictional literature, and thus its aesthetic mediation, signifies, to some extent, a domestication and contributes to the construction of a "fundamentalist imaginary."

As Foxman's immediate rejoinder to Hirst's suggestions shows, in an area so fraught with the perils of offending the sensibilities (religious, political, and emotional) of so many one has to tread softly. Certainly, any serious literary rendering of fundamentalisms demands not only a thorough knowledge of the respective tenets and sentiments, and the larger context, but also a deft hand at "aestheticizing" the fundamentalist other, for, indeed, to the authors whose novels I discuss here, it is the "other" they engage with in their fiction, as none of them have fundamentalist leanings themselves. In fact, as Jonathan Webber notes, "fundamentalism is in principle a category imposed from the outside rather than a self-descriptive category."[71] Fictional, that is, aesthetic constructions of "fundamentalists" and "fundamentalisms," no less seem to be imposed from the outside. Yet, one may wonder whether "fiction-writing" (in the traditional sense) and the inside narrative construction of what appears to outsiders as fundamentalisms are really mutually exclusive or whether they are not, after all, the same thing in different guises—and if so, whether the moral category introduced by Angel, and insisted on by Cheyette, may not be essential to the "aesthetics" of fundamentalism.

In all the novels discussed here, fundamentalisms fail—as a desirable counterlife or as a redemptive project. Yet the "fundamentalist imaginary," generated by these texts as an aesthetic construct, emerges as an "interstitial space" in which the authors attempt to initiate, and engage in a dialogue (even if only a virtual one) in which fundamentalists are given a voice, which sometimes may even appear to be uncomfortably persuasive. That the preferred mode of representation appears to be the satirical, steering wide of anything that might be (mis-)construed as mere caricature, may be due to this ambivalence.

Finally, it may be interesting to note that the focus of the Jewish American authors consistently is narrowed toward Israel, toward the emergence of Jewish fundamentalism in this country, and toward Jewish American involvement in it. The Jewish American texts therefore seem much more "parochial" in outlook than the Israeli novel. Louvish (who, it is true, was born in Scotland and currently lives in London and whose work certainly defies easy categorization[72]) widens the scope of his fiction to embrace the global clash of fundamentalisms among which Jewish fundamentalism, spectacularly upstaged in his novel by U.S. "imperialist fundamentalism," is only one of many—and this may be due to some extent to the entrenched position from which he is writing.

NOTES

1. David Hirst, "Pursuing the Millennium: Jewish Fundamentalism in Israel," *The Nation*, February 2, 2004; quoted from the website of *The Nation*, http://www.thenation.com/doc.mhtml%3Fi=20040216&s=hirst (retrieved July 29, 2004).

2. Abraham H. Foxman, in a letter to the editor of *The Nation Online*, February 6, 2004; quoted from the website of the Anti-Defamation League, http://www.adl.org/media_watch/magazines/20040206 TheNationOnline.htm (retrieved July 29, 2004).

3. Ian S. Lustick, *For the Land and the Lord: Jewish Fundamentalism in Israel* (New York: Council on Foreign Relations, 1988; 2nd ed. 1994). The phenomenon was recognized and discussed much earlier in Israel. Lustick draws on a number of older publications in Hebrew; see his bibliography. For an exposition of studies on Jewish fundamentalism in Israel in Hebrew, see also Israel Shahak and Norton Mezvinsky, *Jewish Fundamentalism in Israel* (London: Pluto, 1999), 150–63.

4. Ibid., 3. The same argument is reiterated, and even intensified, by Shahak and Mezvinsky, who criticize Lustick for neglecting "important parts of ideology" and for being "apologetic"; see Shahak and Mezvinsky, *Jewish Fundamentalism*, vi and, for their criticism of Lustick, 57.

5. Ibid., x.

6. Since the first publication of Lustick's book, e.g., the collection of essays *Jewish Fundamentalism in Comparative Perspective: Religion, Ideology, and the Crisis of Modernity* (1993) was edited by Laurence J. Silberstein, a second edition of Lustick's book appeared in 1994, and in the same year was also published Peter Demant's short *Jewish Fundamentalism in Israel: Implications for the Mideast Conflict* (1994). In some more recent publications a comparative perspective is endeavored, as, e.g., in Karen Armstrong's *The Battle for God: Fundamentalism in Judaism, Christianity and Islam* (2000), Richard T. Antoun's *Understanding Fundamentalism: Christian, Islamic, and Jewish*

Movements (2001), and David S. New's *Holy War: The Rise of Militant Christian, Jewish and Islamic Fundamentalism* (2002).

7. Alvin H. Rosenfeld, "The Progress of the American Jewish Novel," *Response* 7 (1973): 115–30.

8. Miriyam Glazer, "Male and Female, King and Queen: The Theological Imagination of Anne Roiphe's *Lovingkindness*," *Studies in American Jewish Literature* 10 (1991): 81.

9. See also, e.g., Meredith Goldsmith, "Thinking through the Body in Hasidic Culture: Reconciling Gender, Sexuality, and Jewishness in the Fiction of Pearl Abraham," in *Jewish Women's Writing of the 1990s and Beyond in Great Britain and the United States*, ed. Ulrike Behlau and Bernhard Reitz (Trier: WVT, 2004), 247 and esp. note 1. Among religious Jews in America an increasing drift toward tradition is perceptible; see Marc Lee Raphael, *Judaism in America* (New York: Columbia University Press, 2004).

10. See Lustick, *For the Land and the Lord*, 5. For a more recent and comprehensive discussion of the relation of religious fundamentalism and political extremism see Leonard Weinberg, *Religious Fundamentalism and Political Extremism* (London: Cass, 2004).

11. Ibid., 6.

12. Ibid., 9–10.

13. See, e.g., Shahak and Mezvinsky, *Jewish Fundamentalism*, 1–4, which claims that it is "rooted in Jewish history" (1). Not surprisingly, perhaps, Islamic fundamentalism also thrived after the defeat, from the Arab perspective, of 1967. See, e.g., James Piscatori, "Islamic Fundamentalism in the Wake of the Six Day War: Religious Self-Assertion in Political Conflict," in *Jewish Fundamentalism in Comparative Perspective: Religion, Ideology, and the Crisis of Modernity*, ed. Laurence J. Silberstein (New York: New York University Press, 1993), 79–93.

14. Lustick, *For the Land and the Lord*, 41.

15. Ibid., 45.

16. Ibid., 62.

17. Ibid.; for Gush Emunim activism, see, e.g., 65–71.

18. Ibid., 6–7, where he states that Haredim "do not engage actively in politics," 6, Menachem Friedman distinguishes between conservative (Haredi) and innovative (nationalist-religious) Jewish fundamentalisms; see his "Jewish Zealots: Conservative versus Innovative," in *Jewish Fundamentalism in Comparative Perspective*, ed. Silberstein, 148–63. Shahak and Mezvinsky, especially, emphasize the rise of Haredi fundamentalism; see their *Jewish Fundamentalism*, 23–54.

19. Peter A. Huff, "Haredim," in *Encyclopedia of Fundamentalism*, ed. Brenda E. Brasher (New York and London: Routledge, 2001), 207.

20. Shahak and Mezvinsky, *Jewish Fundamentalism*, 16, 19–22.

21. Ibid., 43.

22. Glazer, "Male and Female, King and Queen," 81.

23. Ibid., 82.

24. See, e.g., Axel Stähler, "Mothers in Israel? Female Jewish Identities and *Eretz Yisrael* in the Works of Jewish Women Writers of the Anglo-American Diaspora: Anne Roiphe, Tova Reich and Linda Grant," in *Jewish Women's Writing*, ed. Behlau and Reitz, 204.

25. This and some of the following paragraphs are a revised and extended version of my "Mothers in Israel," 204–06.

26. Anne Roiphe, *Lovingkindness* (1987; New York: Warner Books, 1997), 2. Subsequently cited parenthetically in the text.

27. Suzy Durruty, "Dédoublement identitaire et ennemis intérieurs dans *Loving Kindness* de Anne Roiphe," *Annales du Centre de Recherches sur L'Amerique Anglophone* 21 (1996): 43.

28. A change in Annie's attitude is intimated when she throws away a prayer book given to her by Sarai's rabbi, which she then, however, recovers: "I couldn't leave it there," Roiphe, *Lovingkindness*, 253.

29. For attempts at distinguishing between fundamentalism and Orthodoxy, see, e.g., James Davison Hunter, "Fundamentalism: An Introduction to a General Theory," in *Jewish Fundamentalism in Comparative Perspective*, ed. Silberstein, 28–29 and, more broadly, Aaron Kirschenbaum, "Fundamentalism: A Jewish Traditional Perspective," in *Jewish Fundamentalism in Comparative Perspective*, ed. Silberstein, 183–91.

30. See also Roiphe, *Lovingkindness*, 206–07: "Another of those fool kids you Americans can't seem to raise right come to lurk around the yeshivas looking for someone to take care of them, searching for the meaning of life you Americans couldn't give them. It's your materialism, your chaos, your divorce rate, your drug scene, your porno magazines, your cutthroat competitiveness and you're shipping it to us, every crazy Jewish kid whose parents ran out of insurance for the mental hospital takes a trip on El Al and finds God . . . We are in need of true Zionists, of people of learning and technology and democratic principles, and what do you send us, your broken, drug-riddled, starry-eyed, wiped-out dropouts. And what do they do when they get here? They breed and make more of themselves, exactly what we don't need, thank you very much."

31. Tova Reich was herself raised in an orthodox home, went to yeshiva, and continues to study (in the religious sense). See Blossom S. Kirschenbaum, "Tova Reich (1942)," in *Contemporary Jewish-American Novelists: A Biocritical Sourcebook*, ed. Joel Shatzky and Michael Taub (Westport, CT: Greenwood Press, 1997), 305–13.

32. See Roger Griffin, "Fascism," in *Encyclopedia of Fundamentalism*, ed. Brenda E. Brasher (New York and London: Routledge, 2001), 176.

33. Tova Reich, *The Jewish War: A Novel.* Library of Modern Jewish Literature (1995; Syracuse, NY: Syracuse University Press, 1997), 13. Subsequently cited parenthetically in the text.

34. Gen. 19:11–12.

35. Gen. 17:8.

36. See Gen. 22:14: "And Abraham called the name of that place Jehovah-jireh: as it is said *to* this day, In the mount of the LORD it shall be seen"; Jehovah-jireh literally means "God sees."

37. See, e.g., Roiphe, *Lovingkindness*, 17–19 and 194–95.

38. Reich, *Jewish War*, 90. Subsequently cited parenthetically in the text.

39. Ella Shohat, "Columbus, Palestine and Arab-Jews: Toward a Relational Approach to Community Identity," in *Cultural Readings of Imperialism: Edward Said and the Gravity of History*, ed. Keith Ansell-Pearson, Benita Parry, and Judith Squires (London: Lawrence and Wishart, 1997), 100.

40. See Hayden White, *Metahistory: The Historical Imagination in Nineteenth Century Europe* (Baltimore, London: Johns Hopkins University Press, 1973) and his *Tropics of Discourse: Essays in Cultural Criticism* (Baltimore, London: Johns Hopkins University Press, 1978).

41. See Reich, *Jewish War*, 102, 106–07.

42. The fortified mountain above the Dead Sea was held in the Great Revolt against Roman rule from 66 to 70 CE and beyond, until 73 CE, by zealots. In his *De bello Judaico*, Flavius Josephus gives an extended account of the Roman siege, and of the fall, of Masada, see *Josephus*, trans. Henry St. J. Thackeray, vol. 3; *The Jewish War, Books IV–VII* (London: Heinemann and Cambridge, MA: Harvard University Press, 1957), vii, 280–406.

43. See, e.g., Reich, *Jewish War*, 177 and 247. In Jonestown, too, more than 900 people died, among them 270 children.

44. For Eleazar's speeches, see Josephus, *War*, vii, 320–88 and particularly vii, 327–28: "Maybe, indeed, we ought from the very first . . . to have read God's purpose and to have recognized that the Jewish race, once beloved of Him, had been doomed to perdition."

45. For the concept of the Shechinah, see *Encyclopaedia Judaica*, s.v. "Shekhinah", vol. 14, cols. 1349–54.

46. See, for instance, Glazer, "Male and Female," 87 and Gershom Scholem, *On the Kabbalah and its Symbolism*, trans. Ralph Manheim (New York: Schocken Books, 1965), 106–08.

47. For a similar assessment see also Andrew Furman, *Israel through the Jewish-American Imagination: A Survey of Jewish-American Literature on Israel, 1928–1995* (Albany: State University of New York Press, 1997), 190–91.

48. Philip Roth, *The Counterlife* (1986; New York: Vintage International, 1996), 147. Subsequently cited parenthetically in the text.

49. See, e.g., *Lovingkindness*, 206–07.

50. Melvin Jules Bukiet, *Strange Fire: A Novel* (New York: Norton, 2001), 156. Subsequently cited parenthetically in the text.

51. For an in-depth assessment of "The Real Significance of Baruch Goldstein," largely based on sources otherwise inaccessible to non-Hebrew speakers, see the eponymous chapter in Shahak and Mezvinsky, *Jewish Fundamentalism*, 96–112.

52. Shahak and Mezvinsky, *Jewish Fundamentalism*, 6.

53. Ibid., 11; see also, for the alleged superior value of Jewish lives in fundamentalist thought, ix, 58, 62, 153–54.

54. Ibid., 22, 153–54.

55. Bukiet's *Strange Fire* was published in spring 2001. It may be worthwhile noting that Roth's *The Counterlife* and Reich's *Master of the Return* both appeared before the fatwa was pronounced on Salman Rushdie.

56. See, e.g., Louvish, *Days*, 146.

57. Ibid., 131 and 125 where he refers to the *maladie humaine*.

58. Tariq Ali, *The Clash of Fundamentalisms: Crusades, Jihads and Modernity* (London, New York: Verso, 2002). However, Ali's reference is one of disagreement and he argues polemically against Huntington's concept of the "clash of civilizations," see 281–83.

59. Of course, the phrase of the "new world order" is topical in the context of the First Gulf War and was used by George Bush (in reference to Winston Churchill) in various speeches in the aftermath of the "Cold War" and the Iraqi invasion of Kuwait in August 1990. See, e.g., Huntington, *Clash of Civilizations*, 31.

60. A fifth Blok novel, The Fundamental Blok, is in preparation; see http://www.simonlouvish.com/unpublished.htm (retrieved July 14, 2004).

61. Bryan Cheyette, "Madness now and to come," *TLS* (October 14–20, 1988): 1154.

62. For the related concepts of the "Hidden" or "Last Imam" and the "Mahdi," see, e.g., the respective entries by David Cook and Jeffrey Kaplan in *Encyclopedia of Fundamentalism*, ed. Brenda E. Brasher (New York, London: Routledge, 2001), 232–33 and 291–92. The expectation of the return of the Hidden Imam is similar to Jewish messianism, as is the notion of promoting redemption by the establishment of a just messianic society; see David Cook, "Imam, the Last," *Encyclopedia of Fundamentalism*, ed. Brasher, 233.

63. Teddy Jamieson, "Miracle Worker," *The List* (April 4–17, 1997), 91.

64. Louvish refers repeatedly to the crusades; see, e.g., Louvish, *Days*, 3–13, 94 *et passim* and to intra-Christian schisms, see, e.g., Louvish, *Days*, 95–96.

65. Tariq Ali, in his *Clash of Fundamentalisms*, refers to alleged U.S. imperialist fundamentalism as "the mother of all fundamentalisms," 281. See also the headline of a newspaper clip quoted by Louvish, *Days*, 209: "WASHINGTON'S JIHAD."

66. Louvish, *Days*, 311. Subsequently cited parenthetically in the text. According to Shi'ite apocalyptic beliefs the Last Imam will "appear in Mecca, at the Ka'ba, and gather a band of 313 followers to himself," Cook, "Imam, The Last," 232.

67. Cf. Gen. 8:13–22.

68. Jens Brockmeier and Donal Carbaugh, "Introduction," in *Narrative and Identity: Studies in Autobiography, Self and Culture*, ed. Jens Brockmeier and Donal Carbaugh (Amsterdam, Philadelphia: John Benjamins, 2001), 10.

69. Cheyette, "Madness now and to come," 1154.

70. Shahak and Mezvinsky, *Jewish Fundamentalism*, 150.

71. Jonathan Webber, "Rethinking Fundamentalism: The Readjustment of Jewish Society in the Modern World," in *Studies in Religious Fundamentalism*, ed. Lionel Caplan (London: Macmillan, 1987), 101. In the Jewish context, as Webber also points out, both Hebrew and Yiddish lack a word for "fundamentalism." In the monumental English-language *Encyclopedia Judaica* of 1970–1971 no entries for "Fundamentalism" or "Haredi(m)" are included.

72. Louvish, born in 1947 in Glasgow, soon afterward immigrated with his parents to Israel; during the war of 1967 he served as a military cameraman; in 1968 he left Israel to visit the London School of Film Technique; since then he has been living most of the time in London, but in the "Emerging Voices" series of new international fiction of Interlink Books he "represents" Israel.

PART II

BEYOND THE BINARY: LITERARY INTERVENTIONS IN POLARIZATION

CHAPTER 5

DECONSTRUCTING FUNDAMENTALISMS IN HANIF KUREISHI'S *THE BLACK ALBUM*

WENDY O'SHEA-MEDDOUR

I

At the Hay Literature Festival in 2003, Hanif Kureishi described a scene of horror: a "place of darkness" where "the authorities" can "dehumanise others," a site in which "abuse takes place." The torture chamber to which he refers is "silence": the place "where words can't go." According to Kureishi, the forbidden, the sacred, and the unspeakable must all be represented in art, for the alternative is tyranny and madness. He identifies the artist as the figure capable of exposing (in order to dismantle) this site of horror: "theatre, or poetry, or dance, the novel, or pop" are the "places" where it is possible to speak of the "darkest and most dangerous things," thereby preventing, or at least stalling, the dehumanization of others. If an artist attempts to restrain his expression, he becomes complicit in a brutal process of torture and incarceration: "The person who doesn't want to hear his own words," Kureishi argues,

> is prisoner, prison and the law. Real dictators in the world are a picture, too, of dictators within individuals, of certain kinds of minds.[1]

An artist who silences or refuses to listen to the "words inside his own body" is accused of reflecting and perpetuating dictatorial societies in which "free speech" is denied. For many, the idea that the body is a source of language rather than a product of language is problematic, but to stay with Kureishi's theory, it is clear that he considers the unrestrained "talk" of the artist to be an essential "performance" of liberation.[2] Unsurprisingly, the experimental artist who gives free reign to the words that emerge from *within* is highly esteemed:

> Speaking from themselves and sensibly refusing to do advertising, they do nonetheless speak for some of us, and they take the punishment on our behalf too. In the absence of other convincing figures, like priests or leaders, it is tempting to idealise artists and the culture they make.[3]

As artistic expression is identified as a means of destroying silence, disrupting dictatorship, and dismantling scenes of torture, it inevitably becomes a scene of punishment. In a Nietzschean move, Kureishi names artists as culture's *only* convincing figures: individuals willing to "take punishment on our behalf."[4] Salman Rushdie, Kureishi's friend and mentor, clearly inhabits the subtext of this speech. Like many artists, Kureishi was deeply affected by Khomeini's fatwa against the author of *The Satanic Verses*. He explained to interviewers: "There were all these blokes who wanted to kill this friend of mine, and I wanted to know why, so I went and found them." Thus began his "research" on "Muslim 'fundamentalism.'" It involved going "around the colleges and mosques nearby," and talking to "these kids, who were 20 or 21, at college doing engineering and computer studies and stuff, about why they were such raging fundamentalists."[5] The result was Kureishi's second novel, *The Black Album*.

In an interview in *The Guardian* called "Faith, Love and Fundamentalism" Kureishi described *The Black Album* as "an attempt to write a book about ideology, about Islam; about a young man who is drawn to that, struggles with it and finally rejects it."[6] When the book was first published in 1995, it was released into cultures in which the dominant politics of representation encourages readers to assume that a Muslim-sounding name on the jacket of a novel, in combination with an image of an Indian-looking man (a smiling Kureishi strikes a thoughtful pose on the back cover), qualifies the author to speak for the Muslim South Asian "other." In Anglo-American contexts, the works of "post-colonial authors" are repeatedly subject to such representational readings. But when speaking to an Indian audience, for whom the reception of postcolonial authors is of course different, Kureishi insisted that he was not trying to speak for "the Muslim other": "I am not a Muslim at all. I'm an observer, a humanist; I'm interested in the way men and women

relate to one another. Religion is a business. *I came from a British intellectual family;* we were encouraged to think for ourselves" (my italics).[7]
In other words, he is a self-proclaimed and stridently secular British free-
thinking liberal. This is often overlooked by readers and critics in the
West. As Kureishi acknowledges, his initial success resulted from the
assumption that he could function as a "cultural translator": someone
who could make sense of the British Muslim Asian "other." There was
little advantage in proclaiming either his British or his secular, liberal
credentials. Besides, prevailing attitudes in British culture meant that few
would hear.

II

The struggle to resist the dominant politics of representation facing the
postcolonial author in Anglo-American culture is endlessly played out in
Kureishi's work. The realist aesthetic, currently privileged in contemporary Western culture, promotes a reading practice in which a character
(or community) from an ethnic or religious minority, when portrayed in
a novel, play, or film, is read as "representative." One way in which the
artist can challenge the onslaught of the stereotype is to counter it with
an array of "positive images." But as Shohat and Stam argue in
Unthinking Eurocentrism, this approach remains caught within an essentialist trap. By offering only positive representations of minority groups,
texts will appear unconvincing, monolithic, and dull. Moreover, instead
of distorting and undermining existing power structures, texts invert and
repeat them. The effort to evade the dictates of the realist aesthetic
clearly marks Kureishi's work. His novels and screenplays are full of
British characters with complex cultural and racial subject positions that
defy singular definitions. (Jamila, in *The Buddha of Suburbia,* would be
a good example. As an Indian, British, Muslim, bisexual, feminist, wife,
she is difficult to read as an "authentic" example of any one of these
subjectivities.) Self-conscious fictional characters, aware that their artistic
expression will be considered "representative" of their race or religion,
often police both their behavior and their work accordingly. In Kureishi's
critical essays and in the lives of his fictional characters, one can trace
an unresolved tension between the desire to experience unrestrained artistic expression and the desire to "protect" one's cultural location from the
tyranny of the stereotype.

A condensed exploration of this tension is played out in *The Buddha
of Suburbia.* At a meeting of their drama group, the protagonist, Karim,
and a black actress called Tracey battle out two opposing conceptual positions. Tracey complains that Karim's characterization of his Pakistani

Muslim uncle Anwar (who goes on "hunger strike" to force his unwilling daughter into an "arranged marriage") will reinforce the idea that "black people" are "irrational, ridiculous" and "hysterical."[8] She considers Karim a traitor and maintains that responsibility to one's culture is paramount. Karim, on the other hand, balks at any form of "censorship" and believes that "Truth" should have a "higher value" than loyalty to one's race or culture.

Although both positions are rendered sympathetically, the text suggests that both are naïve and problematic. While Tracey considers Karim's approach to be politically irresponsible, her desire to reductively "protect *our* culture" (my italics) reveals that her position is complicit with existing power structures. Despite the fact that she and Karim have little in common either racially or culturally (other than their Britishness), she views both herself and Karim through the reductive lens of dominant white culture—she refers to "*our* culture" and "*us*" "blacks." Inadvertently, she repeats what she accuses Karim of doing: reinforcing the "picture" of "what white people already think of *us*" (180). Karim's position is similarly flawed. The fact that this argument is staged in front of an exploitative and powerful white director (the "High Court Judge Pyke") emphasizes that his ideological position regarding the freedom of the artist cannot escape the glare of existing power structures. The text also reminds the reader that Karim's "frantic" need to "freely" express himself is based on the fear that the white director might sack him should he fail to come up with a *convincing* "black" character. The naïveté of Karim's position is further underscored by the fact that, for his first acting role, Karim is cast as Mowgli and asked to darken his skin and put on an Indian accent to appear more "authentic." Even when Karim and Tracey establish themselves as successful actors in New York, they are still subject to the gaze of the white director. Their Britishness remains invisible to others, and *authentic* "ethnic entertainment" is put on to make the "black British" feel at home: seated in the front row they watch in bewilderment as "dark-skinned" dancers with drums and "a black man" naked "from the waist up" fling themselves around for their benefit (223–24). In other words, the novel does not let us forget that Karim's desire to express himself freely—however noble his intent—cannot be isolated from the external power structures for which he performs.

Unfortunately, there is a crucial, obvious point that the text fails to acknowledge in its representation of this argument: that the libertine desire to place "free artistic expression" above all else is a highly cultural and relatively modern Western tradition, and should not be mistaken for a neutral, "free," or apolitical concept. Nevertheless, *The Buddha of Suburbia* does suggest that the privileging of aesthetic realism and its almost tyrannical transformation of the singular into the general (specifically with regard to "minority" groups) is a reading practice that renders the binary opposition between censorship and the freedom of expression obsolete. For even if one accepts the problematic notion that it is possible for an author or actor to "freely express" a single character, the actual moment of expression will negate the artist's intention because the character will be "read" as a "representative" figure the instant the work is released into a culture in which the realist aesthetic holds sway. Both Tracey's and Karim's responses to the realist aesthetic demand are unsatisfactory. By ignoring the realist aesthetic, one falls victim to it. But by heeding it, one restricts artistic potential and fails to escape its confines.

Although Tracey and Karim's debate remains a binary one, it is with a sigh of relief that many have identified the presence of a third option within Kureishi's work: his novels are full of characters with plural and fluid subjectivities that resist traditional aesthetic demands for realistic representation. Relatively unified and singular identities, so typical of many realist novels, are rejected in favor of multiple, and often contradictory, subject positions. Exit the English man who loves football, blondes, pie and chips, and all things British, and enter the Pakistani/Irish, line-dancing, Buddhist-Muslim member of the British National Party (BNP). This foregrounding of hybridity makes it almost impossible for a careful reader to view Kureishi as a "cultural translator," as someone on "the inside" who can explain and communicate the "truths" of multicultural Britain. By introducing characters with plural and contradictory subjectivities, Kureishi mobilizes a particular technique of resistance. It is this literary tactic that has caused critics such as Gayatri Spivak to praise Kureishi for his experimentation with "subject-effects."[9]

Undoubtedly, discontinuous subject-effects are one way of resisting reading practices promoted by essentialist identity politics and aesthetic realism. *The Buddha of Suburbia* employs them to great effect. But this trademark strategy is virtually abandoned in *The Black Album*. With the exception of the protagonist, Shahid Hasan, and his immediate relatives—who are liberal, British/Asian "free-thinkers" exploring a range of subject positions—most of the other characters (particularly the young Muslim ones) attempt to inhabit singular subject positions and, as such, are left to the mercy of the stereotype. Does this novel experiment with a different formula of resistance? Does the nature of subject positions such as "Muslim fundamentalist" preclude the possibility of plural subjectivities?

Or is Kureishi only willing to defend "liberal" subjects against the burden of representation?

III

The Black Album is the story of a young student, Shahid, who becomes a member of Riaz's Muslim brotherhood while also having an affair with his lecturer, Deedee Osgood. Meetings after those in the mosque in the day are followed by scenes of drugs, music, and experimental sex at night. At the beginning of the novel, Shahid is an "invisible" subject whose only desire is to "belong."[10] He is a subject-effect with whom we are familiar from Kureishi's earlier work. But in order to become a visible subject in the world of *The Black Album,* he must attain a unified identity and choose between what are presented as two mutually exclusive subjectivities: that of the "Islamic fundamentalist" and that of the "liberal fundamentalist." The first subject position is promised if he dedicates himself to Riaz's Muslim brotherhood, the second if he gives himself, both physically and mentally, to Deedee Osgood. The narrative is structured around these two crudely expressed and excessively polarized forms of fundamentalism. The reader follows Shahid as he journeys (mostly on the London underground) between the two points of identification. It is important to stress that I do not believe that such static, essentialist, fundamentalist categories exist "out there" in the real world.[11] Nor am I arguing that Kureishi holds this to be the case. This latter line of enquiry is of little interest. Recent poststructuralist theories have undermined the significance of "authorial intention" by revealing that this literary approach depends on the metaphysical assumption that fixed meanings reside in the head of the author and can be accessed via the text. To hinge a reading on Kureishi's "belief" about fundamentalism is therefore somewhat of a dead end. While *The Black Album*'s monolithic representation of Islamists is clearly vulnerable to a reading that reinforces the dominant culture's prejudices about Islamic fundamentalists, it is interesting to note that, during the first half of the novel, a similar case could be made about the representation of liberal fundamentalists. In other words, at times, *The Black Album* fails to protect a range of its characters from essentialist readings. In fact, it actively encourages such readings. Therefore, before looking at where the novel eventually takes us ideologically, let us focus on the ways in which subjectivity and fundamentalisms are both constructed and deconstructed in the novel.

If the plots in Kureishi's novels usually resist essentialist readings because they focus on characters that experience an array of coexisting subjectivities, *The Black Album* is clearly atypical. There are no devout British-Indian Muslims who love Scottish shortbread, martial arts, Bart Simpson, and scuba diving. Nor are there any liberal feminists who attend embroidery classes, lunches at the Masonic Lodge, and Sunday Mass. The characters must choose a subject position, and Shahid is fairly unique even in a place of indecision. Plural and sometimes-contradictory subjectivities are edged out of the text in favor of characters that strive to experience a singular and unified subject position. This does not mean that characters in *The Black Album* experience only one type of subjectivity—far from it. But in order to enjoy what is presented as a "fundamentalist" identity, they must reject or suppress all other subjectivities. This results in a culture of identity exchange.

By looking at the characters' attempts to conform to singular subjectivities, it becomes clear that *The Black Album*'s stance on subjectivity is not dissimilar to that in Kureishi's previous work. Those who choose "fundamentalist" subjectivities do so at their cost. Chad, the once-pimping, drug-dealing, pop-music fanatic, suppresses and guards against his former subjectivities to become an Islamic fundamentalist. His "withdrawal" from music is a painful one, and his arduous attempt to "police" himself against his own laughter is equally grueling. (Even the group's leader, Riaz, writes poetry secretly so as to conceal what may be perceived as unnecessary "frivolity" [57].) Members of Riaz's Muslim brotherhood constantly regulate themselves against any form of pleasure and engage in a host of clichéd behavior and activities, including unquestioning allegiance, self-righteousness, book burning, and petrol bombing. In fact, they are described as much akin to robots: Chad behaves as if "someone had activated a motor in his stomach" (10), while Riaz eats as though "he were fuelling a machine" (4). However, those who identify with an extreme form of liberal hedonism do not fare much better. Deedee Osgood lives out an endless repetition of sexual experimentation, violent fantasies, drug highs, and house parties; a life depicted as having loneliness and physical harm at its core. Dr. Andrew Brownlow, a fundamentalist Marxist, is also damaged by his loyalty to a singular and apparently exhausted subjectivity: once an articulate intellectual, he is now reduced to a series of stammers and stutters. Like the young Muslims, he is depicted as being mechanical and "thumps himself on the head as if to repair a connection" (26).

With the exception of Shahid, who swings (often unconvincingly) between two identity poles—"One day he could feel passionately one thing, the next the opposite" (122)—the stereotype traps all characters that are committed to a singular identity. Extreme liberals, hedonists,

Marxists, and Islamists are all condemned to a life of caricature because, by identifying with a unified subjectivity, they have made themselves vulnerable, the novel suggests, to essentialist readings. To varying degrees they are all portrayed as mindless, misguided, childish, and self-destructive. Kureishi's familiar narrative technique of resistance, one that emphasizes heterogeneity and specificity, is abandoned. Instead, characters motivated by the desire to experience a unified subjectivity are left to the mercy of essentialist stereotypes. This is a fate from which some are rescued. Others are not.

IV

Although *The Black Album* is constructed around two drastically over-simplified binary oppositions and populated with characters rendered defenseless against essentialist readings, the text simultaneously deconstructs and undermines the stability of what it constructs as the poles of Islamic and liberal fundamentalism. In order to look at this further, it is helpful to refer to what Jacques Derrida would identify as the mark of "the trace." The trace is that which undermines metaphysical laws of contradiction by revealing that a pure concept ("the one") is always already contaminated by characteristics of its excluded opposite ("the other"). In Derrida's words:

> The outside, "spatial" and "objective" exteriority which we believe we know as the most familiar thing in the world, as familiarity itself would not appear without . . . the nonpresence of the other inscribed within the sense of the present . . . The trace, where the relationship with the other is marked.[12]

With regard to *The Black Album,* the concept of the trace enables us to explore the ways in which the text repeatedly draws attention to similarities between apparently opposing fundamentalist subject positions.

As one might expect in a plot that revolves around the activities of a group of simplistic, book-burning, petrol-bombing Muslims, the text is full of references to bombs, massacres, and explosions. However, although there is a sinister backdrop of unexplained bomb explosions in London (associated with Islamic fundamentalism by textual inference), only one explosion is explicitly blamed on Riaz's Muslim brotherhood. The language of terrorism is far more central to the depiction of Deedee Osgood. On her first "date" with Shahid, she drops "a bomb on her tongue" (47) and pressurizes him to do the same. Moments later, they arrive at a silver warehouse surrounded by "barbed wire," "sentries," and "security cameras." It resembles "a prison yard," and "some kids" attempt to climb the surrounding fence like "refugees." Having spent some time in this "inferno," amid "scream[s] of pleasure," they go on to an "end-of-decade" house party where "big men" search "Shahid, putting their hands down his trousers" (51). Inside, "bodies" are spread across the floor "as if they had been massacred." Terrorism, violence, and self-destruction, terms so familiar in cultural representations of Muslim fundamentalism, are repeatedly used to describe Osgood's liberal fundamentalist lifestyle. This constitutes just one instance of the trace. The theme of childishness is another example. Osgood's husband, Dr. Brownlow, a disillusioned Marxist, accuses Muslims of having an "infantile dependence on God." Kureishi's caricatured Muslim brotherhood clearly conforms to this stereotype. When they prepare to defend a Muslim family against racist attacks, they don "duffle coats and woolly hats." One member of the group is described as looking "as if his mother had dressed him for school on the day" (67). And when their leader, Riaz, is absent, we are told that the group becomes "childish" and "forgets the reasons for their actions" (107). However, the suffocating "freedom of instruction" (22) that Deedee offers is similarly infantilized. A rather disconcerting link between sexual experimentation and childhood is repeatedly made. At a party in "the White Room," a woman who is "naked except for high heels and a large plastic penis strapped to her thighs" struts between others who are "dressed as babies" (50). On one of the many occasions when Shahid is depicted "playing with himself," the pleasures of "pornography" are likened to those of "children's books" (124). In the middle of an explicit sex scene, Deedee and Shahid both tuck "their legs in the air like babies" and after "turning herself into pornography," Deedee falls to sleep in a fetal position "with her legs pulled up, sucking her thumb" (176, 100). In this manner, both Muslim and liberal fundamentalist positions are presented as being childlike and vulnerable. But in many ways, the brothers in their duffle coats are far less disturbing than the instances in which masturbation, pornography, sexual experimentation, and childhood innocence are combined.

Shahid frequently marks the site of fracture at which the binary oppositions between "fundamentalist" liberalism and Islamism deconstruct, and parallel incidents are juxtaposed to undermine the differences between what appear to be polar opposites. For example, there are only three memorable occasions in the text when Shahid is shown to be "on his knees." The first takes place in Shahid's room. "Afraid" that "his ignorance" about Islamic history or basic Muslim rituals "will place him in a no man's land" at a time when "every one was insisting on their identity" and "coming out as a man, woman, gay, black, Jew" (76), he asks for his friend Hat's instruction. In line with the text's suggestion that Islam is for the intellectually vacant, Hat teaches Shahid (and the unfamiliar reader) only the "actions" of Muslim prayer. Intellectually unsatisfied, Shahid attempts to offer his own form of secular prayer:

> While praying, Shahid had little notion of what to think, of what the cerebral concomitant to the actions should be . . . so, on his knees, he celebrated to himself the substantiality of the world, the fact of existence, the inexplicable phenomenon of life, art, humour and love itself—in murmured language, itself another sacred miracle. He accompanied this awe and wonder with suitable music, the "Ode of Joy", from Beethoven's Ninth, for instance, which he hummed inaudibly.[13]

The reader's perception of Muslim prayer would have been very different if Hat had informed Shahid that his "actions" should be accompanied by the recitation of verses from the Qu'ran, both preselected and individually chosen, which celebrate the substantiality of the world and the universe, the fact of existence, the awesome phenomenon of life, death, the hereafter, spiritual contentment, justice, and love itself—to be murmured in the Arabic language, itself another sacred miracle. This awe and wonder was to be accompanied by praises for the Creator, to be uttered both audibly and inaudibly. Instead, the implication is that there is no "cerebral concomitant" in Muslim prayer, and Shahid's attempt at spiritual submission remains rather unconvincing. It is followed by a far more persuasive effort at the feet of Deedee Osgood:

> Suddenly, she sat up and licked her lips. He shrank back. "You're looking at me as if I were a piece of cake. What are you thinking?" "I deserve you. I'm going to like eating you. Here. Here I said." On his knees he went to her.[14]

The final instance of kneeling occurs when Deedee offers Shahid a rather humiliating ultimatum—he must "leave his friends to God" if he wishes to be with her:

> His trousers had fallen around his ankles, resting in the wet; his pants were around his knees, his arms across his chest. The stink of vomit rose around them. She laughed. "I like looking at you like that . . . Say this: I am an atheist, a blasphemer and a pervert. Say it on your knees in a toilet."[15]

While Riaz's group "assume" that Shahid is their "possession" and require him to stop thinking and mindlessly submit himself to God, Deedee's drive for ownership is, as the above example illustrates, often more degrading. She applies kisses to Shahid as if he were one of her herd, "*stamping* him with love" (108), and frequently uses her drug-induced confidence to dominate her young lover. The language of sexual experimentation, drugs, and religion become interchangeable. After spending time popping pills and conjuring up "the fantasy Deedee masturbates to" on the Northern Line (103), Shahid begins to resent the "illusions he's been subject to! What torrents of drug-inspired debris he had allowed to stream through his head! What banal fantasies he believed were visions!" (108). When Shahid is tired of sexual fantasies and wants to attain Islamic conviction, the text suggests that he must swallow religion like one of his pills: he "grasped" that he must "follow the prescriptions and be patient" (80). The reader is constantly reminded that intoxication and addiction are central to Shahid's experience of both spiritual and sexual pleasure.

Dressing up constitutes another instance of the trace. While "the brothers" give Shahid a salwar kamiz to wear, Deedee orders him to put on makeup and parade naked (109, 98). The consecutive nature of these events serves to emphasize that Shahid's body is, in both arenas, a physical place of contestation. The tube provides yet another link between polarized visions of fundamentalisms. Not only does it carry Shahid between the two subject positions with speed and ease, the effects of both saturate it. At one station, "a bomb had exploded on the main course of Victoria Station" (84); at another, "the platform of Baker Street was Arcadia itself" (103). Like Shahid, the London tube appears to be a site in which both Riaz's version of Muslim fundamentalism and Osgood's version of liberal fundamentalism vie for dominance.

V

By exploring these instances of the trace, it is possible to see how Kureishi's text might undermine and complicate dominant culture's assumptions about Muslim "fundamentalism." At its most challenging moments, *The Black Album* reminds us that secular liberalism could just as convincingly be described as having a fundamentalist core. It exposes a form of liberal fundamentalism so often invisible because it is "naturalised" by the existing hegemony. By exaggerating and then collapsing the binary opposition between Islamic and liberal fundamentalists in this way, the trace marks the site at which the novel occasionally opens up exciting ways of thinking about the heterogeneity of both Muslim and liberal subjectivities. But as the novel progresses, the possibility of exploring varied or complex Muslim subjectivities is closed off.

Without exception, the Muslim characters in the novel are dim-witted. Riaz's Muslim brotherhood is little more than a bumbling, disorganized, and inane scout-group. And the novel offers only one explanation of the possible appeal of Islam to young British youth: it is a direct response to vitriolic racism. One of the key members of the group, Chad, was adopted by white racists, and the "sense of seclusion drove him mad. He wanted to bomb them" (89). He is described as a drug-dealing pimp, "spring loaded, a gun about to go off," until he meets Riaz, converts, and changes his name to Muhammad Shahabuddin Ali-Shah. The text implies that Riaz, the leader of the group, had similar experiences. Riaz had "little physical presence," and Shahid "imagines him in the corner of the school playground, his hands across his face shying from the bullying blows" (143). Shahid also suffered:

> Even when he vomited and defecated with fear before going to school, or when he returned with cuts, bruises and his bag slashed with knives, she [his mother] behaved as if so appalling an insult couldn't exist. And so she turned away from him.[16]

In *The Black Album,* the mosque promises one irresistible thing to all these victims of racism. It is an "uncompetitive, peaceful, meditative" place where "race and class barriers had been suspended" (109). There is no attempt to engage with the complex range of conceptual positions that Islamic thought offers to subjects of the modern world. The appeal of Islam is explained as a result of and protection against racism, nothing more.

Although on the decline after the "sacred" "aubergine exhibition," the fatwa against Rushdie's *Satanic Verses* is the event that really kills off *The Black Album*'s play with the trace. From this point on, Deedee is rescued from hedonist excess and becomes the bastion of free speech, free choice, and free thought. Once she starts teaching "the book," the narrative surrounds her with a pink and rosy haze. The spaced-out, aging teacher who deals out drugs to vulnerable students and issues orders from vomit-soaked toilets is all forgotten. Instead, she is described as being "so brightly alive; how people enjoyed her classes" (184). Shahid fondly recalls that she "always stimulated him to think" and "told him, don't do anything you don't want to do—not ever" (156). We also discover that she provided a safe haven for a young Muslim girl who ran away from her parents because "religion treated women as second-class citizens." (The girl, after engaging in "discussion with her parents," commits suicide [191].) While Deedee comes to embody freedom and intellectual stimulation, the Muslim groups are characterized by mindless violence and buffoonery: they are not "afraid to speak," they just have "nothing to say" (152). Their apparent inability to reason is exacerbated by the fact that the reader is given no justification for their anger against *The Satanic Verses.* On the contrary, "Islam" is presented as a suffocating blanket of "certainty" that forbids thinking and demands mindlessness. (One need only look at the heated debate and variety of opinion on a few Islamic websites to disrupt this harmonic and monolithic representation.) When Shahid argues that literature disturbs us and makes us think, Riaz responds: "Must we prefer this indulgence to the profound and satisfying comforts of religion?" (153). When Shahid pleads: "Riaz, there are so many questions I have," he is told: "Dismiss them! . . . Just believe in the truth!" (146). The "stupidity" of the brothers becomes a significant theme:

> The stupidity of the demonstration appalled him. How narrow they were, how unintelligent, how . . . embarrassing it all was.[17]

The reader is very clearly aligned with Shahid when he asks: "Surely, brother, there must be more to life than swallowing one old book?" (226). This is reaffirmed by Kureishi in his essay "The Carnival of Culture," in which he rallies liberals to fulfill their "human duty to inform them [young Muslims] that there is more than one book in the world."[18] For Shahid, it becomes a question of "to think or not to think." This choice is articulated by Zulma, his sister-in-law: "They will slaughter us soon for thinking. Have you stopped thinking, Shahid?" (156). When Zulma drags Shahid out of one of Riaz's meetings, he is "gladdened by the sudden freedom" (155). After contact with his Muslim "friends," Shahid rushes for an antidote with increasing speed—usually finding it in the arms of Deedee, some porn, a pill, or a stiff drink. Although I am reluctant to conflate the novel's narrator with the novel's author, it is difficult not to notice the similarities between these episodes and Kureishi's response to his own "meetings" with "young 'fundamentalists.'" In *The Word and the Bomb* he writes: "I found these sessions so intellectually stultifying and claustrophobic that at the end I'd rush into the nearest pub and drink rapidly, wanting to reassure myself that I was still in England."[19] England is defined as the place where you can do what you want: a sentiment echoed by the central character in Monica Ali's *Brick Lane:* "'This is England,' she said. 'You can do whatever you like.'"[20] However, this freedom is restricted to those who fully adhere to liberalism, and it is made very clear that Riaz is someone who does *not* belong to this country. When Shahid asks him if he "likes living in England," he replies, "This will never be my home . . . I will never entirely understand it," whereas for Shahid, England "suits me. There's nowhere else I will feel more comfortable" (146). By the end of the book, the Muslim "fundamentalists" have been referred to as "throat-cutters" (203), "book-burners" (189), and petrol bombers. And immediately after the demonstration against *The Satanic Verses,* Shahid hears that there "has been another bombing in the City: many roads had check-points. He knew it would be wrong to think that everything would be alright" (189). What started as a bumbling scout-group has become a real and sinister threat to the English "way of life."

Throughout *The Black Album* it is emphasized that the Muslim fundamentalist threat is not only incomprehensible to liberal sensibilities, it is characterized by its incomprehensibility. Their inability (or unwillingness) to think is what defines them. Kureishi's failure to engage with or offer a convincing account of Islamism closes down one of the most exciting possibilities of the trace. As Bobby Sayyid argues in *A Fundamental Fear,* Western literary and intellectual engagement with Islamism rarely moves beyond "cultural essentialism and particularism." "Accounts of Islamism," he observes, are largely dominated by two fundamentalist icons: "book burners" and "suicide bombers" (5). This is clearly true of *The Black Album.* Quoting Robert Young's definition of "postmodernism" as "European culture's awareness that it is no longer the unquestioned and dominant centre of the world,"[21] Sayyid suggests that one could

> see in Islamism an attempt to articulate modernity that is not structured around Eurocentrism. That is, to take seriously the Islamists' claims to being a movement dedicated to a level of denial of the West, but not to read in this rejection of the Western an attempt to establish "traditional" agrarian societies.[22]

In other words, both the Islamist and the postmodern intellectual are concerned with decentering the West, and both share an incredulity toward Western metanarratives. Furthermore, contemporary manifestations of Islamism cannot be entirely separated from contemporary manifestations of postmodernism. They have emerged within overlapping conceptual air space:

> The appeal and power of the Islamist projects are due to the way in which they are able to combine the deconstructivist logic of the postmodern critique of modernity with an attempt to speak from another centre, outside the orbit of the West . . . the logic of Islamism is threatening because it fails to recognize the universalism of the Western project.[23]

Islamism is, of course, very different from the postmodern condition in the sense that it is centered around a specific metanarrative—a difference Sayyid is aware of and discusses in depth—but Islamism and postmodernism share the desire to "decolonize the forms of European thought," undermine the "absoluteness of any Western account of history," and mobilize a rigorous critique of "the Eurocentric premises of Western knowledge."[24] Unfortunately, the Muslims in *The Black Album* would have trouble spelling, let alone reflecting on, any of these issues. Consequently, the deconstructive potential of the trace fails to go beyond superficial and ideologically biased points of intersection. The reader is only encouraged to identify similarities between liberal and Islamic extremism in the form of infantile dependence, addiction, intoxication, and dressing up. Kureishi's unwillingness to step outside a Eurocentric liberal framework or engage with Islamism in any serious way means that the Muslim characters can only be read as unthinking, unquestioning, and incapable of reasoned logic.

One of the most interesting things about *The Black Album* is its strict code of crime and punishment. In nineteenth-century novels, the adulteress must meet with a grisly death—we expect no less. But the didactic conclusion in the final chapters of Kureishi's novel is equally harsh. The Muslim groups are humiliated and eventually self-destruct (Shahid's big brother holds a knife to Riaz's throat and later forces him to undress, while the terrible screams of Chad can be heard when a petrol bomb explodes in his face). Meanwhile, Shahid and Deedee are returned to what is presented as a postmodern safe haven and go on a romantic excursion to the seaside.

As well as punishing the Muslim fundamentalist characters for their transgressions, the narrative also keeps a strict rein on the moderate liberal reader. Chapter 10 illustrates this well. The reader is written into the position of a complicit voyeur while the previously self-conscious Deedee "splays" her fingers and shows Shahid

> her cunt. He picked up the candle and, holding it close, peered in. He was so pleased, and the drug, making her smiling face waxy, rendered her in magazine soft-focus; without losing her soul she was turning herself into pornography.[25]

Deedee goes on to perform tricks with a "deodorant bottle"—details are not spared: "She invited him to watch while she lifted one leg and pressed the finger into the muscle of her arse until it disappeared." For those who are uncomfortable with being aligned with the narrator in this way, the text quickly disciplines them by presenting them with the sinister alternative. As Deedee, exhausted from her antics, falls into a faintlike swoon, Shahid recalls a conversation that he had with Hat and Riaz:

> Hat had stated that homosexuals should be beheaded, though first they should be offered the option of marriage. Riaz had become interested and said that God would burn homosexuals forever in hell, scorching their flesh in a furnace before replacing their skin as new, and repeating this throughout eternity . . . Riaz's hatred had been so cool, so certain. Shahid had wanted to mention it to Deedee but was nervous that it might distract her. Was Riaz not, though, his friend? If only Shahid could understand where such ideas came from.[26]

This conversation may well have "distracted" Deedee (and possibly resulted in unfortunate anatomical consequences), but its strange position within the narrative serves a clear purpose. It functions as a sort of electric parameter fence. Readers who question the merit or narrative pleasure of Kureishi's pornographic scenes are quickly shocked back into the mainstream "liberal" position. The text suggests that disloyalty to liberal values (extremist or otherwise) will result in a world in which barbaric, homophobic, Muslim "fundamentalists"—with their Ian Paisley–style tirades—will gain power. This textual arrangement leaves the reader little alternative than to accept the inclusion of the pornographic narrative: we, like Shahid, are encouraged to defend the right to peer into Deedee's "cunt" or face what is presented as a frightening and incomprehensible alternative: the "cool hatred" of the Muslim "fundamentalist." In this manner, the floating liberal reader is herded back into the fold.

The Black Album is a very moral tale that offers one safe conceptual space in which characters and readers can exist. They must have total conviction in uncertainty. Both Deedee and Shahid experience these moments of postmodern ephiphany:

> How could anyone confine themselves to one system or creed? Why should they feel that they had to? There was no fixed self; surely, our several selves melted and mutated daily. There had to be innumerable ways of being in the world.[27]

The Black Album stridently suggests that Muslims cannot experience "innumerable ways of being in the world" within the framework of Islam. Instead, they are molded into one large and lumpy, mentally challenged, cliché. The Hollywood-style ending offers only one alternative to this unattractive representation of Muslimness: a romanticized and secular embrace with "undecidability." The novel implies this is a neutral and liberating position that allows one to escape reductive subject positions. In a moment of revelation, Shahid reflects: "Now he would embrace uncertainty. Maybe wisdom would come from what one didn't know, rather than from confidence" (227). He is depicted as being free of those who are "devoid of doubt" and finally shares Deedee's desire not "to be certain anymore" (91, 97).

Clearly, there is a problem with the didactic manner in which post-modern uncertainty is prescribed. As any good theorist will tell you, once postmodern doubt becomes the new belief, it is no longer post-modern. This is a mistake that Derrida would never have made, and was one of the reasons why he "took pains to make deconstruction as impossible to essentialize as deconstruction made everything else."[28] Narrative strategies that discipline the wavering liberal reader, in com-bination with the punishments accorded to Muslim characters and rewards visited on postmodern believers, illustrate why Kureishi's com-pulsory "postmodern doubt" is just another fundamentalist dogma.

Ziauddin Sardar and Merryl Wyn Davies put it neatly when they complain that "dogmatic secularism is so sure of its doubt that it neg-lects to notice it has become a certainty":

> It is hard for the doubter to conceive that this freedom can itself be an act of force, an imposition, in effect, upon others. Doubt is not a Western invention: all traditions incorporate some notion of doubt. But perpetual doubt and its host, secularism, are purely Western inventions; they are the product of a particular history unique to Europe—a history with book-burning and suppression of thought at its core.[29]

In a rather poststructuralist move, Sardar and Davies conclude that "if fun-damentalism simply connotes that part of our final vocabulary we are not willing to concede, the difference between non-fundamentalists and funda-mentalists collapses" (15). The bleak fate of the Muslim characters in *The Black Album* definitely suggests that the particular version of postmodernist liberalism on offer has "a fundamentalist core." Although the binary oppo-sitions in the text initially appear ripe for the effects of deconstruction to take place, it is difficult to avoid the fact that the novel is overwhelmingly conservative. The norms of secular liberalism are allowed to nestle cosily in the concluding chapters of the novel, while those who dare to differ become increasingly inarticulate and come to a sticky end. The complete silencing of the rationale of the Muslim group is perhaps the inevitable result of the novel's conservatism. To quote Sardar and Davies:

> When one's ideology, in this case secular fundamentalism, becomes the yardstick by which reality is measured, one exists in a totally insulated

space that permits no counter-reality . . . It is not possible to understand the position of the other side, let alone comprehend its arguments, when one's own value, secularism, is seen as the value to which all other values must defer.[30]

This helps to explain why all the Muslims in *The Black Album* are monolithically dull and alien to sophistication, their behavior no more than an irrational response to racism. It also helps us to understand why critics such as Ruvani Ranasinha argue that Kureishi is "singularly ill-equipped to give insight into a group which decries the lifestyle he so cherishes."[31]

In *The Word and the Bomb*, Kureishi claims that "fiction writers" can prevent "prejudices becoming institutionalised or an acceptable part of the culture."[32] These are noble sentiments. But when Kureishi describes "the truly religious" as being "terrifying to us [liberals] and almost incomprehensible" and identifies "body-hatred" and a "terror of sexuality"[33] as one of the causes that leads "religious people not only to cover their bodies in shame but to think of themselves as human bombs," it becomes difficult to see how his work can do anything other than perpetuate prejudice. By failing to admit the possibility of heterogeneous, complex, and nuanced Muslim subjectivities, *The Black Album* reveals itself to be bound and blinkered by a very rigid form of secular liberal fundamentalism.

NOTES

This research was funded through a Postdoctoral Research Fellowship with The British Academy. I am also grateful to Professor Catherine Belsey for reading an earlier version of this chapter.

1. Hanif Kureishi, "Loose Tongues and Liberty," *The Guardian,* June 7, 2003. Edited version of his speech at the Hay festival.
2. Ibid.
3. Ibid.
4. Ibid.
5. Hanif Kureishi, *The Black Album* (Portland, Oregon: Powell's Books); see http://www.powells.com/cgi-bin/biblio?inkey=1-0684825406-4-43k.
6. Interview with Kureishi, "Faith, Love and Fundamentalism," *The Guardian,* November 5, 2001; see http://books.guardian.co.uk/departments/general-fiction/story/0,6000,586724.
7. See Ray Deonandan, "The Source of the Rage," February 24, 2002, http://www.podium.on.ca/kureishi.html. The article originally appeared in *India Currents Magazine,* February 1996.

8. Hanif Kureishi, *The Buddha of Suburbia* (London: Faber and Faber, 1990), 180. Subsequently cited parenthetically in the text.

9. Gayatri Chakravorty Spivak, "In Praise of *Sammy and Rosie Get Laid*," *Critical Quarterly* 31, no. 2 (1989), 80–89. For further discussion of Kureishi's work, see "The Burden of English," in *Orientalism and the Postcolonial Predicament: Perspectives on South Asia*, ed. Carol Breckenridge and Peter van der Veer (Philadelphia: University of Pennsylvania Press, 1993), 134–57.

10. Hanif Kureishi, *The Black Album* (London: Faber and Faber, 1995), 13 and 5, respectively. Subsequently cited parenthetically in the text.

11. For a sophisticated discussion of the term "fundamentalism," see Bobby Sayyid's, *A Fundamental Fear: Eurocentrism and the Emergence of Islamism* (London, New York: Zed Books, 1997), 15.

12. Jacques Derrida, *Of Grammatology*, trans. Gayatri Chakravorty Spivak (Baltimore, London: Johns Hopkins University Press, 1976), 71, 47.

13. Kureishi, *The Black Album*, 77.

14. Ibid., 95–98.

15. Ibid., 133.

16. Ibid., 61.

17. Ibid., 188.

18. Hanif Kureishi, *The Word and the Bomb* (London: Faber and Faber, 2005), 100.

19. Ibid., 99.

20. Monica Ali, *Brick Lane* (London, New York: Doubleday, 2003), 413.

21. Robert Young, *White Mythologies: Writing, History and the West* (London, New York: Routledge, 1990), 19.

22. Kureishi, *The Black Album*, 105.

23. Ibid., 120.

24. Young, *White Mythologies*, 19.

25. Kureishi, *The Black Album*, 119.

26. Ibid., 99.

27. Ibid., 228.

28. http://en.wikipedia.org/wiki/Jacques_Derrida.

29. Ziauddin Sardar and Merryl Wyn Davies, *Distorted Imagination: Lessons from the Rushdie Affair* (London: Grey Seal, 1990), 12–13.

30. Ibid., 6.

31. See Ruvani Ranasinha, *Hanif Kureishi* (Devon: Northcote House Publishers, 2002), 88 and 82, respectively. In a similar vein, Tariq Modood has claimed that, in *The Black Album*, Islam is portrayed as a "radical assault upon British values, a threat to the state and an enemy to good race relations." See Modood, *Not Easy Being British: Colour, Culture and Citizenship* (London: Runnymede Trust, 1992). Meanwhile, and clearly writing from a firmly Western liberal perspective, Bart Moore-Gilbert acknowledges that *The Black Album* might infer "that there is no such thing as a moderate Muslim" (148), but praises Kureishi for critiquing elements of cultural "fundamentalism" which, in his words, "disregard internationally-agreed

standards of human rights" (211). This argument is problematic for obvious reasons, the least of which is the principle that "one's freedom ends when another's begins." Moore-Gilbert, *Hanif Kureishi: Contemporary World Writers Series* (Manchester: Manchester University Press, 2001), 210.

32. Kureishi, *The Word and the Bomb,* 100 and 87, respectively.

33. It is interesting to note that, historically, one of the recurrent criticisms of Muslims in European narratives centered on their "lascivious sensuality." See Rana Kabbani, *Europe's Myths of the Orient: Devise and Rule* (London: Pandora Press, 1988), 6. While some religious traditions have considered sex to be sinful, Islam is far from coy when it comes to such matters. Sex within marriage is viewed as both a duty and a charity for which you can attain spiritual reward. Kureishi appears to conflate these differences when he refers to "religious peoples' . . . terror of sexuality."

CHAPTER 6

FROM ENLIGHTENMENT TO THE PRISON OF LIGHT: REVERTING TO PARSI FUNDAMENTALISM IN ROHINTON MISTRY'S *FAMILY MATTERS*

CATHERINE PESSO-MIQUEL

Most of the characters in Rohinton Mistry's *Family Matters* (2002) are members of the Parsi community in Bombay. The main story line covers roughly six months, from August 1995 to early 1996. There is a forty-page epilogue at the end, situated five years later, in 2000. The novel focuses on a spectacular reversal—one of the adult characters, forty-three-year-old Yezad Chenoy, veers, in the space of a few months, from a modern, "enlightened," indifferent skepticism toward traditional Parsi beliefs and rituals to an intransigent, fanatical endorsing of the most orthodox tendencies of the Parsi religion. My aim is to analyze the subtle way in which the narrative voice chronicles this reversion and its causes: if Mistry's own distaste for fundamentalist attitudes does transpire, it is in a discreet, oblique way, through the use of contrasting structural devices and multiple focalization. Thus, the narrative conveys a certain sense of pessimism and fatalism in the face of the reversibility of beliefs: bigotry can be an acquired and cultivated taste rather than the result of indoctrination at an early age, and "reform" is an unstable, reversible process. The narrative gives a great deal of importance to rabble-rousing forms of Hindu nationalism and sectarianism, which serve as a background and a foil to the description of orthodox Parsi attitudes. Problematically, the same word, "fundamentalism," is commonly used to refer to both types of behavior: to both the "private" cultivation of difference and (superior) "apart-ness" and the "public" use of hatred and collective violence against other groups.[1] This portrayal of religious and political agitation will be the first point I shall tackle, before moving on to the structural devices and symmetrical patterns that dramatize the act of "reverting," the last point being devoted to the analysis of the various factors that could account for this "reactionary," regressive journey.

A BACKGROUND OF COMMUNALISM AND VIOLENCE: DRAMATIZATION OF SHIV SENA AGITATION

There are many references in the novel to the riots and communal violence that occurred in India in the wake of the destruction of the Babri Mosque in Ayodhya in 1992.[2] The only Muslim Indian portrayed here is Husain—a peon and a victim of the 1992 riots. He is a Bombayite whose family was ruthlessly destroyed by fanatical "goondas" (thugs) spurred on by the Shiv Sena, a regional Hindu-chauvinist party in the state of Maharashtra. These events are filtered through the mind of Yezad, who was not an eyewitness but who was told the story by someone else. Paradoxically, in spite of the distance thus created, the reader is led to identify strongly with the victims:

> [Yezad] would remind himself about the peon's story, . . . goondas setting people on fire . . . Husain and his Muslim neighbours watching as their chawl went up in flames, wondering where his wife and three sons were . . . and then four burning figures tumbling down the steps of the building, their smoking hands beating at the flames . . . while the goondas sprinkled more kerosene from their cans over Husain's family.[3]

In this reticent account, the constant aposiopeses create gaps, allowing the reader to picture the horror.

The Shiv Sena, like other nationalist Hindu organizations, insists on creating a confusion between the Indian nation and Hinduism, and on rejecting members of other religions as foreigners. The Shiv Sena was behind the drive to change the name of its city from the Portuguese, "foreign" Bombay to Mumbai, the name of a local Hindu goddess. Mistry describes the brutality of the Shiv Sena, its "sticks-and-stones method of political persuasion" (141)—the organization represents a constant menace lurking in the background, threatening people like Husain with down-right violence and wealthier people with extortion. The Hindu extremists are often referred to as brainless bullies (43–44) or as members of an organization intent on spreading hatred of minorities (31–32). The Shiv Sena, as a member of the ruling coalition,[4] is portrayed as being "in a constant fit of censorship and persecution" (273). At one point a suspicious stranger is surprised by the inhabitants of a building in the act of noting down names from the building directory; he then slips away quietly. He is not, as the reader might expect, someone planning a burglary, but a "Sainik," a Shiv Sena activist, listing names and addresses to find Muslim homes to attack, "planning ahead for next time" (106). In one of her essays, Arundhati Roy showed that along with this particular sort of "canvassing," modern technology was used to find the targets of attack: "The leaders of the mob had computer-generated cadastral lists marking out muslim homes, shops, businesses, and even partnerships."[5]

Mistry dramatizes the collusion between institutional powers and the perpetrators of communal violence. Indeed when Husain's boss, Mr. Kapur, is killed by Shiv Sena activists, Husain wants "the police to catch the dogs who killed Kapur sahab," but recounts that when he told the policemen his story they intimidated him: "They said it was not right to connect Shiv Sena, there was no evidence. One policeman laughed in a very bad way. He said, 'You Muslims, always trying to blame Shiv Sena'" (405). Such a climate explains why minorities should feel threatened and wish to close ranks in order to develop a strong sense of identity and belonging and is presented as a factor that contributes toward Yezad's "complete about-face" (302). Moreover, Mistry deftly weaves the Shiv Sena element into his main plot: Yezad is tempted to manipulate and use communal violence for his own benefit, and is then led to rue it deeply.

In *The Moor's Last Sigh*, Salman Rushdie also treats the theme of fundamentalist Hindu agitation, and he draws a vitriolic portrait of Bal Thackeray, the leader of the Shiv Sena, which becomes in the novel "the Mumbai Axis," a name intended to evoke Mr. Thackeray's admiration for Hitler. When asked on television whether he wanted to be the Hitler of Bombay, Thackeray boasted he was the Hitler of the whole of Maharashtra, and wanted to be the Hitler of the whole of India.[6] Rushdie calls the character based on Thackeray "Raman Fielding": the surname comes from the name of an English novelist and the first name, Raman, alludes to the clever manipulations of the "Mumbai Axis", which has put the emphasis on the cult of *one* divinity, Rama (an incarnation of Vishnu), and on *one* revealed narrative, the *Ramayana*, and has encouraged "mass puja" to gather mobs necessary for the persecution of Muslims: "A single, martial deity, a single book, and mob rule: that is what they have made of Hindu culture, its many-headed beauty, its peace," thunders one character in Rushdie's novel.[7] The same character expresses the idea that this is a recent phenomenon: "This fundo stuff is really something new" (338). Rushdie invents episodes in which the hero and narrator of the novel actively participates in ugly acts of intimidation and violence committed by Fielding's followers:

> And shall I tell you how—at the local feudal landowner's invitation—we visited a village near the Gujarat border, where the freshly gathered red chillies stood around the houses in low hills of colour and spice, and put down a revolt of female workers? But no, perhaps not; your fastidious stomach would be upset by such hot stuff. Shall I speak of our campaign against those out-caste unfortunates, untouchables or Harijans or Dalits, call them what you please, who had in their vanity thought to escape the caste system by converting to Islam? Shall I describe the steps by which we returned them to their place beyond the social pale? (308)

Although this is a first-person narrative, its effect is to alienate the reader, to prevent identification of the reader with the provocative, mocking narrative voice, whereas Mistry's mediated account of Husain's plight is calculated to arouse the reader's compassion and have him adhere to the tale. In Rushdie's treatment, preterition replaces aposiopesis and the reader's disgust is compounded by the lurid evocation of the sexual titillation added to the communal bullying: the red chillies are here meant to play the same part as the infamous corn cob in Faulkner's *Sanctuary* and to serve as a grotesque distortion of the "spicy love" theme associated with Aurora and Abraham Zogoiby, the Moor's parents ("Aurora da Gama at the age of fifteen lay back on pepper sacks, breathed in the hot spice-laden air, and waited for Abraham," 88).

In such a climate, all sorts of parties and groups rise and thrive, a fact that both Mistry and Rushdie dramatize. Stopped by a demonstration, Nariman wonders which party it is, and Jal shrugs off the question: "BJP, JD, VHP, BSP,[8] doesn't matter, they're all the same" (Mistry, 60). Rushdie's Moor draws the same conclusion: "Fielding, too, was making allies, with like-minded national parties and paramilitary organisations, that alphabet soup of authoritarians, JP, RSS, VHP"[9] (Rushdie, 337). Bal Thackeray had expressed outrage when India banned *The Satanic Verses*, arguing that his was a free country, but he had no scruples in getting *The Moor's Last Sigh* banned in Bombay and Maharashtra.

Soon after this, the Shiv Sena put pressure on the national government, and the book was banned nationally.[10]

In *Family Matters* the sympathetically portrayed Husain is the only representative of the Muslim minority in India. Mistry uses the synecdochical method, concentrating on one fictional individual, appealing to the reader's imagination and empathy, to give an idea of the atrocities committed against one community. Indeed rabid nationalist Hindus treat Muslims as strangers in their own land; they use them as scapegoats, in an attempt to crystallize a strong feeling of Hindu identity in the majority of Indians.[11] The destruction of the Babri Masjid was preceded by a long, intense campaign of mobilization organized by the BJP,[12] which repeatedly provoked communal riots between Muslims and Hindus, causing hundreds of deaths. This exploitation of religion for political and communal goals was commented upon by Corbridge and Harriss in *Reinventing India*:

> The Babri Masjid was transformed into a potent symbol of the way in which the Hindu majority was "threatened" by the Muslim "Other." As Hansen[13] points out, it came to stand for the violated rights of the Hindu majority within the paradigm of "equal rights of communities" laid down within the Constitution, while making Ram "into a metaphor of the essential Hinduness of Indian culture."[14]

Mistry has chosen to represent Muslims as victims, which of course they were, in this case, and not to mention (because, after all, this was not his subject) the backlash led by some Muslims against Hindus after the destruction of the Babri Masjid and the accompanying riots, in India as well as in neighboring countries with a Muslim majority. The denunciation of ricochet Muslim violence against Hindus in Bangladesh, however, is the subject of Taslima Nasrin's 1993 novel, written in Bengali, titled *Lajja* (which means "shame"). This novel did nothing to soften the attitude of Muslim fundamentalists or of the Bangladeshi government toward Nasrin, against whom several *fatwas* have been issued, and who now lives in exile.

Unlike Mistry, Rushdie insists on the reciprocity of communal violence and uses a much more intellectual, distanced point of view, even though, again paradoxically, this is a first-person narrative and the narrator is personally involved in the killings:

> There comes a point in the unfurling of communal violence in which it becomes irrelevant to ask, "Who started it?" The lethal conjugations of death part company with any possibility of justification, let alone justice.

They surge among us, left and right, Hindu and Muslim, knife and pistol, killing, burning, looting, and raising into the smoky air their clenched and bloody fists. Both their houses are damned by their deeds; both sides sacrifice the right to any shred of virtue; they are each other's plagues. (365)

Arundhati Roy also insists on the lethal reciprocity of violence, remarking that there is little to distinguish the two sides bent on slaughtering each other and that they "worship at the same altar" and are "both apostles of the same murderous god, whoever he is" (18). However, Rushdie wrote his remark before the rise to power of a Hindu nationalist movement and Roy, writing more recently, is careful to point out that "there *is* a fundamental difference between a pogrom such as the one taking place in Gujarat now and the burning of the Sabarmati Express in Godhra"[15]: indeed no one knows "who exactly is responsible for the carnage in Godhra," whereas the pogrom against the Muslims "has at best been conducted under the benign gaze of the state and, at worst, with active state collusion." Therefore, Roy concludes, "either way the state is criminally culpable," and as a citizen she feels that she has been made complicit in the Gujarat pogrom: "It is this that outrages me. And it is this that puts a completely different complexion on the two massacres" (24).

FUNDAMENTALISM AS A CYCLICAL PATTERN OF REVERSION

The main story line in *Family Matters* unfolds slowly: apart from the forty-page epilogue at the end, the book contains twenty chapters, covering a six-month period in 458 pages. The Chenoys (husband, wife, and two sons), who live in a tiny two-room flat, have to make room for Nariman Vakeel, Mrs. Chenoy's father, who suffers from Parkinson's disease. The story of Nariman's life is told in installments, parts of which are made distinct from the rest of the text by being printed in italics: the episodes correspond to the old man's memories, dreams, and nightmares. Mistry develops Nariman's story in counterpoint to Yezad Chenoy's, and Yezad's relationship with his own son repeats a tragic pattern that affected Nariman, whose parents pressured him into leaving the woman he loved (Lucy Braganza, a Goan Christian). He did marry, according to his father's wishes, "a good Parsi girl," but he then kept up a tormented relationship with Lucy. Their love story follows two archetypal plots: first the tragic Romeo-and-Juliet pattern of love thwarted by parental enmity, and then, once Nariman yields to parental pressure, the Hamlet/Ophelia pattern of rejection and female madness.

At the beginning of the novel, Yezad is portrayed as a skeptic, full of jokes and humor, who blunders clumsily through the Parsi prayer rituals and mocks his wife's pious delight in the respect of traditions: "Yezad did not believe in [religious observances][;] he said . . . loban smoke was merely one way to get rid of mosquitoes" (25). When his son, after hearing about his grandfather's tragic love affair, asks whether "there [is] a law against marrying anyone who [isn't] a Parsi," Yezad answers, "Yes, the law of bigotry" (42).

By the end of the novel, five years later, Yezad's easy laughter, associated with his skepticism and liberalism (25), is gone; he "hardly smiles, let alone laughs" (465), and his is a "doom-laden face" (481). He catches his elder son, Murad, in the company of a non-Parsi girl and forbids him to see her: "The rules, the laws of our religion are absolute, this Maharashtrian cannot be your girlfriend" (482). The liberal, modern man who rejected "the law of bigotry" has become filled with blind reverence for the ancient laws of a "three-thousand-year-old religion" (132), and this is emphasized by Nariman's reaction of mute distress to the rituals imposed in the house by his son-in-law. The smoke of frankincense fills him with despair. His daughter explains to Yezad that her grandparents' intransigence over Nariman's love affair with Lucy had led him to give up his religion: "He used to call it the religion of bigots. He hasn't stepped inside a fire-temple in forty years" (444). But Yezad is totally oblivious to his father-in-law's anguish and his objections to the observance of religious rites. A tragicomic scene is enacted as Yezad's tyrannical prayers enter into conflict with their neighbor Daisy's compassionate performance, on her violin, of Nariman's favorite love song. When Nariman is finally soothed by the music, Yezad, symbolically blinded to his surroundings, claims the victory: "Yezad opened his eyes. He held out his hands towards the settee to indicate the calm that the vibrations of his praying had wrought" (447).

The echoes and structural devices ("law of bigotry"/"religion of bigots") are not gratuitous: an effect of ironical circularity is created, with the young Murad reenacting Nariman's battle against his own father, a staunch orthodox Parsi and author of an angry and self-righteous campaign of letters against the "ignorant" Reformists (132). In one of the flashback passages, the ideas of Nariman's father are made very clear: he writes a letter to the editor of the *Jam-e-Jamshed*, the Parsi newspaper, to denounce the "ignorance of mischief-making priests" who perform the navjote ceremony for children with one non-Parsi parent, thus compromising "the purity of this unique and ancient Persian community, the very plinth and foundation of its survival" (132). This provokes his Reformist Parsi neighbor to write a letter accusing him of being "a rabid racist who, in his maniacal quest for purity, wouldn't think twice about eliminating the spouses and offspring of intermarriage" (133). As Jehangir, Yezad's younger son and the narrator of the epilogue, explains, Murad's sarcastic comments ironically echo those of a younger Yezad: "Murad's jokes are like the ones Daddy himself used to crack when we were small . . . And I also remember conversations Daddy and Grandpa would have, about the silliness of slavishly following conventions and traditions" (468). Now Yezad, like extremist Hindus (273), is puritanically engaged in "campaigns to be waged against films or publications that have given offence" (466).

This tragic pattern of repetition is a powerful structural device within the novel, and it is emphasized by further effects of symmetry and contrast, which clearly indicate where the sympathies of the author go. At the beginning of the novel, Yezad's sister-in-law, Coomy, is portrayed as a devout Parsi who scrupulously respects all the rituals and ceremonies of her religion. She is also characterized as an unmarried woman with a humorless, petty, scheming mindset, whose dreams betray her sexual frustration (74). She owns a glass cabinet that Yezad and his wife, Roxana, jokingly refer to as her "shrine" and make fun of, and for which the narrator also uses religious vocabulary:

> "Shrine" was their secret word for the clutter of knickknacks, toys, and glassware that packed the shelves *venerated* by Jal and Coomy. Their *sacred icons* included a clown with ears that waggled . . . a white fluffy dog with a bobbing head . . . and a battery-operated Elvis . . . When they acquired a new toy, they would demonstrate it proudly, then perform its solemn installation behind glass. All that was missing in this *ritual,* according to Yezad, was incense, flowers, and the chanting of prayers. (27, my italics)

At the end of the novel, Yezad appropriates Coomy's cabinet, and he too uses it, literally this time, as a shrine: filled with his "holy items," the cabinet stands within the pure, protected space mapped out by Yezad in his own living room (499) and is linked to the fundamentalist obsession with purity and impurity: the "purity" of the community ("We are a pure Persian race, a unique contribution to this planet, and mixed marriages will destroy that," 482) and the "impurity" of women ("Daddy has passed the menstruation laws . . . Mummy must not enter the drawing-room at all while she has her period," 493). Yezad has fully embraced the most literal interpretations of his creed, those of the orthodox, who frown upon the "modern" women who do not wear saris ("The orthodox believed that once a girl began menstruating she had no business wearing a frock," 307). The puritanical attitude toward sex is also a strategy to avoid exogamy; Yezad and his orthodox friends have decided to campaign "to reintroduce a strict policy of excommunication. Parsi men and women who have relations with non-Parsis, in or out of marriage, will suffer the consequences" (467). In fact, Mistry's portrayal of Yezad's fundamentalist reflexes link up with responses common to many religious extremists, whatever their creed: a puritanical attitude (like that of the Shiv Sena against men's magazines, which they claimed were "endangering Indian morals with nudity and sex and vulgarity," 273), a stern rejection of exogamy to protect the "purity" of the group, and the assertion of a patriarchal authority over women and the younger generations. Yezad's insistence on endogamy and his refusal to accept a "parjaat" girl, however charming, is very similar to the attitude of the Pakistani father described in Ken Loach's film *A Fond Kiss* (2004). This character is a Pakistani living in Scotland for whom it is unthinkable that his son should marry "a gori." The woman involved is an Irish Catholic, and her fanatical parish priest has exactly the same attitude toward her lover: he cannot conceive that she will marry a non-Catholic unless he converts to Catholicism or promises to bring up the children in the Catholic faith. The end of the film shows that Loach favors "hybridization" against "purity." Similarly, Salman Rushdie plays with the notion of "bastardization" in his novels: the Indian Spanish Jew, Abraham Zogoiby, is in fact the descendant of Boabdil the Moor: "*My mother who insists on the purity of our race, what say you to your forefather the Moor?*" (82, author's italics) Both Ken Loach and Rohinton Mistry seem to have chosen their camps in the old argument for "impurity" as Rushdie defines it:

> The argument between purity and impurity, which is also the argument between Robespierre and Danton, the argument between the monk and the roaring boy, between primness and impropriety, between the stultifications of excessive respect and the scandals of impropriety, is an old one; I say, let it continue. Human beings understand themselves and shape their futures by arguing and challenging and questioning and saying the unsayable; not by bowing the knee, whether to gods or to men.[16]

The fixation on "purity" often provokes a maniacal obsession with bodily cleanliness and the threat of pollution.[17] Hari Kunzru, in *The Impressionist*, draws a comical portrait of a Hindu who is "terrified of pollution"[18] and who devotes a great deal of energy to maintaining "impermeable boundaries between himself and the world's filth" (31). As for Mistry's Yezad, he feels "real panic" when his son, fresh from the hairdresser's, wanders absentmindedly toward his father's "shrine," the cabinet, approaching within less than fifteen feet. Yezad shouts "through gritted teeth": "You are in the prayer space in your impure state. After a haircut, you are unclean till you shower and wash your head . . . Fifteen feet away, I told you! The minimum distance!" (463), which provokes the son to ask him sarcastically where he got this figure ("Did Zoroaster whisper it in your ear?" 463). Later on, Murad ironically suggests that "the League of Orthodox Parsis could invent a Purity Detector, along the lines of the airport metal detector" (486). Of course, Yezad had found the figure in one of the sacred Parsi texts, which he now reads literally and reverently, a habit that for Terry Eagleton is a touchstone of fundamentalism:

> [Fundamentalism] is basically a textual affair. Fundamentalists are those who believe that our linguistic currency is trustworthy only if it is backed by the gold standard of the Word of Words. They see God as copperfastening human meaning. Fundamentalism means sticking strictly to the script, which in turn means being deeply fearful of the improvised, ambiguous or indeterminate. Fundamentalists, however, fail to realise that the phrase "sacred text" is self-contradictory. Since writing is meaning that can be handled by anybody, any time, it is always profane and promiscuous. Meaning that has been written down is bound to be unhygienic . . . Fundamentalists are really necrophiliacs, in love with a dead letter. The letter of the sacred text must be rigidly embalmed if it is to imbue life with the certitude and finality of death.[19]

One could argue that Yezad's fundamentalism, unlike Hindu activism, is limited to the private sphere and does not resort to violence. But proportionally, and potentially, the violence is there, because Yezad threatens "to throw Murad out of the house if he does not live by his rules" (493). This threat cannot be taken idly in a novel that insists heavily on the theme of insecurity linked to the fear of redundancy and homelessness in a city like Bombay. Yezad has become exactly like Nariman's father, with the same willingness "to trade familial happiness for narrow beliefs" (133). The interests and freedom of one individual have to give way to the interests of the group, the community.

Mistry uses other examples of negative "cycles" as a way of underscoring his main theme; thus, when a Canadian official of Japanese origin prevents Yezad from immigrating to Canada,[20] Yezad remembers the xenophobia and racism suffered by Japanese immigrants during World War II in Canada, where they were interred in camps as potential enemies. Yet one of them shows racism toward an Indian would-be immigrant, and Nariman comments: "We always assume that people who suffer atrocities acquire a greater than average capacity for compassion. But there is no such guarantee" (254). In fact the cyclical pattern within the Vakeel/Chenoy family can be read as a paradigm for a tendency common to different forms of fundamentalism throughout the world. The belief in the superiority of one group over the others, whether from a racial or a religious point of view, or both, inevitably leads to a rejection of tolerance. Thus, when asked whether he wants to continue the Parsi custom of keeping tokens of every religion, by taking from the wall the holy pictures that used to hang there ("Sai Baba, Virgin Mary, a Crucifixion, Haji Malang, several Zarathustras, Our Lady of Fatima, Buddha," 485) Yezad chooses to dispose of them: "All the non-Zarathusti[21] images must go—in a Zarathusti home, they interfere with the vibrations of Avesta prayers" (491).

Mistry uses patterns of reversal in the subplots as well. Thus, when Mr. Kapur's wife convinces her husband to give up his dreams and illusions about changing Bombay and fighting corruption, Yezad, who also used to discourage him (158), is disappointed, which amuses his boss: "We've completely reversed—I sound like you, you sound like me" (302). Elsewhere recurrence is used as a form of poetic justice: when Mrs. Kapur humiliates Yezad by making him empty his desk before her, Yezad is reminded of a servant boy his father had dismissed years ago, forcing him to show his meager belongings before leaving, to make sure he was not making away with anything (427).

FACTORS OF REVERSAL

GUILT: THE MACBETH SYNDROME

Yezad is guilty of a form of hubris, since twice he thinks he can force the hand of fate. First he gambles indispensable household money on Matka, an illegal numbers game, and second he agrees to let two actors impersonate Shiv Sena activists in an attempt to spur Mr. Kapur into running in the municipal election. Later, when Mr. Kapur dies at the hands of genuine Shiv Sena thugs, Yezad feels that his interference has made him directly responsible for the murder. Like Macbeth,[22] he is filled with horror and guilt, a literary parallel suggested in the banter of the actor, Gautam:

> "Understood," said Gautam. "Basically, Mr. Kapur needs to experience an epiphany. So we must convey more than just present danger to him and his shop. We must transcend the here and now, move beyond this bank and shoal of time,[23] and let him glimpse the horrors of a society where the best lack all conviction while the worst are full of passionate intensity."[24] (332)

Gautam likes to pepper his speeches with grandiloquent quotations, but the latter also have an ironical dimension. The lines from Shakespeare, spoken by a Macbeth who is talking himself into action and murder, allude directly to Mr. Kapur's inability to decide whether he should run in the elections, and more indirectly they point to the fact that the impersonation plan will have a tragic outcome. As for the quotation from Yeats, it bears directly on the situation in Bombay, where the Hindu extremists are full of passion and violence, whereas the "best," like Yezad or Mr. Kapur, are indecisive and lack any religious or political commitment. The quotations thus point to one of the motives for Yezad's later endorsement of a fanatical conviction: religion has become for him a release from secret guilt, a path to atonement and redemption.

LAYING DOWN THE LOAD

Yezad's reversal can also be explained by his sense of economic insecurity, a theme developed by Mistry in his previous novels, *Such A Long Journey* and *A Fine Balance*, which develop the threat of poverty and homelessness, the fear of losing what little income and security one has in a country where millions of people survive as best they can, "renting" a doorstep or a strip of pavement on which to lie down at night. In *Family Matters* Husain, the poor peon, has to vacate his kholi at 7 a.m. because he rents it on a twelve-hour basis, "time-sharing" it with a factory worker who is on night shift; Husain is "aware that he [is] more fortunate than those who [rent] eight-hour rooms" (139).

Bombay is consistently portrayed as a polluted, poisoned city where deep breathing is hazardous and where motorcyclists wear breathing masks; this provides Yezad with an image to picture his deep need of escapism ("Wouldn't it be great if there were a mask to filter out the world's problems," 306). In the midst of his financial worries, weighed down by the crushing responsibility of having to earn a salary for a family of four and his suffering father-in-law, Yezad gradually discovers that his own neglected religion provides that mask, that filter. The fire-temple is an "oasis" "in the harsh desert this city had become" (364), a "sanctuary in this meaningless world" (359), a place where, very symbolically, the priest rubs his back "as though he were physically removing something, pulling strands of stress out of his tortured being" (340). Mistry skillfully suggests the attraction, for Yezad, of surrendering again to the sensations of peace and pleasure of his childhood ("The dustoorji was wearing his full prayer garb, the robes fragrant with sandalwood smoke.

The smell brought a wistful smile to Yezad's face," 308). Mistry himself is obviously moved by the aesthetic beauty, the peace, and the sense of belonging linked to the Parsi religion, and he conveys this nostalgic feeling in a stirring, fluid, beautifully poised sentence:

> How comforting to see the figure in the flowing white robe, see him moving, unhurried, employing the various silver utensils in the ceremony, performing the mystical gestures that were repeated five times each day, performed with an elegance that could come only with the cumulative grace of generations and centuries, so that it was encoded in blood and bone. (342)

Little by little, Yezad yields to the temptation of this soothing retreat from the world, from reality. When, through Coomy's death, his material worries are definitively solved, the respite seems to have become permanent, as if a Parsi form of Providence had intervened in his favor. But, with Coomy's flat, Yezad seems to have inherited her literal, bigoted devotion to the Parsi religion, along with her pettiness, her fussiness, her inability to be happy, and her bullying attitude toward her brother, Jal (462).

Mistry's novel makes it very clear that "enlightenment" and "modernity" are not to be taken for granted: the belief that cultures and human groups can be mixed and can enrich one another is an easily reversible tenet. At the level of a society, or at the individual level, cycles occur, steering people back toward the temptation of a stable, reassuring world in which the weight of moral responsibility, of the freedom to choose, of the agony of unanswered questions, is taken off their shoulders. Religion has an answer for every doubt, every question: the *truth* has been revealed once and for all. In a self-reflexive statement that mirrors the novel we are reading, Mistry suggests that Yezad's story is paradigmatic, universal: "No matter where you go in the world, there is only one important story: of youth, and loss, and yearning for redemption. So we tell the same story, over and over. Just the details are different" (228).

EXISTENTIAL INSECURITY AND THE SEARCH FOR A FATHER FIGURE

The priest who relieves Yezad's feeling of stress is a fatherly figure, and Yezad's first tentative visit to the fire-temple brings back memories of childhood and of his father. The image of the father is associated with that of the clock presented to him as a reward for an act of courage (232). For the depressed Yezad, for whom "nothing made sense" (296), his father's clock is a cherished object, "the one remembrance of his childhood home, of his father" (374):

> How comforting its ticking, reassuring, like a steady hand guiding the affairs of the universe. Like his father's hand that held his when he was little, leading him through the world of wonder and upheaval. And his father's words, always at the end of the story, *Remember your kusti prayers: manashni, gavahshni, kunahsni—good thoughts, good words, good deeds.* (375)

The clock as described here evokes the eighteenth-century representations of a benign creator, the "clockmaker" of a well-ordered universe in which everything has a place and works like clockwork; it is also associated in the character's mind with images of a pious father, exhorting him to observe the rites of his religion. The mention of the clock sends the reader back to an earlier episode in which Yezad tells his sons the story of how his father was rewarded with the clock and sets it up as an example of conduct for them. But Mistry ironically chooses to juxtapose with this edifying tale of filial piety an evocation of bitter conflict between generations, since on the same page Yezad hears Nariman shouting in his dreams, reenacting the trying conflicts of the past: "You disgrace the role of fatherhood!" (234)

Yezad does not allow his sons to wind the precious clock (231), and this detail creates a parallel with the clockwork toys that Coomy will not allow her nephews to touch (28). Coomy projects onto her beloved showcase and its toys all her frustrations; to her ears the sound of the clockwork toys being wound is "as familiar as the breath of a cherished infant" (28). This is also a form of compensation for the loss of her father: Nariman says that if his stepchildren are obsessed with the showcase and the toys, it is because of the death of their father when they were young and the unhappiness of their childhood. The text suggests that with the glass cabinet, Yezad inherited a tendency toward infantile behavior and the search for a parent figure: "Wounded by Murad's taunt, however, Daddy turned to [Mummy], his expression a child's who has been slapped without warning. And when mummy sees him like this she behaves like a protective mother" (464). Yezad's yearning for an orderly and meaningful world causes a regression in him. Religion has the same effect as the old photographs shown to him by Mr. Kapur, "a strange effect, as though he were living in two time zones, six decades apart. But it was a pleasant, reassuring feeling" (153). The pictures are "like magic," "capturing time" (225), and Yezad wishes he could manage "to slip into Mr. Kapur's old photographs." Later he will enjoy "the time-less quality" of his religion, "the fire burning, the same fire his parents had gazed upon, and his grandparents, and great-grandparents" (341). The symbol of the clock is again in the background when Mr. Kapur uses the common phrase "nobody can turn back the clock" (302), because this is exactly what Yezad tries to do. It is significant that after Mr. Kapur's death, his widow deprives Yezad of another outlet for his feelings of nostalgia by pettily demanding that he return the photos given to him by her husband (428). Moreover his vision of paradise is one in which a benevolent father figure satisfies every need, and shoulders the weight of responsibility: "Grandpa is in heaven . . . Dada Ormuzd is providing for him now. Clothes, ice cream, pudding, everything" (477).

Of course the benevolent father figure is a feature in all the major monotheistic religions, both an infantilizing figure and a paradigm of the legitimacy of patriarchal power, the authority of the father over his family being the reproduction, on a smaller scale, of the relationship between God and the believers. Tariq Ali shows how the Muslim religion inherited and inverted the tradition of polyandry present "in pagan Arab society, where women played a central role in commerce, tribal politics and sex."[25] In their famous book *The Madwoman in the Attic*, Sandra Gilbert and Susan Gubar quoted Edward Said's reflection on the words *author* and *authority*,[26] in which Said pointed out the links between writer, deity, and maleness in the form of the *pater familias*. The author fathers his text as God fathered the world. Perhaps we could read the choice of narrative voices in *Family Matters* as an oblique comment on this conception of "authority": Yezad is not given the dignity of being the narrator, since the first part of the story is a "third person" narrative, whereas Jehangir cultivates his own voice by becoming the narrator in the final part. In other words, Mistry subtly dissociates the tyrannical *pater familias*, in thrall to a single truth, from the figure of the author, bestowed on the "liberal" Jehangir, who believes in the relativity of truth and chooses at the end to pronounce a different "truth" in order not to hurt his mother.

AN INSECURE IDENTITY

In a self-reflexive, intertextual exploration, Mistry develops the idea that his characters suffer from an excess of English culture, or rather a delu-sion concerning the very nature of Englishness and English culture. Yezad scoffs at his younger son's fascination for Enid Blyton's reassur-ing universe of carefree summer holidays. A few Indian authors[27] have explained that India lacks a sufficient production of children's fiction; children's books published in India tend to be "useful" and educational, but they do not cater to children's imaginations, leaving the door open for "the lovely world of those books" (216), the world of "Enid Blyton" (a synecdoche for outmoded Western children's literature). When his wife protests that Enid Blyton is harmless and fun, Yezad retorts that it does "immense harm": "It encouraged children to grow up without attachment to the place where they belonged, made them hate themselves for being who they were, created confusion about their identity" (97). Mistry's novels, in fact, provide an answer to Yezad's wish: "What they needed was an Indian Blyton, to fascinate them with their own reality" (117). Interestingly, Mistry also situates himself within a double literary tradition, by playfully weaving together allusions to Shakespeare and to Salman Rushdie. This is particularly apparent in Mr. Kapur's skit on John of Gaunt's bitter panegyric of England[28] in *Richard II*:

> This beautiful city of seven islands, this jewel by the Arabian Sea, *this reclaimed land*, this ocean gift transformed into *ground beneath our feet*, this enigma of cosmopolitanism where races and religions live side by side and cheek by jowl in peace and harmony . . . (160, my italics)

The allusion to Rushdie is both explicit, since Mistry uses the title of one of his novels (*The Ground Beneath Her Feet*, 1999), and implicit, since the reclamation of land in Bombay is a major theme both in *Midnight's Children* and *The Ground Beneath Her Feet*. In the latter novel, Rai's father (V. V. Merchant) has turned Bombay into a hobby and a passion, just as Mr. Kapur does in *Family Matters*.

But postcolonial issues are only one aspect of the complex question of identity in India. Another factor behind Yezad's reversion is the pressure exerted on minorities. Yezad is very conscious of the threat of dissolution of a very old community in the variegated mosaic of India, and there is subconscious guilt at work here also. Interestingly, Yezad first thinks of the legacy of the Parsi community in "progressive" terms of business (338), in keeping with Dr. Fitter's eulogy of "the [Parsi] forefathers, the industrialists and shipbuilders who established the foundation of modern India" (51).[29] But later, Yezad's interest in the community becomes more conservative, and his library becomes confined to sacred Parsi texts and books on Zoroastrianism (463), the teachings of which he takes quite literally, taking his cue, for example, from the Vendidaad to define the exact measurements of the "pure" prayer space that must be protected from pollution (462).

REACTING TO PRESSURE

In *Brick Lane* Monica Ali dramatizes the fact that "young ones will always rebel," and she places a paradoxical question in the mind of one of her characters: "If the parents are liberal then how can [their children] rebel except by becoming illiberal themselves?"[30] Writers often portray a "positive" youthful rebellion—a rejection of tradition to embrace modern, liberal, "enlightened" ways: thus, in *The Satanic Verses*, Salman Rushdie created characters who are the London-born teenage daughters of Bangladeshi parents, and very much westernized,[31] but Mistry and Ali focus more on the reversion to traditional beliefs and fundamentalist attitudes among youths who feel they must rebel against the open-minded and liberal principles of their parents.

In France the issue of girls wearing *hijab* in school divides politicians and citizens, and a controversial law that forbids "ostensible" religious signs in school has been passed. Two of the girls who were expelled from their schools in October 2003 for refusing to take off their "veil," Lila and Alma, are the daughters of Laurent Lévy, Jewish by birth but not by creed, and of an Algerian (Berber) Catholic woman. The girls' Muslim "fundamentalism" (in fact a rather fanciful creed they worked out for themselves) is for them a way not only of "returning to their roots" but also of rebelling against parental authority and values. They were interviewed on television, their smiling faces were plastered on magazine covers and front pages of newspapers all through the autumn of 2003, and they seemed to relish the attention and the limelight. Yet this publicity contradicts the very meaning of the veil, which is intended to make women inconspicuous, invisible, and "protected."[32]

Ali also shows that you can be pressured by other groups into adopting a certain attitude; they can make you feel obligated to demonstrate loyalty to one camp or the other, to "take sides," whether you want to or not. Chanu, a Bangladeshi immigrant in London, is caught between Muslim fundamentalist pressures on the one hand and racist right-wing propaganda on the other:

> If [Chanu] had a Lions Hearts [anti-immigrant, anti-Muslim] leaflet in his hand, he wanted his daughters covered. He would not be cowed by these Muslim-hating peasants. If he saw some girls go by in hijab he became agitated at this display of peasant ignorance. Then the girls went out in their skirts. (219)

Family Matters methodically explores what, from a "humanist" point of view, can only be assessed as a backtracking, a negative reversal, since the ultimate failure of Yezad's quest is easily demonstrated. The cyclical nature of the plot and the structural device of circularity epitomize the fact that Parsi fundamentalism works as a stifling, lethal enclosure; thus, in the sentence "his progeny had been properly welcomed into the Zoroastrian fold" (28), the image seems positive but the word "fold" also evokes a snare, an entrapment. Yezad's fascination for the eternal fire of the Parsi religion, burning "in the sacred chamber," "demarcated by a marble threshold" (341), traps him into an illusion of peace, followed by a perverse burrowing into more and more orthodoxy and unhappiness (499). The rejection of enlightenment in favor of the eternal fire turns out to be a prison, albeit a prison of light. When he is first drawn back into the "fold," Yezad delights in the "pure clang" of the bell in the fire-temple: "It was ringing out life, thought Yezad, it was ringing hope, and his heart sang with the bell" (343); in the epilogue the gloom and doom of fanaticism and puritanism have won him over: he "never whistles,[33] never joins in with songs," and "says music disturbs him" (465). He had hoped, by returning to the fire-temple, to be relieved of a heavy load, yet this hope was vain, for he now "sits as though he is carrying a secret burden, whose weight is crushing him" (465). As a child Yezad had been fascinated by the inner sanctum of the fire-temple, which only a select few, "in a state of ritual purity," could enter, and he had fantasized about entering the forbidden space, "Dadaji's private place." Powerfully attracted but filled with "reverent fear," he had worried that he might stumble, that "a part of him, a hand or a finger, would accidentally cross the prohibited barrier, with some terrifying consequence" (341). Murad unwittingly uses a very similar image when he reviles his father's fanaticism: "'He's gone over the edge,' says Murad. 'Deep into the abyss of religion'" (493). The ending of the novel is deeply ambiguous: Jehangir's brave lie in the last line, "Yes, I'm happy" underlines the absence of a happy end, creating the sense of a dead end, a blind alley; at the same time, it underlines the new "authority" acquired by the young Jehangir, which defies that of the Father and the sacred text, thus creating the sense of a way out of the blind alley, a way "forward."

As portrayed in this novel, Parsi orthodoxy is really fundamentalist, urging a strict, uncritical respect for age-old rites, texts, and practices—that is to say, the blind perpetuation of an unadulterated tradition—whereas Hindu nationalism distorts and twists tradition to suit its political needs. Parsi orthodoxy works inwardly, and only affects a small community, unlike Hindu nationalism, allied with paramilitary power and actively engaged in ultraviolent persecution, destruction, and murder. Yet the two forms of behavior are linked, because Hindu nationalism exploits the very fear that prompts fundamentalist beliefs: minority communities' fear of disintegration and assimilation into an alien culture. It also exploits the undemocratic fundamentalist belief in the superiority of one community over another. The propaganda of the BJP purposely harps on the "threat" posed by the relatively small Muslim community in India by grossly exaggerating its birthrate and demographical growth. This is intended to cause fear, to enhance the sense of a Hindu "identity," and to increase the number of people voting for the party.

Mistry's portrayal of fundamentalist Parsis might be read as a synecdoche for the human race, for which there is no chance of a linear march toward "progress," toward the unreachable goal that Rushdie's Moor wistfully yearns for, "the triumph of the impure, mongrel, conjoining best of us over what there is in us of the solitary, the isolated, the austere, the dogmatic, the pure; of love as democracy, as the victory of the no-man-is-an-island, two's company Many over the clean, mean, apartheiding Ones" (289). No chance, because history stutters and stammers, constantly repeating itself, and the only "revolution" available is a literal one, *id est* not a "leap forward" but a rotation, a complete circle reverting back to the starting point.

And yet Mistry's pessimism is not total, because he explicitly places his novel within the postindependence Indian literary tradition of "committed" literature, intent on creating a memory of what must not be forgotten, intent on overcoming communalism and hatred based on differences of religion. Many contemporary Indian novels still harp on the Partition of 1947, and Mistry's novel can be read as a different, but similar way of shouldering the load of Sisyphus. It is difficult not to see in the narrator's following comment on "Indian authors" a self-reflexive assertion of Mistry's own sense of commitment, both ethical and aesthetic:

> Yezad felt that Punjabi migrants of a certain age were like Indian authors writing about that period, whether in realist novels of corpse-filled trains or in the magic-realist midnight muddles,[34] all repeating the same catalogue of horrors . . . But Yezad's silent criticism was always followed by remorse. He knew they had to keep telling their story, just like the Jews had to theirs, about the Holocaust, writing and remembering and having nightmares about the concentration camps and gas chambers and ovens, about the evil committed by ordinary people, by friends and neighbours, the evil that, decades later, was still incomprehensible. *What choice was there, except to speak about it, again and again, and yet again?* (151, my italics)

NOTES

1. For a developed reflection on the definition of the word "fundamental-ism," see Terry Eagleton's grimly humorous article, "Pedants and Partisans," *The Guardian*, February 22, 2003.
2. On December 6, 1992, in the wake of a nationwide campaign to "arouse the pride" of Hindus, mobs of Hindu nationalists demolished this old mosque, said to have been built on the site of a Hindu temple devoted to the cult of Ram, and announced their intention of replacing it with a huge Hindu temple (Ram Mandir).
3. Rohinton Mistry, *Family Matters* (London: Faber and Faber, 2003), 144. Subsequently cited parenthetically in the text.
4. Before the May 2004 elections, which brought the Congress party back to power.
5. Arundhati Roy, "Democracy: Who Is She When She Is at Home?" *War Talk* (Cambridge, MA: South End Press, 2003), 21. Subsequently cited parenthetically in the text.
6. Quoted by Anthony Spaeth in "Rushdie Offends Again," *Time*, September 11, 1995, 53. In *Family Matters*, Yezad is accused by his son Murad of having the same notions of "purity" as Hitler (482).
7. Salman Rushdie, *The Moor's Last Sigh* (London: Jonathan Cape, 1995), 338. Subsequently cited parenthetically in the text.
8. Bharatiya Janata Party (the Indian People's Party), Janata Dal, Vishwa Hindu Parishad (Universal Hindu Association), and Bahujan Samaj Party.
9. Janata Party and Rashtriya Swayamsevak Sangh (literally, the National Self-Help Group, a right-wing Hindu cultural guild, the ideological support of the BJP).
10. Cf. John F. Burns, "Another Rushdie Novel, Another Bitter Epilogue," *The New York Times*, December 2, 1995.
11. Muslims were to be viciously targeted again ten years later, with the mass rapes and killings orchestrated in the state of Gujarat in March 2002, under the impetus of Gujarat's chief minister, Narendra Modi, who was triumphantly elected in the regional elections of Gujarat in December 2002 (but fell in the elections of May 2004).
12. Bharatya Janata Party, the nationalist Hindu party that stayed in power in India, with a coalition of regional parties from 1998 to May 2004.
13. T. B. Hansen, *The Saffron Wave: Democracy and Hindu Nationalism in Modern India* (Princeton: Princeton University Press, 1999), 174.
14. Stuart Corbridge and John Harriss, *Reinventing India: Liberalization, Hindu Nationalism and Popular Democracy* (Malden, MA: Blackwell Publishers, 2000), 133.
15. Fifty-eight Hindu passengers were burned alive on the Sabarmati Express in Godhra in March 2002, allegedly by Muslims, but in the absence of any concrete evidence different theories prevail, which blame an angry Muslim mob, a plot by the Pakistani Intelligence Services, a plot by

Hindu extremists to set off the Hindu backlash that followed, and so on (cf. Roy, "Democracy," 120).

16. Salman Rushdie, *Imaginary Homelands* (London: Granta, 1991), 394–95.

17. Interestingly, as Tariq Ali quips in *The Clash of Fundamentalisms* (London: Verso, 2002), 37n, the "ethnic cleansing" carried out by Catholic Spain against Jews and Muslims after the *Reconquista* caused a breakdown in personal hygiene, because baths, being associated with Islam and sensuality, were destroyed, and the spies of the Inquisition kept a look out for people who appeared too keen on personal ablutions, a sure sign in their eyes that the latter were imperfect converts who had remained secretly loyal to their old faith.

18. Hari Kunzru, *The Impressionist* (London: Penguin Books, 2003), 31. Subsequently cited parenthetically in the text.

19. Eagleton, "Pedants and Partisans."

20. Emulating his creator, who was born in Bombay and emigrated to Canada, where he has lived since 1975.

21. Yezad despises the word "Zoroaster," which for him is a "Greek perversion" of Zarathustra (463).

22. Thus Yezad is again set in parallel with Coomy, who is portrayed as a mock avatar of Lady Macbeth (109).

23. *Macbeth*, 1. 7. 5–6.

24. W. B. Yeats, "The Second Coming," lines 7–8.

25. Ali, *The Clash of Fundamentalisms*, 63.

26. Sandra Gilbert and Susan Gubar, *The Madwoman in the Attic* (New Haven: Yale University Press, 1984), 4. Their quotation is taken from Edward W. Said, *Beginnings: Intention and Method* (New York: Basic Books, 1975), 83.

27. Twenty Indian writers were invited to France in November 2002 to give conferences and take part in debates. The event was organized by "Les Belles Etrangères," an organism sponsored by the French Ministry of Culture to promote foreign literature translated into French.

28. William Shakespeare, *The Tragedy of King Richard II*, 2. 1. 40–66.

29. In *The Ground Beneath Her Feet*, Rushdie portrayed a Parsi in this vein: the westernized, anglophile, classicist scholar Sir Darius Xerxes Cama.

30. Monica Ali, *Brick Lane* (London: Doubleday, 2003), 219. Subsequently cited parenthetically in the text.

31. Salman Rushdie, *The Satanic Verses* (London: Viking, 1989), 244–245.

32. See Chahdortt Djavann, *Bas les voiles!* (Paris: Gallimard, 2003), 22.

33. Jehangir used to love his father's "invincible" whistle, "like a cheerful umbrella" under which "the world was safe and wonderful" (288).

34. One of Mistry's discreet and humorous allusions to Rushdie and his "Booker of Bookers," *Midnight's Children*.

CHAPTER 7

DOUBLING OF PARTS: ARUNDHATI ROY AS NOVELIST AND POLITICAL CRITIC

SUSANNE PETERS

INTRODUCTION

If the influential claim that postcolonial literature is to be understood as an allegorical reconstruction of the nation[1] holds true, one might argue that it could perhaps be extended to include an allegorization of fundamentalist beliefs. If we regard fundamentalism as an integrative—albeit deplorable—phenomenon within the overall context of nationhood, the metaphorical level of the notion of a nation ought to accommodate reactionist beliefs as well, if only to complete the picture. With particular reference to India, there are many subtexts of the notion of a nation that still present vast potential for the persistence of fundamentalist beliefs. The treatment of women and children, the status of members of the so-called lower castes, and the exclusion of outcasts from society are just a few that I will concentrate on in this chapter.

It is a well-known commonplace that writers of all ages and nations address social injustices that may spring from fundamentalist, reactionist motivations, but to envisage the scope with which such subject matters are treated in contemporary Indo-Anglian/Anglo-Indian fiction, it is worthwhile to take a brief look at the recent works of successful writers such as Romesh Gunesekera, Bharati Mukherjee, Michael Ondaatje, and Salman Rushdie, and then discuss Arundhati Roy's position among these in more detail.[2]

In Gunesekera's much-acclaimed first novel, *Reef* (1994), fundamentalist thought remains rather securely encapsulated below the surface texture of the narrative, and yet, it makes its presence felt through a number of opaque allusions, such as to the real cause of Dias's death, which is withheld from the reader throughout the novel. Any kind of political involvement of the protagonist-cum-narrator, Triton, is characteristically foreclosed in an often-used perspicuous sentence that formulates his unswerving stance in all matters of active political engagement, as this excerpt from a dialogue with Wijetunga, a member of a revolutionist/reactionist group, demonstrates: "'You know, brother, our country really needs to be cleansed, *radically.* There is no alternative. *We have to destroy in order to create . . .*' I said, 'But I am only a cook.'"[3] In Gunesekera's later novels, such as *Heaven's Edge* (2002), the male protagonist again encounters members of fundamentalist groups on a person-to-person level, but we cannot locate any intellectual reasoning within the narrative that directly tackles fundamentalist stronghold positions or their objectives. Instead, fundamentalists are generally referred to as "warlords and their cronies,"[4] a characteristic feature that makes it considerably more difficult—at least for a Western reader—to grasp the degree and level of the narrator's (or even the author's) involvement with politics. Although the male protagonist physically fights reactionists, criminals, and fundamentalists in defense of his ideals—if not his life—the outcome is less clear; his lover is killed in combat, and with her all of his reasons for survival seem to have also died. In Mukherjee's novel *Jasmine* (1989), the female protagonist's husband dies in a bomb attack staged by Hindu fundamentalists, an incident that causes great emotional trauma and motivates her migration to America to escape "feudalist" entrapment as a neglected widow. In her more recent novel *Desirable Daughters* (2002),[5] on the other hand, Mukherjee locates fundamentalist views—as far as they can be aligned with feudalism—within the realm of myth as well. Although she thus seems to broaden her historical perspective, the female protagonist's husband is again victimized and almost killed in a firebomb explosion that carries the handwriting of violent fundamentalists. However, in the novel it is also thought feasible that the explosion was caused by "ordinary" criminals. Hence, it seems an elusive undertaking to qualify fundamentalism in Mukherjee's novels, as fundamentalist motives and opinions are hardly ever reflected in them. It is perhaps in Ondaatje's novel *Anil's Ghost* (2000) that we find the most deeply unsettling narrative involvement with what fundamentalists are prepared to do to people's bodies and to people's minds. The political oppression of those who oppose governmental positions, the disturbing omnipresence of torture and murder, and the despicable disposal of their bodies are mostly presented from a scientific or medical viewpoint that is rather reminiscent of Roy's factual narrative voice, which I will describe later. In Ondaatje's novel, the forensic expert Anil Tissera dedicates herself to the restoration of some kind of integrity to victims of torture by giving them a (fictitious) identity. Here, the concepts of individuality and identity are radically endangered, as the skeleton that is being forensically examined by her is not only given a name ("Sailor") but also has its face remodeled. *Anil's Ghost* is a powerful and compelling allegorization of a nation in a barbaric state in the tight grip of fundamentalists. Rushdie's *Midnight's Children* (1981) most explicitly features the body as an allegory of the nation. Here, it is grotesquely deformed, yet equipped with sensuous abilities that far outreach those of ordinary human beings. As the grotesque body degenerates, the nation cracks up too. Rushdie's antifundamentalist agenda then includes the option to renegotiate both history and identity on a national level, as his dissolution of the clash between Eastern and Western cultures deconstructs the myth of fundamentalist identity.[6] These few examples show that although there is a wide range of narrative concepts in Anglo-Indian fiction that deal with fundamentalist positions, they do so by focusing on affected, physical–personal points of view and by exhibiting the inflictions on the human body caused by fundamentalist violence rather than by reflections on political issues.

Among this group of writers, Roy's way of dealing with fundamentalism continues in this vein, yet it is particular in that she seems to have re-created the perspective from which the effects of fundamentalism are experienced in the most radical sense. In *The God of Small Things,* the belief in the caste system forms a major part of a wider fundamentalist, reactionary, and patriarchal network of beliefs that guide the treatment and social status of women, children, and subordinates. Although India's caste system was officially abolished in 1947, it still blocks the social advancement of many individuals. Over 150 million people, mainly untouchables and dalits, still lead a miserable existence, without proper access to jobs, schooling, or health care.[7] These conditions are firmly placed within the referential context of the novel, and if we understand the term *fundamentalism* to denote movements that seek to return to orthodox, feudal value systems, the power of India's caste system can also be seen as a reactionist opposition to modernism, social reforms, individuality, and particularly liberalism.[8]

Although such obstinacy need not be conceived in temporal terms, it is an intriguing way of thinking about fundamentalism, because we can then apply what Foucault wrote on the history of imprisonment practices.[9] In his analysis of corporeal punishment practices in Europe from the Middle Ages onward, Foucault links up several movements in the history of humane thinking: corporeal punishment and torture are seen as the workings of a power mechanism that is itself aligned to both the development of humanistic ideals and the development of a collective sensibility. Until the end of the eighteenth century, Foucault argues, the bodies of those who transgressed the law were subjected to a kind of "official" punishment that was often staged as an event, sometimes even turned into a public spectacle and a supposed necessary, though not always effective, deterrent. In the nineteenth century, an economy of suspended rights came into existence, in which the object of penalization was no longer the delinquent's body. As the punishment was no longer corporeal but spiritual, the body was slowly replaced by the soul. Though the body was restricted in its movements, the delinquent imprisoned or subjected to hard labor, he was no longer tortured. Instead, the soul was made to suffer by psychological forms of disciplinary actions. Foucault thus places the history of corporeal punishment within a matrix between the history of power and the history of humane thought—a perspective that also applies to *The God of Small Things*. The murder of Velutha in Roy's novel, the banishment of Ammu from the village society, the sexual abuse of Estha, and the reenactment of these traumatic events in the Kathakali theatrical performance that is attended by the grown-up twins can thus be read as phenomena that appear to have their roots in a different age of the history of the human soul. To put it in another way: Roy's *The God of Small Things* and, one might add, Ondaatje's *Anil's Ghost* depict violence as precisely such anachronistic occurrences that, according to Foucault, have long ceased to be practiced. If what Foucault describes for the European context also applies to Anglo-Indian writing, it is the anachronism of violence, the radical reversal of humanistic thinking, that seems to endanger the concepts of individuality and identity. Fundamentalists have held strong positions in the long history of the repression of individuals and social groups, even whole nations, and their anachronism is perhaps one of the most obvious arguments against their exertion of violence as the expression of power. Foucault's arguments can also be read in view of one of the most pressing concerns of writers such as Roy and Ondaatje, which is to rescue human and humane sensitivity: a defense of the soul. Within this historically oriented context, we can understand fundamentalism as an anachronistic phenomenon of strong antiliberalist provenance that is opposed to modern values of humanity, social equality, and freedom of choice. To complement such *ex negativo* descriptions, fundamentalism can also be constructed around an excessive or exclusive exertion of power—and this is, I hope to show, also Roy's position.

Arundhati Roy—novelist, political critic, and popular campaigning activist—has so far published only one novel, *The God of Small Things,* which won the prestigious Booker Prize in 1997. It became an international success and has been translated into more than forty languages, selling well over 6 million copies. Despite such international acclaim, Roy has not published another novel since. Instead, using the media attention she gained for her novel, she has increasingly voiced her concern with global and local power politics, of which three collections of essays give evidence: *The Cost of Living* (1999), *Power Politics* (2001), and *War Talk* (2003). A number of important interviews have been conducted that deal with her ambition and concerns in more detail.[10] Issues she frequently deals with include the destructive effects of globalization, terrorism, U.S. hegemony, racism, environmental concerns, and pollution. Her political activism is currently aimed at the dams built in India that displace hundreds of thousands of people and destroy their villages and their culture. Her voice is often aggressive, her rhetoric relying on short main clauses, and there is a general lack of elaborate or background argument. At times her nonfiction makes a difficult read, as it does not offer to lead or guide the reader, but simply tries to get the messages across.

"I believe that all the beauty of human civilisation—our art, our music, our literature—lie beyond these fundamentalist positions." This is how Roy replied to Bush's notorious statement "You are either with us or with the terrorists" after the 9/11 attacks on the United States. In her critical and often provocative writing, Roy tackles a wide range of fundamentalist phenomena—regarding gender, race, caste, and religion, as well as global and local politics. She addresses fundamentalism's many facets and voices her protest on various levels, often employing different channels of communication. In *The God of Small Things,* Roy's concern to speak out for the oppressed is communicated in a deeply sensitive and subjective, yet vulnerable, convincing manner.[11]

CONCEPTUALIZING SENSITIVITY AS AN ANTIDOTE TO FUNDAMENTALIST BELIEFS

The history of the twins, Rahel and Estha, is told on two narrative levels, one of which relates the traumatic events that happen during a relatively short period of about two weeks in 1969, when the children are seven years old. The twins' half-English cousin, Sophie Mol, arrives on a visit from London and then accidentally drowns as the twins attempt to escape from their home after a quarrel with their mother, taking Sophie with them. The untouchable, Velutha, whom the children adore and who is also their mother's lover, is beaten to death by a troop of policemen in front of the children. The second narrative level relates how twenty-three years later, Rahel returns to Ayemenem to meet her brother, Estha, who was sent back by his father and needs looking after because he does not speak. Both adults appear to still suffer from their traumatic childhood experiences and are depicted as extremely solitary, withdrawn characters: Estha is mute, and Rahel, though of a seemingly stronger disposition and whose voice we often take to be the narrator's, is unable to sustain a normal male–female sexual relationship. At the end of the novel, the twins transform their relation as siblings into an incestuous bond, which can be regarded as both a consequential consummation of their lifelong unity and a renewal of their long-lost ability to express emotions, poised as a bulwark to fend off the still-painful reality of the world outside them. However, the novel ends with a structurally ambivalent turn back to the private history of Ammu and her lover, Velutha, to her promise to meet again "tomorrow." This can be read as a repetition and thus an insistence on the possibility of love, but at the same time, love seems forever postponed into the future. Factually, the lovers never meet again, although, at the moment of speaking, they could not have known that.

Fundamentalism is often topical in *The God of Small Things*, and it forms an alliance with related discourses that lay down the laws by which the protagonists (and the other characters that populate the novel) are to abide, yet mostly refuse to do: discourses of a globalized entertainment industry that is finding its way into the local Indian culture in the form of materialistic paraphernalia, Elvis Presley hairstyles, and the film *The Sound of Music* that the family go to see before they collect Sophie from the airport.[12] However much the children love the movies, for them the cinema becomes a site of corruption and sexual abuse. The treatment of women in the novel can also be related to the realms of reactionist/fundamentalist beliefs, as women have a very fixed specter of tasks and roles to fulfill as either mothers and grandmothers or aunts and obedient, servile wives, but they are never considered independently of their assumed roles.[13] They are neither considered to be lovers, nor are they seen as consumers of materialistic goods. If they do not accept these offers of identification presented to them by the dominant patriarchal culture they are a part of, if they do not abide by its laws and codes of behavior, they are punished by being expelled from society. This is what is done to Ammu after her love affair with Velutha has been discovered. She is separated from her children and sent away to fend for herself. The children themselves are separated too, and they are not even allowed to stay in each other's company after the horrifying events of Sohpie's and Velutha's deaths.

One important example of such immediate and severe punishment for the transgression of laws is the narration of the murder of Velutha, which is for the most part communicated to the reader in a mechanical, unemotional, and seemingly detached voice that borders on satire. The murder of the untouchable Velutha by a group of policemen is the most significantly distressing event described in the book. Velutha is wrongly accused of having raped Ammu (with whom he is having a love affair) and having abducted her children (who fled from home because of an argument with their mother). These reasons are, however, only the official side of things. In reality, he is punished for not acting his part as "untouchable," for his allegedly disrespectful liaison with a member of one of the "touchable" upper classes of Ayemenem. This is made quite clear from the beginning of the novel through the abundance of metaphorical allusions to the laws by which all the characters have to abide. The event is narrated, however, by a voice that seems rather unemotional, a voice that does not tell the readers about the pain and the shame, but that seems to focus, even linger, on rather mechanical details ("Blood barely shows on a Black Man").[14] Thus, the episode vividly brings to life what fundamentalism does to people's bodies and to people's minds: as the children witness the murder, they watch "dinner-plate-eyed" (308), but what they see is related in a manner that appears to be stripped of feelings. This of course also means that the impression the children get is simply too much for them to bear. Neither do they cry, nor do they attempt to interfere. In this sense the function of reliance of the narrative voice on mechanical aspects of the event ("The sober, steady brutality, the economy of it all" [308]) becomes clear: because of the inconceivability of what is taking place, the event can only be related by fragments and details rather than by the whole sight—which, nevertheless, the reader is finally called upon to imagine, as the policemen themselves step back to admire their work, to take in the whole picture of the miserable sight of a smashed body: "They stepped away from him. Craftsmen assessing their work. Seeking aesthetic distance" (310). The idea that there is no way for the children to express what they feel, that there is no outlet for their impression, is then taken up in the idea of their acting a part in a play they do not understand.

The events that the children experience have marginally different effects on each of them. While Estha is sexually abused (an event that is even more drastic because it takes place under the eyes of those who were there to look after him) and while he is the one who betrays Velutha in a futile attempt to save his mother from disgrace, Rahel seems to fare slightly better. She manages to acquire a stronger personality, although, in the words of a school report, she "doesn't know how to be a girl" (17) after these events and is disruptive and unruly throughout the years of her youth. The betrayed Estha, on the other hand, who is unbeknownst to himself turned into the betrayer instead of being the betrayed, is filled with a sense of guilt that never leaves him and that gradually and then finally numbs him. Thus he becomes an active participant in what the narrator calls "History": the painful injustices of those in power toward those who are powerless. The end of the novel features another event of transgression. The incestuous reunion of the twins is the breaking of a strong taboo, and, after their mother's out-caste love affair, another transgression of the laws of love, of "who loves who, and how, and how much," that reverberates throughout the novel—but it is also a celebration of the twins' emotional survival in an otherwise hostile environment.[15] Thus, the importance of the overall concept of sensitivity and sensibility in the novel may be viewed as an antidote and a cathartic restorative against the harmful effects of fundamentalism's many faces.

From this follows that its repercussions are experienced from "below" or from "within," from the minor perspective of the victim(s). The novel is more concerned with the expression of emotions and feelings and family and sexual bonds. The impact of fundamentalism is so effectively communicated to the reader precisely because its presentation is not intellectual, as it seems to insist on the physical and psychological concerns of the body rather than on conventional rhetoric.[16] This specific approach is complemented by the point of view from which the story is largely told: a reconstruction of a child's perspective, namely that of the seven-year-old twins who suffer a lifelong trauma from witnessing the murder of the man they loved. Of course, this reconstruction is only one of the voices we listen to as we read along—yet it is one that is easily distinguishable, because it does not interpret actions: it experiences and performs them.[17]

The male characters' brutality in pursuing their goals is linked to the male's over the female, over the lower castes, and over children. Fundamentalist belief is portrayed as a rationalization of the (necessary) fear of the powerless. It also signifies the functioning of the law: after all, as Rahel's cynical narrative voice adds, you cannot make an omelette without breaking the egg.

KATHAKALI: ACTING AS A METAPHOR FOR HISTORY AND IDENTITY

As Roy counterbalances individual experience and the effects of history against the idea of "live performance" in her novel, she also explores a triangular relationship between history, fiction, and performance. Her metaphor for this relationship is a traditional Indian dance that reenacts ancient Hindu myths: the Kathakali that originates in Kerala, where the novel is set.

Kathakali is an elaborate and spectacular performance art that is usually performed at night in temples, lasting six or seven hours. It tells stories from Hindu mythology and is performed to live musical accompaniment, though the stories are mainly communicated visually and in a densely structured manner. The bodies of the actors are dressed in exuberant, colorful costumes; their makeup is painstakingly applied, following precise rules. Kathakali actors take years to perfect their art; they view their performance not as a part of life, but as life itself. Over the years, they train their bodies to control the magnificent movements.[18] The difference between this traditional Kerala performance art (or dance) and Western concepts of acting is hinted at in the novel itself: "Ironically, his [i.e. the Kathakali dancer's] struggle is the reverse of an actor's struggle—he strives not to enter a part but to escape it" (231).

A performance of this dance is attended by the grown-up twins in the novel and it forms an important link between Roy's conceptualizing of the body as a mediator between the spheres of outside/public and inside/private on the one hand, and her understanding of history on the other, not only in the private context of the protagonists, Rahel and Estha, but also in a more general, public sense. In the Kathakali dance too, the actor's body communicates the history of events, and he does it from a private point of view, not a public one, as one might have expected. Although the events are sectioned off in single stories, in sets of visual displays and prescribed movements, and although they are fictive, they still relate the truth: "It didn't matter that the story had begun, because Kathakali discovered long ago that the secret of the Great Stories is that they *have* no secrets . . . They don't deceive you with thrills and trick endings. They don't surprise you with the unforeseen" (229, author's italics).[19] This alternative history in live performance, contrary to the "real" one that is to be experienced, is not threatening, and it brings the twins together after Rahel's return to Ayemenem, as they both sit by a sleeping elephant and watch the performance that lasts all night, without needing to acknowledge each other's presence.

As Rahel and Estha sit quietly through the Kathakali performance, both their cultural history and their cultural identity are revealed to them through stories. However, at one point the performance seems to get out of control, partly because of the trancelike stance the actor has hyped himself up to, and partly because of the actors' humiliation at having to perform truncated stories in front of tourists for a living. In the cathartic act of watching the Kathakali performance, Rahel and Estha see a kind of theatrical reenactment of their own fate, of the rule of the love laws, of Estha's abandonment, and, at the end of the performance, of the horror they witnessed twenty-three years earlier. The only difference, as is explained by the narrator, is the difference between the "brutal extravagance" of the performance art and the "savage economy" (235) of the murder of Velutha. Again, Rahel and Estha become history's witnesses, again they are trapped in stories that are and are not their own, "(t)hat had set out with the semblance of structure and order, then bolted like a frightened horse into anarchy" (236). "History in live performance" then reveals itself twice to the twins. Once, as children, they form the "under-age audience" (309), witnessing the murder of a man they loved. History has lessons to teach, as is foretold by the narrator much earlier in the novel:

> While other children of their age learned other things, Estha and Rahel learned how history negotiates its terms and collects its dues from those who break its laws. They heard its sickening thud. They smelled its smell and never forgot it. History's smell. (55)

There are more lessons of this kind the children have to learn, as "Blood barely shows on a Black Man" and "It smells, though" (310). The lessons translate history back into a matter of perception. History wrongs people, and although this may not be outright visible, one can hear it and smell it: these are surer ways of knowing that some wrong has been done than offers of explanation. In their attempt to stall their fear, the children think up some guidelines by which they hope to manage to survive. The first one is "Anything Can Happen To Anyone"; the second runs "It's Best to be Prepared" (267). The lesson they learn as they watch the Kathakali performance is very similar to these: because the events performed in the temple are so closely related to their own experience twenty-three years ago (the only difference being "brutal extravagance" against "savage economy"), they learn that history still has the same awful smell.

The metaphor of play-acting is also used to describe the role of the children in Velutha's murder:

> A pair of actors trapped in a recondite play with no hint of plot or narrative. Stumbling through their parts, nursing someone else's sorrow. Grieving someone else's grief.
> Unable, somehow, to change plays. Or purchase, for a fee, some cheap brand of exorcism from a counsellor with a fancy degree, who would sit them down and say, in one of many ways: "You are not the Sinners. You're the Sinned Against. You were only children. You had no control. You are the *victims,* not the perpetrators."

It would have helped if they could have made that crossing. If only they could have worn, even temporarily, the tragic hood of victimhood. Then they would have been able to put a face on it, and conjure up fury at what had happened. Or seek redress. And eventually, perhaps, exorcize the memories that haunted them.
But anger wasn't available to them and there was no face to put on this Other Thing that they held in their sticky Other Hands, like an imaginary orange. There was nowhere to lay it down. It wasn't theirs to give away. It would have to be held. Carefully and for ever. (191, author's italics)

The pair of actors trapped in a scenery they do not understand is reminiscent of the theater of the absurd—without any discernible logic or causal string that connects the separate scenes, bare of a narrative or a story line that would allow them to assign their worries to a natural cause, to compartmentalize or even to locate their fear. All this is denied them, which is why they cannot get over what they had to endure.

On another level, this reading of the acting metaphor provides us with information about the role of fiction for Arundhati Roy. It seems that fiction helped her to exorcize a pain that she felt in view of India's "wrongfooted history," with all the brutality of its still-existing caste system, its treatment of women and children, and the effects of fundamentalism. Unlike her protagonists, she was able to lay down her "sticky orange," and once she finished her novel, she could profoundly change her strategy in her fight for the oppressed.

SURPASSING THE THEATRICAL MODE:
"FICTION DANCES OUT OF ME"

The theatrical mode of the Kathakali performance and its metaphorical link to Roy's concept of history cannot simply be extended to her involvement with politics. The focus on the body, the preference of sensitivity over reason in *The God of Small Things* discussed so far, seems to foreclose a direct intellectual address of political issues, and it becomes feasible that Roy speaks with a very different voice in her essayistic work. However, there is a relation to be discovered between her mode of fiction and her political activism.

There is a question frequently put to Roy after the success of her novel that seems to indicate a certain amount of irritation on the part of her readers with her outspoken political criticism ever since. Roy's readers seem to expect and even wish for another piece of emotional, sadly enjoyable fiction. The eager wait for another novel, however, seems to be at odds with her geopolitical activism. This is what she said in interview:

> The last question every visiting journalist always asks me is: Are you writing another book? That question mocks me. Another book? Right *now?* This talk of nuclear war [a reference to the ongoing India-Pakistan conflict] displays such contempt for music, art, literature, and everything else that defines civilization. So what kind of book should I write?[20]

Roy herself seems to have provided a subtle answer to that question. In another passage from *War Talk,* she writes:

> Writers imagine that they cull stories from the world. I'm beginning to believe that vanity makes them think so. That it's actually the other way around. Stories cull writers from the world. Stories reveal themselves to us. The public narrative, the private narrative—they colonize us. Fiction and nonfiction are only different techniques of storytelling. For reasons I do not fully understand, fiction dances out of me. Nonfiction is wrenched out by the aching, broken world I wake up to every morning. (45)

Fiction escapes her "for reasons she does not fully understand": perhaps we can enquire into these reasons by considering that in *The God of Small Things,* emotions and feelings are perceived by those who are small, experienced from below or from within the body. The reconstruction of the perhaps most vulnerable point of view imaginable—that of the children—and its complementary other, that of the grown-up Rahel, both stand for the private sphere Roy herself alludes to in the interview. The voice she uses in her essays and political speeches is, on the other hand, a public one. Yet the core issue remains the same: her ambition is to get people to see and to realize the iniquitousness of a "wrongfooted history," and she does that by "doubling her parts": one private and emotional, the other public and intellectual.

THE FACTUAL NARRATIVE

Roy's private emotional voice can be linked to the public anger she expresses in her essays and political speeches, if it is seen as an extension of the emotional perspective in the novel. Sensitivity thus becomes aggression. However, we find examples of the public voice in Roy's novel too, in the rather factual narrative mode she uses, characterized by a voice that relates the events in a seemingly detached, matter-of-fact tone—for example, in the descriptions of the social injustices of India's caste system. As in her compassionate voice we have described above, where we identified a link between sensitivity and aggression based on the expression of emotion in both, we can describe another link from the detached cool voice to the intellectual rhetoric that Roy later employs in her political essays, in which she examines the effects of globalization. Here is an example of such doubling of parts from the novel that can be regarded to be at the roots of Roy's political engagement:

> When the British came to Malabar, a number of Paravans, Pelayas and Pulayas (among them Velutha's grandfather, Kelan) converted to Christianity and joined the Anglican Church to escape the scourge of Untouchability. As added incentive they were given a little food and money. They were known as the Rice-Christians. It didn't take them long to realize that they had jumped from the frying pan into the fire. They were made to have separate churches, with separate services, and separate priests. As a special favour they were even given their own separate Pariah Bishop. After Independence they found they were not entitled to any Government benefits like job reservations or bank loans at low interest rates, because officially, on paper, they were Christians, and therefore casteless. It was a little like having to sweep away your footprints without a broom. Or worse, not being *allowed* to leave footprints at all. (74)

Roy's most pressing concern is an understanding of the "physics of power": a play in which the two spheres of the private and the public are effective. They form a dangerous alliance if the wrongs on the collective level are repeated on the individual level and vice versa:

> There can never be a single story. There are only ways of seeing. So when I tell a story, I tell it not as an ideologue who wants to pit one absolutist ideology against another, but as a storyteller who wants to share her way of seeing. Though it might appear otherwise, my writing is not really about nations and histories, it's about power. About the paranoia and ruthlessness of power. About the physics of power. I believe that the accumulation of vast unfettered power by a state or a country, a corporation or an institution—or even an individual, a spouse, friend, or sibling—regardless of ideology, results in excesses such as the ones I will recount here. (*War Talk*, 46)

In her novel, it is the "Love Laws" that are strongly connected with such physical aspects of public power reaching into and putting the private sphere at risk. Those who transgress these laws have to face the cruel consequences.

I believe that the effectiveness of Roy's strategy results from her ability to address the effects of fundamentalism in two voices. One can be described as emotional and private, making extensive use of a perceptive but childish and naïve, even anti-intellectual, point of view that is designed to lay bare the abyss between love, care, and emotion on the one hand and the cynical attitudes of fundamentalist beliefs, with the violent action that goes with them, on the other. Taking sides with the twins, the readers are brought to see the absurd faces of "wrongfooted" history, fundamentalism, and general oppression of the subaltern. In this sense, there are decisive educational aspects to be found in Roy's writing that rely on the reconstruction of an ultimately private point of view, with which the reader may safely identify, and a rather public, rhetorical, intellectually demanding argument, which asks for more critical distance. Roy herself believes in the inseparability of fiction and nonfiction:

> I don't see a great difference between *The God of Small Things* and my nonfiction. In fact, I keep saying, fiction is the truest thing there ever was. Today's world of specialization is bizarre. Specialists and experts end up severing the links between things, isolating them, actually creating barriers that prevent ordinary people from understanding what's happening to them. I try to do the opposite: to create links, to join the dots, to tell politics like a story, to communicate it, to make it real. To make the connection between a man with his child telling you about life in the village he lived in before it was submerged by a reservoir, and the WTO, the IMF, and the World Bank.[21]

If we link the expression of emotion in the novel to the even more emotional anger in her essays, we might link the factual narrative in the novel to the intellectual rhetoric of her essays. Perhaps it is not surprising that Roy has met with harsh criticism both as a writer of fiction and as a political activist. As a novelist, Roy, who believes in the inseparability of literature and politics, is at times attacked because she does not content herself with being an accomplished author of fiction; while as a political writer, she has been criticized for her daring, passionate, almost ruthless voice.[22] Perhaps it frightens people that an artist, and a female artist at that, capable of conveying sensitivity in the particular way she does in her novel, can also speak such fearless, clear, and accusing words in her public, political writing.

It seems to me that Roy needed fiction to exorcize her own helplessness and the pain she felt in view of the many-faceted fundamentalist beliefs she meets with not only in India but in other countries shaken by humanitarian crises and wars as well. In this sense, she does not need to write another book to help her to formulate the pain that she feels. Instead, she now seeks redress in the real world.

NOTES

1. This is a reference to Fredric Jameson's (1986) phrase "national allegories": "The story of the private individual destiny is always an allegory of the embattled situation of the public national project" (69). Thormann (Janet Thormann, "The Ethical Subject of *The God of Small Things*," *Journal for the Psychoanalysis of Culture & Society* 8, no. 2 (Fall 2003): 299–307) does not agree with the applicability of this claim in the case of Roy's novel. She sees the nation "as something like an absent mediator between the local and the global, figured only through rules governing property, the caste system and the regulation of women, and the regional operations of the Communist party and the police" (306n). The criticism seems justified, if an allegory is taken to be the transformation of an abstract term into a physical image. In Roy's novel, the nation does indeed remain somewhat abstract. However, we are still left with the question of the specific form its representation takes, as the rules and regulations are set and the violence carried out by protagonists in the novel.

2. Obviously, this list just serves to illustrate my point. The fact that all these writers, with the notable exception of Roy, are expatriates, is not the issue here, but would be a topic for a separate study.

3. Romesh Gunesekera, *Reef* (London: Granta/Penguin, 1994), 121. Emphasis not added. Elsewhere I have treated the protagonist's lack of political awareness in more detail (2003).

4. Romesh Gunesekera, *Heaven's Edge* (London: Bloomsbury, 2002), 36. This is characteristically continued in the dialogues that depict opponents as criminals: "War here, like everywhere else, was once about land and identity. But after the death cloud in the south everything changed. You see, we were reshaped by gangsters into new collectives held together only by conscriptions. You could say myopia, no? Not language, not religion, not any of those outmoded notions of nation. After so many years of fighting, violence became ingrained into our way of life. So now we have only thugs for politicians and tyranny in every tribe" (ibid., 37).

5. The second volume of a forthcoming trilogy, titled *The Tree Bride*, is due to appear later this year. Judging from the title alone, which takes its leitmotif from the first volume, one may speculate that the mythical/historical level will feature even more prominently in the new novel.

6. See Klaus Stierstorfer's contribution to this volume.

7. Dalits have formed their own pressure group, which can be consulted under www.dalits.org. See also the detailed study by Oliver Mendelsohn and Marika Vicziany, *The Untouchables* (Cambridge: Cambridge University Press, 1998). The authors explore the construction of the untouchables as a social and political category, the historical background that led to such a definition, and their position in Indian society today. Cf. also the term *homo hierarchicus* as opposed to more individualistic Western concepts of identity coined by Louis Dumont (*Homo Hierarchicus: The Caste System and its Implications* [Delhi: Vikas, 1970]).

8. Gordon Campbell, on the other hand, warns in his contribution to this volume against muddling fundamentalism with radicalism because this might endorse popular prejudice. Of course he is right in demanding accuracy of the concepts we work with, yet we must not forget that to tackle (and perhaps work to overcome) fundamentalism and radicalism, we need to examine their common denominators as well.

9. *Surveiller et punir. La naissance de la prison* (Paris: Gallimard, 1975).

10. The most recent is David Barsamian's collection, *The Checkbook and the Cruise Missile* (Cambridge, MA: South End Press, 2004).

11. Julie Mullaney, *Arundhati Roy's "The God of Small Things": A Reader's Guide.* (New York: Continuum, 2002) discusses Roy's different voices in the light of the concept of "third world womanhood," which itself refers to Spivak's concept of the subaltern. Mullaney highlights the differences among the women characters in Roy's novel, when she writes "[s]he carefully delineates not their false homogeneity as representations of oppressed 'third world woman' but the range of options and choices, whether complicit, resistant—or both—to the dominant order . . . " (11).

12. *The Sound of Music*—a famous mid-fifties musical with its marketing slogan "the happiest sound in all the world" is an important subtext in the novel, as it seems to juxtapose the clichéd world of a delightful musical with the harsh reality that the twins experience in India, particularly Estha's sexual abuse during the visit to the cinema. Catherine Pesso-Miquel, "'Queen Cigars' and 'Peppermint Children': Foreign Arrivals in *The God of Small Things*," *Reading Arundhati Roy's "The God of Small Things"* (Dijon: Editions Universitaires de Dijon, 2002), 23–40 has examined the wider influence of the foreign in the novel.

13. Mullaney aligns Roy's characterization of women with that by writers Sahgal and Desai, "which together paint a devastating critique of the interwoven choices and fates facing generations of Indian women in light of the inherited dominant mythic archetypes of Indian womanhood . . . the cornerstones on which . . . the Indian family and therefore Indian society is built," Mullaney, *Arundhati Roy's "The God of Small Things,"* 2.

14. Arundhati Roy, *The God of Small Things* (London: Flamingo, 1997), 310. Subsequently cited parenthetically in the text.

15. Thormann provides an intriguing (and convincing) psychoanalytic reading of their incest: "But since the Love Law at the origin of any law at all is the incest prohibition, the violation of the incest prohibition in the narrative stands as a measure of the novel's radical interrogation of the foundations of social exchange," Thormann, "The Ethical Subject of *The God of Small Things,*" 300.

16. Thormann seems to agree with me at this point, taking the layout of the text as another signifier for the stress on the body: "Incomplete sentences, separated in the printed layout as separate paragraphs, exaggerate emotion, while sensuous images and metaphors strain against the limits of conventional prose by insisting on the body" (ibid., 301).

17. Examining the children's language within the context of their transgression of the laws of the English language, Thormann argues that they nevertheless transmit family history. The twins break up proper words into syllables and phonemes, form rhymes, and reduce meaning to nonsense phrases. The voice of the narrator "reinvents ordinary language, infusing it with jouissance. It is a writing, like much women's writing, heavy with melodrama" (ibid., 301). One might perhaps consider that one of Roy's favourite authors and famous predecessors in the playful use of words is James Joyce, whose influence on her writing we also need to consider here.

18. For a popular description of Kathakali performance art see, for example, Vidya Bhavani Suresh, *What is Kathakali?* (Chennai: Skanda Publications, 2003).

19. Mullaney interprets the Kathakali performance as a macrostructural comment on Roy's own fiction making, "on the architecture of her own story," in Mullaney, *Arundhati Roy's "The God of Small Things,"* 57, 60. Cf. also 62.

20. Arundhati Roy, *War Talk* (Cambridge, MA: South End Press, 2003), 7. Subsequently cited parenthetically in the text.

21. From Barsamian, *The Checkbook and the Cruise Missile,* 10.

22. I am referring to the ongoing legal case she is involved with because of allegations that her novel is responsible for the corruption of public morality. Cf. the introduction to the above by Naomi Klein (vii). See also http://www.rediff.com/news/nov/29roy.htm and www.rediff.com/news/2001/nov/05spec.htm.

PART III

FUNDAMENTALISM IN POST/MODERNIST CONTEXTS

CHAPTER 8

TARIQ ALI AND RECENT NEGOTIATIONS OF FUNDAMENTALISM

KLAUS STIERSTORFER

INTRODUCTION

This chapter attempts to present a fast-forward version of recent developments in literary negotiations with fundamentalism highlighted by what can hopefully be conceived as writers and texts representative of the points to be made in my literary and literary historical argument. This argument situates the engagement with fundamentalism in literature in English at the threshold between modernist and postmodernist discourses, as well as in the context of explorations beyond the postmodernist paradigm that both revaluate and transcend modernist essentialisms. Before the fast forwarding can begin, however, a kind of origin can be established, if only in etymological terms in English. It points to the Southern United States in the early twentieth century.

In fact, fundamentalism is an American invention, at least where the term itself is concerned. It originates with the twelve-volume paperback sequence titled *The Fundamentals: A Testimony,* funded by the oil magnates Lyman and Milton Stewart between 1910 and 1915 and distributed for free throughout the United States in thousands of copies (3 million eventually) to further a specific vision of evangelical Protestantism. The attributive "fundamentalist" was subsequently coined by the Baptist pastor Curtis Lee Laws (1868–1946) when he co-organized the Buffalo Conference on the "Fundamentals of the Baptist Faith" in 1920. In an editorial after the conference he defined a "fundamentalist" as a person "who still cling[s] to the great fundamentals and who mean[s] to do battle royal for them." What this "battle royal" could look like can be seen with numerous preachers, especially in the Southern States, such as John Franklyn Norris (1877–1952), a.k.a. "The Texas Cyclone." During his sermons, Norris would roam the platform, shouting and weeping, bringing live monkeys to the pulpit to mock Darwinism, and making a name by sermon series in his base at Forth Worth such as "The Ten Biggest Devils in Fort Worth—Names Given."

These "fundamentalists," as they called themselves, went to battle against contemporary developments that, they felt, endangered the very basis of their Christian faith. One such danger came from the Higher Criticism of German provenance, against which the Stewarts had already founded the Bible College at Los Angeles in 1908 to insist on a literal understanding of the Bible. A particular test case was the story of creation, which liberal theologians had begun to read metaphorically in keeping with the findings of evolutionary theory in the wake of Charles Darwin. Premillennial convictions came in, especially triggered by the experience of World War I, which many fundamentalists saw as the beginning of the End.

Here it already becomes clear that fundamentalism can be understood as one reaction against the basic tenets and consequences of modernity and its eventual culmination in modernism: secularization and the "privatization" of religion, the emergence of science as the predominant paradigm, and the experience of general fragmentation and the breakup of traditional systems of belief. Used as a term of affirmation by religious groups that wanted to resist modernism's effects on their way of life and thought, fundamentalism as a label soon lost its attractiveness, however, through its pejorative appropriation by its critics, but also through unintentional self-deprecation. Thus, in the famous 1925 Scopes Trial in Tennessee, the fundamentalist plaintiff William Jennings Bryan became the defendant under questioning by the rationalist lawyer Clarence Darrow. Darrow forced the fundamentalist Bryan, who particularly stood up for a literal understanding of the biblical account of the creation of the world, to concede that "he had never read any critical account of the origins of the biblical text, that he had no interest in any other faith, and that, finally, 'I do not think about things I don't think about' and [that he] only thought about the things he *did* think about 'sometimes.'" (author's italics)[1]

FUNDAMENTALISM AND MODERNITY: O'CONNOR AND VAUGHN

Despite this strong reaction by liberal secularists against what they perceived as a fundamentalist threat, literary reception of the fundamentalist movement remained complex and ambiguous. One of the best examples here is the writer Flannery O'Connor (1925–1964) from Savannah, Georgia. Although a Roman Catholic herself, she strongly identified with the fundamentalist Protestants from her native land, the American South. O'Connor's work was misread as a send-up of fundamentalism by her early critics, but it has now come to be seen as an intervention against the homogenizing consensus religion of the Eisenhower era of the 1950s, perhaps best characterized by his famous bon mot: "Our government makes no sense unless it is founded in a deeply felt religious faith—and I don't care what it is."[2] As Jon Lance Bacon convincingly argues,[3] O'Connor thus shares with contemporaries such as C. Wright Mills, Marshall McLuhan, David Reisman, William Whyte, Vance Packard, or Reinhold Niebuhr a very critical view of what was noisily proclaimed as the "American Way of Life" at the time. This prevalent "secularized Protestantism"[4] was rejected by O'Connor as an abandonment of true faith for hedonism, consumerism, and materialism. As a Roman Catholic, she not only rallied the wool-hat evangelists and pulpit-pounding preachers of her home territory for her cause, which undoubtedly was strongly didactic and religious, but also asserted a Southern identity against what she perceived as the colonization and homogenization emanating from Washington and the North. This latter aspect becomes palpable in her literary work when she counterbalances her religious didacticism by an entirely secular brand of Georgia humor, which is rightly seen in the tradition of Augustus Baldwin Longstreet, Joel Chandler Harris, "Bill Arp," and William Tappan Thompson.[5] On another level, her Catholic heritage may predominate in the religious impulse and message of her two novels and numerous short stories, but it is fundamentalist rhetoric, as Robert Brinkmeyer perceptively observes, that shapes her narratives and gives them their specifically grotesque twists and turns, reminiscent of effects produced on the British stage much at the same time by Harold Pinter in the field of social critique. Brinkmeyer asserts, "[O'Connor's] method—distortion and exaggeration—had its origins in fundamentalist fanaticism."[6] Thus, with reference to her second novel, *The Violent Bear It Away* (1960), O'Connor wrote,

> When I write a novel in which the central action is a baptism, I am very well aware that for a majority of my readers, baptism is a meaningless rite, and so in my novel I have to see that this baptism carries enough awe and mystery to jar the reader into some kind of emotional recognition of its significance. To this end I have to bend the whole novel—its language, its structure, its action. I have to make the reader feel, in his bones if nowhere else, that something is going on here that counts. Distortion in this case is an instrument; exaggeration has a purpose, and the whole structure of the story or novel has been made what it is because of belief.[7]

For all its outlandish aspects and lack of balance, fundamentalism for O'Connor was a valuable resource that fed and inspired her narrative style. At the end of the day, it is the atheistic rationalist Rayber in *Violent Bear It Away* who emerges in the end as the most uprooted or grotesque personality, even compared to the abnormal and weird behavior of the fundamentalist Tarwater.

Beyond O'Connor's highly original vision, writers in her tradition have not generally continued her ultimately positive stance toward the evangelicals and roaming preachers among their countrymen and to the kind of social order they envisaged. Preferably, the dark side of fundamentalism is highlighted, as instanced in recent years by the Alabama writer Elizabeth Dewberry Vaughn (born in 1962), whom critics immediately placed in the O'Connor tradition[8] because of her own evangelical upbringing and her intense thematic interest in the fundamentalist culture of the Southern States. Both her novels, *Many Things Have Happened Since He Died* (1992) and *Break the Heart of Me* (1994)[9] explore the place of women in the part of Southern American social structure informed by the tenets of Christian fundamentalist patriarchy. In Vaughn's transgressive way of writing, the female protagonists of both works illustrate the lack of a voice for women, indeed their active silencing in the American South's fundamentalist culture, in stories rife with child abuse, violence, and marital rape. As Gloria Cronin points out, the legacy of the fundamentalist tradition here emerges as "violence, guilt, horror, and distortion[10]"; any redemption Vaughn's female protagonists can find is in the liberation from this kind of religion and its sociopolitical structures and comes entirely from the women's power to endure and survive.

The difference between O'Connor's positive approach to fundamentalism and Vaughn's emphatic critique can also be explained, I would argue, against the further development of fundamentalism in the United States. As fundamentalists had lost ground from the 1925 Scopes Trial onward and, having lost the Prohibition battle as well, faded from public view in the 1930s, O'Connor can almost be said to have resurrected a culturally and politically latent tradition of little significance at the time she wrote in the 1950s and early 1960s. Vaughn, by contrast, referred to a brand of fundamentalism that, by the 1990s, had resurfaced as an impressive cultural and political influence under the guise of the "New Christian Right," boosted 1970s onward by such organizations as the "Moral Majority" founded by Richard Viguerie, Paul Weyrich, and Howard Phillips, who were perhaps the most influential pioneers of the new movement. Although the actual political clout of U.S. fundamentalism today remains, for all its important coterie within the Republican Party, a contentious issue,[11] its social virulence and high-profile activities, beyond doubt, witness numerous teacher harassments for including the "wrong" kind of literature in the canon of the school curriculum and violent forms of protest against abortion clinics[12] as its most unsavory outcrops. The New Christian Right fundamentalists may look very different from their 1920s ancestors, as Steve Bruce aptly puts it: "Old-time religion was now a smooth presenter in a glossy chat show, not a sweaty redneck tent preacher in bri-nylon."[13] Nevertheless, the Bible and especially its literal readings of the creation story, the role of women, and the lack of tolerance toward people with a different cultural or religious outlook remain the same.

Meanwhile, more important changes had, however, shaken the discussion of fundamentalism worldwide: comparable movements in other religions had made their appearance on the global stage. Although Jewish and Hindu fundamentalisms have also played their part, it is Islam and its fundamentalist groups that have quickly occupied the limelight position in the Western media.

FUNDAMENTALISM AND POSTMODERNISM: SALMAN RUSHDIE

Analysts of fundamentalism generally acknowledge the problematics involved in extending the concept to other, non-Christian, religions and sects. Etymologically, this development was pinpointed in 1957 by the OED, which quoted a journalistic reference to Hindu fundamentalism in India. However, the use of the word achieved wider currency only from the 1970s onward, and it is the Iranian revolution of 1979 that, in the eyes of most commentators, cemented the word "fundamentalism" in today's derogatory sense and mainly in association with Islam. While the differences between such widely disparate groups as the American New Christian Right, Hezbollah, the Feddayin, al Qaeda, or Saudi Wahhabism are obvious, it is, in Karen Armstrong's view, a "strong family resemblance"[14] that persuades most scholars to stick to the cover-all term for want of better alternatives. In this sense, Almond, Appleby, and Sivan present a working definition:

> "Fundamentalism" . . . refers to a discernible pattern of religious militance by which self-styled "true believers" attempt to arrest the erosion of religious identity, fortify the borders of the religious community, and create viable alternatives to secular institutions and behaviors.[15]

Thus, although reformist tendencies can be found at any period in history, fundamentalism's quarrel with secularization and the specific and unique concepts of society and culture produced by Western modernity place its beginnings firmly in the twentieth century. It is a reaction against modernism, and its relationship to modernity as a whole can therefore be described as "symbiotic"[16] or, I would even suggest, "parasitic." The reason I would, in fact, prefer parasitic is that fundamentalisms cannot be credited with simple, wholesale rejection of modernity. Apart from their conceptual reaction, fundamentalists of all kinds tend to use scientific arguments to prop up their arguments. Thus, many anti-Darwinist statements, for example, were formulated according to strictly rational premises, often engaging evolutionists on their own scientific ground. What is more, all major fundamentalist movements heavily rely on technology, particularly in mass communication as well as, invidiously, in the arms and explosives sector, which only modern science has made possible. In fact, as Sami Zubaida succinctly argues, "Western political theory is the necessary precondition for Khomeini's *Al-Hukumah Al-Islamiya* (Islamic government),"[17] which is very strongly based on concepts of "the people" as a revolutionary force entirely unknown to the Islamic tradition.

Nevertheless, distinctions have to be made, the most important of which is, again, based on specific kinds of linkage to modernism. It clearly separates "Western" fundamentalism from its "other," mostly Islamic, variants. U.S. fundamentalism, as we have seen, originated in the early twentieth century as a reaction to developments in Western culture. This holds partly true for Islamic cultures as well, since some of these developments can be seen occurring on a parallel level in Islamic countries, thus providing equally "indigenous" causes for Islamic fundamentalism. Here, however, Bruce perceptively points out a second factor:

> But modernization has also been thrust upon Islamic countries from the outside [through Western colonization]. That is, Islamic fundamentalism is a response both to the modernization of their own societies and to the influence of the West.[18]

The distinctive constellation that Islamic fundamentalism sets out to oppose has been aptly labeled Kemalism by Bobby S. Sayyid, as for him, "Kemal Ataturk can be presented as an icon marking the culmination of various projects of westernization" in the Islamic world.[19] In this sense, modernism is not only perceived as an internal threat to traditional Islamic identity but can also be projected as foisted onto Islamic culture from the outside by colonial and imperial hegemonies.

From this perspective, the massive Islamist vituperation against Salman Rushdie's work, of which Khomeini's fatwa was only the most drastic incident, can be further illustrated. Writing as a professed atheist,

Rushdie used a subversive slant in his narratives to hit the foundational concepts of Islamist identity from inside the tradition of Islam itself as well as from the outside, thereby threatening the clearly drawn border lines established in defense against "westoxification." What he thought about fundamentalism is most explicitly demonstrated by the narrator of *Shame* (1983), Rushdie's metafictional view of Pakistan's recent history:

> Few mythologies survive close examination, however. And they can become very unpopular indeed if they're rammed down people's throats.
>
> What happens if one is force-fed such outsize, indigestible meals?— One gets sick. One rejects their nourishment. Reader: one pukes.
>
> So-called Islamic "fundamentalism" does not spring, in Pakistan, from the people. It is imposed on them from above.[20]

A few pages earlier in the book, the same narrator, referring to Georg Büchner's *Dantons Tod,* had already given his dialectic view of the world:

> This opposition—the epicure against the puritan—is, the play tells us, the true dialectic of history. Forget left-right, capitalism-socialism, black-white. Virtue versus vice, ascetic versus bawd, God against the Devil: that's the game. (254–255)

But he immediately qualifies this Manichaean division:

> "The point is," one of my friends argued, "that this opposition exists all right; but it is an internal dialectic." That made sense. The people are not only like Robespierre. They, we, are Danton, too. We are Robeston and Danpierre. The inconsistency doesn't matter; I myself manage to hold large numbers of wholly irreconcilable views simultaneously, without the least difficulty. I do not think others are less versatile. (256)[21]

Mixture and impurity are thus the key words in Rushdie's fictional universe, as he pursues and expounds them, for example, in *Midnight's Children* with regard to history, in his famous concept of the chutnification, and in *The Moor's Last Sigh,* with regard to genealogy, as Moraes Zogoiby describes himself in irreverently fumbling puns:

> I . . . was raised neither as Catholic nor as Jew. I was both, and nothing: a jewholic-anonymous, a cathjew nut, a stewpot, a mongrel cur. I was—what's the word these days?—*atomised.* Yessir: A real Bombay mix. (author's italics)[22]

Beyond Rushdie's outright, antithetic rejection of fundamentalism, and his general subversion of purity as an identity principle, as it was later taken up and further developed by Amin Maalouf,[23] his championship of impurity was specifically hurtful to Islamic fundamentalists in two distinct yet connected areas.

First, he repeatedly undercuts the distinction between Orient and Occident, colonizer and colonized, and *East, West,* as programmatically set forth in the title of his short story collection of 1994, and dramatized in Zogoiby's Jewish-Portuguese-Indian genealogy in *Moor's Last Sigh.* The projection of the danger of secularization onto the Western imperial colonizer is, however, a cornerstone in the edifice of Islamic fundamentalism, and if the East-West divide does not hold, both the clear-cut contours of the enemy and those of fundamentalist identity are under imminent threat.

Second, this external unraveling of Islamist foundational concepts was massively aggravated when Rushdie also injected his visions of impurity into the tradition of Islam itself, and here indeed at the Qur'an as the very core of this tradition. The quarrel is well known and need not be repeated here. The bone of contention lay primarily in the way Rushdie depicted, via the dreams and fantasies of the deracinated Indian film star Gibreel Farishta, the life of Muhammad, suggesting a lecherous, charlatanistic side to Allah's prophet, as well as implying that the Qur'an was tainted by heathen, that is satanic, influence in the so-called Satanic Verses[24] that Rushdie's namesake, Salman the Persian, had smuggled in. Defending himself years later in *Imaginary Homelands,* Rushdie once again expressly portrayed himself as the champion of impurity:

> The *Satanic Verses* celebrates hybridity, impurity, intermingling, the transformation that comes of new and unexpected combinations of human beings, cultures, ideas, politics, movies, songs. It rejoices in mongrelization and fears the absolutism of the Pure. *Mélange,* hotchpotch, a bit of this and a bit of that is *how newness enters the world.* It is the great possibility that mass migration gives the world, and I have tried to embrace it. *The Satanic Verses* is for change-by-fusion, change-by-conjoining. It is a love-song to our mongrel selves.
>
> Throughout human history, the apostles of purity, those who have claimed to possess a total explanation, have wrought havoc among mere mixed-up human beings. Like many millions of people, I am a bastard child of history. Perhaps we all are, black and brown and white, leaking into one another, as a character of mine once said, *like flavours when you cook.* (author's italics)[25]

To sum up, Rushdie's mixing up of pure fundamentalist thought has appeared on three levels: on the universally human, in that he argues in *Shame* that nobody is a monolith but always a mixture of an epicure and a puritan; on the cultural level, in his deconstruction of the East-West divide; and on the level of Islamic tradition, where impurities are discovered in the most sacred centers of faith. A fourth level could, although implied in the former, be added, as perhaps the one ultimately most unsettling to fundamentalists: the disrespect with which Rushdie's fiction approaches the divide between past and present: for him, the past is not a closed-off, static, and sempiternally immutable domain. His rewritings and interventions, as in Gibreel's historical dream-excursions into the distant past, open what Lowenthal has labeled the "foreign country" of the past[26] for renegotiation and new understandings, thus depriving fundamentalist faith of its power base in questioning its hegemonic command over history.

While O'Connor and Vaughn, for all their disagreement over Southern fundamentalism, intellectually stayed within the modernist tradition insofar as their novels can be read as a narrative critique of a cultural tradition that at the same time shaped an identity pattern—a renegotiated religious attitude in O'Connor's case and a newly asserted independence for women in Vaughn's instance—Rushdie leaves this common ground. His celebration of mixture and mongrelization is not an identity pattern in itself, but only a precondition for the generation of ever-new, unpredictable identities. He provides questions, not the answer, as he clearly places himself within the postmodern paradigm:

> This rejection of totalized explanations is the modern condition. And this is where the novel, the form created to discuss the fragmentation of truth, comes in . . . The elevation of the quest for the Grail over the Grail itself, the acceptance that all that is solid *has* melted into air, that reality and morality are not givens but imperfect human constructs, is the point from which fiction begins. This is what J.-F. Lyotard called, in 1979, *La Condition Postmoderne*. The challenge of literature is to start from this point, and still find a way of fulfilling our unaltered spiritual requirements . . . But while the novel answers our need for wonderment and understanding, it brings us harsh and unpalatable news as well. It tells us there are no rules. It hands down no commandments. We have to make up our own rules as best we can, make them up as we go along. And it tells us there are no answers; or, rather, it tells us that answers are easier to come by, and less reliable, than questions. If religion is an answer, if political ideology is an answer, then literature is an inquiry; great literature, by asking extraordinary questions, opens new doors in our minds. (author's italics)[27]

Not all authors dealing with fundamentalism are, however, satisfied with formulating questions. If Huntington's dyadic worldview of a clash of civilizations is correct, then a "third way" for negotiating common ground on a global stage is urgently needed. But does this imply an abandonment of Rushdie's postmodernist stance? Here, the recent work of Tariq Ali suggests itself as a particularly influential and complex example.

FUNDAMENTALISM BEYOND POSTMODERNISM?—TARIQ ALI

Born in 1943 in Lahore in what was then British-occupied India, and later exiled from Pakistan, Tariq Ali has been active on the political left in Britain as a writer, commentator, broadcaster, filmmaker, and playwright for many years now. Recently, his various commitments have, however, become focused on an engagement with fundamentalism, the Islamic heritage, and the East-West conflict. He is both an analyst, notably in his major recent work on the subject, *The Clash of Fundamentalisms* (2002),[28] and a novelist, in his "Islam Quintet," of which four volumes have been published so far.

Clash of Fundamentalisms is a mixture of Ali's own biography and experiences, as well as a historical survey of important phases in history, from the founding of Islam, which Ali finds crucial to the present fundamentalist clash of the book's title. Ali's approach has its populist elements, as witnessed in the two telling cover collages and a reprinting of the well-known satirical map from the *Economist* in its title pages. Between them, these illustrations do, however, sum up well the central tenets of the book. It asserts a fundamentalist quality in the recent U.S.-Islamic battle scenarios, while laying much of the blame on Zionism and British and U.S. imperialism, as well as these nations' heavy-handed diplomacy and lack of understanding for Islamic concerns. Ali can be reproached for representing the United States in a monochrome fundamentalist picture, neither giving dissenting voices in the United States itself enough hearing nor showing the necessary differentiation in the background to U.S. fundamentalism, the actual influence of fundamentalist groups in the United States, or the very different nature of these U.S. groups when compared with their Islamic counterparts—precisely the kind of differentiation that he wants to bring to his readers' attention when it comes to the Islamic world and the context from which its fundamentalisms spring. Ultimately, this is part of the message of the book, which is mainly, Ali announces, "an attempt to explain why much of the world doesn't see the [American] Empire as 'good'" (ix). He writes,

> In the clash between a religous [*sic*] fundamentalism—itself the product of modernity—and an imperial fundamentalism determined to "discipline the world," it is necessary to oppose both and create a space in the world

of Islam and the West in which freedom of thought and imagination can be defended without fear of persecution or death. (ix)

While the book thus is hardly worth its paper for readers interested in balanced information on the United States, and I am not the specialist to judge Ali's representation of Islamic historical contexts, it is the third space between the world's fundamentalisms he mentions in this quotation that is the interesting part here. And it is precisely this third space, I would argue that Ali finds so painfully wanting in today's global cultural geographies and that he only hints at en passant in the book as his utopian vision for Kashmir,[29] but that he purposively sets out to create and people in his fictional work. *Clash of Fundamentalisms* therefore remains a useful intertext for Ali's efforts, which spell out some of the historical and political convictions underlying his work, but it is mainly the "Islam Quintet" where his antifundamentalist utopias can be found projected and woven into history.

The four novels that so far have appeared of the planned "quintet"[30] are set in historically significant moments of what is mainly Christian-Islamic history, periods where the contacts between Occident and Orient were particularly intense. *Shadows of the Pomegranate Tree* (1991), the first novel, starts in A.D. 1500 during the final years of the Reconquista in Al-Andaluz; *The Book of Saladin* (1998) tells the story of Saladin and the fall of Jerusalem to Muslim forces in 1187; *The Stone Woman* (2000) takes place around 1900 during the last, declining years of the Ottoman Empire; and *A Sultan in Palermo* (2005) is set against the history of mid-twelfth-century Sicily under Norman rule. Throughout, the stories are told from the Islamic point of view and thus constitute, on a metafictional level, a rewriting of Eurocentric history, much as, for instance, Maalouf did in his 1984 history *The Crusades through Arab Eyes*. In each novel, persons, usually of Muslim denomination, of outstanding wisdom and mundane tolerance are contrasted with purist firebrands of a fundamentalist bend. In *Shadows,* it is the barbaric, book-burning inquisitor Ximenes de Cisneros who stands against the conciliatory Don Inigo Lopez de Mendoza, the mayor of Granada. In *Saladin,* the extreme poles are occupied, on the one side, by Saladin himself as the icon of the wise and ideal ruler and by his favorite wife, the brilliant Jamila, who is well versed in secular philosophy and has a lesbian affair with Halima, a later arrival in Saladin's harem; on the other side, there is the despised Richard "the Lion-Arse," as he is called, and Bertrand the Cathar (the sect using the Greek adjective for "pure" as their name), who first shows himself averse to all temptations of the flesh, but eventually is found out to have a penchant for sadistic practices with young men. In *Stone Woman,* the members of the Young Turks movement are described as "people who wanted to recreate a pure and modern empire" (109), while old Iskander Pasha himself seems to epitomize the complexities of the old Ottoman mentality. In *Sultan,* finally, the wise but dying Sultan Rujeri of Siqillya, a.k.a. King Roger II of Sicily, is opposed by the firebrands of both the Muhammadan and the Christian communities.

In these novels, Ali's search for a third space develops into an extension and imaginative representation of contact zones between the religions,[31] where peaceful coexistence is possible through mutual tolerance and the absence of fanatics and where Oriental sensuality and a sometimes almost florid richness of both vocabulary and subject seem to allow glimpses of a decidedly Islamic brand of Paradise, as in the pre-Conquista Al-Andaluz or twelfth-century Sicily.

However, the idea of a third way also applies to the novels' inner-Islamic cartography, establishing another space between the fundamentalists on the one hand and those who give in to the Orient's decline and the rise of Western modernity on the other, as symbolized by the four traumatic losses central to the novels: the loss of Al-Andaluz, of Jerusalem (though remedied by Saladin), of a foothold in Sicily, and of the Ottoman Empire. In an argument pervading all four novels, Ali's shrewd move is to claim precedence in modernity and the virtues propounded by liberal humanism for the Islamic world. In the history of ideas, it was the 300 Arabic manuscripts that Cisneros could be prevailed upon to exempt from his book burning in Granada that were to "pave the way for the Renaissance" (*Shadows,* 2). In the development of religious policy, it was the Islamic governments and administrations, in Al-Andaluz, at Saladin's court, as in the Ottoman Empire, that stood for tolerance and openness. In cultural matters, it is the Christians who always appear as the barbarians: burning books, indiscriminately killing their defeated enemies, and lacking all understanding for other cultures and religions;[32] Ali's novels are full of independent-minded, strong women in direct opposition to today's stereotype of Islamic chauvinism; the Muslims' art of cooking is far more sophisticated (*Shadows,* 96–97) and their superiority of hygiene has become a matter of religious identity, as Yazid's nurse Ama complains when she tells the boy about his great-uncle Miguel's conversion and establishment as a bishop:

> "He has turned his back on us. On everything. Did you notice that this time he was stinking, just like them?" Yazid began to laugh again. . . .
> Even his father had joined in the laughter when Ummi Zubayda had described the unpleasant odours emanating from the Bishop as being reminiscent of a camel that had consumed too many dates. "Did he always

stink?" "Certainly not!" Ama was upset by the question. "In the old days, before he sold his soul and started worshipping images of bleeding men stuck on wooden crosses, he was the cleanest person alive. Five baths a day in the summer. Five changes of clothes. I remember those times well. Now he smells like a horse's stable. Do you know why?" Yazid confessed his ignorance. "So that nobody can accuse him of being a Muslim under his cassock. Stinking Catholics! The Christians in the Holy Lands were clean, but these Catholic priests are frightened of the water. They think to have a bath is a betrayal of the saint they call the son of God." (*Shadows,* 10)

What is more, Ali's stories proclaim the Islamic cultures he describes as the pioneers of enlightened secularism, as the religious life of all his protagonists is underdeveloped or nonexistent. In *Shadows,* the boy Yazid, on whom the story centers, does not understand his nurse's lack of enthusiasm for chess. In an emblematic gesture indicating a generational transition from old religion to enlightened rationality at this historical moment of the dawning Renaissance, Yazid thinks, "Was not chess infinitely superior to the beads she was always fingering?" (6) However, Ali's undoubted heroine, both from a feminist point of view and in the context of enlightenment, is Jamila, Saladin's favourite wife. In a central discussion with Ibn Yakub, the scribe/narrator of the book, Jamila explains part of her argument against life after death:

Ibn Rushd [i.e., Abul-Waleed Muhammad Ibn Rushd (Averroës), 1128–1198] and his friends in Anadalus, who have studied, understood and developed Greek philosophy, are also inclined to doubt. Divine revelation in all our great Books is one type of wisdom. It relies on tradition to create a set of rules, a code of conduct, by which we must all live. But there is another kind of wisdom, as the ancient Yunanis taught, and that is wisdom which can be demonstrated to all without recourse to the heavens. That wisdom, my tutor at home once taught me, was called Reason. Faith and reason often clash, do they not Ibn Yakub? I'm glad we agree. Unlike reason, divine truth can never be proved. That is why faith must always be blind, or else it ceases to be faith. (125)

In a wider context, Ali's move here is apt to solve the dilemma as outlined after Sayyid and others above:[33] By appropriating humanism and the move to enlightenment and rationality as rooted in Islamic tradition and thus reclaiming a significant share in the origins of modernity for the Islamic cultures, Ali opens a way for an Islamic acceptance of modernity without simultaneously being co-opted into a Western hegemonic and potentially imperial project. A secular Islamic modernity without the dangers of "westoxification" is Ali's quintessential argument that he pursues in his Islam quintet as well as in his *Clash of Fundamentalisms*. Islamic culture has all the advantages of history, but it lacks proper government, and this is what Ali's mouthpiece, Al-Zindiq, points out as the reason for the loss of Andalusia; however, it can easily be inferred by the reader to hold true for Islamic history to the present, even in the confrontation with what Ali sees as a global U.S. imperialist presence. Here is Al-Zindiq's analysis:

> No amount of religion can succeed in changing the ways of kings unless it is based on something more, on something which our great teacher Ibn Khaldun called solidarity. Our defeats are a result of our failure to preserve the unity of al-Andalus. We let the Caliphate collapse and in its place we let poisonous weeds grow, till they had covered every inch of our garden. The big lords pounced on al-Andalus and divided it amongst themselves. Each became a big fish in a tiny pond, whereas exactly the opposite process was reshaping the kingdoms of Christianity. We founded many dynasties, but failed to find a way of ruling our people according to the dictates of reason. We failed to establish political laws, which could have protected all our citizens against the whims of arbitrary rulers. We who led the rest of the world in the realms of science and architecture, medicine and music, literature and astronomy, we who were a privileged people, could not find the road to stability and a government based on reason. That was our weakness and the Christians have learnt from our mistakes. (127–128)

With this approach, Ali clearly takes a step beyond Rushdie's position, as adumbrated above. Where Rushdie always follows the unique and specific, the unmistakable singularity of an individual's fate and mixture of identities, many of Ali's characters become emblematic for ideas and visions. While Rushdie's emphasis on hybridity and transcultural migration only sets a framework for unpredictable cultural creativity and novelty beyond all hegemonies and systems of governance, Ali is much clearer and definitive when it comes to the social and cultural propositions underlying his novels. Where Rushdie, the nonbeliever, can only find minor, contingent footholds on uncertain ground,[34] Ali, the nonbeliever, ventures to reestablish a framework of secular government and social order of an emancipated Islamic secular culture and nonfundamentalist Islamic identity as a model equal to the prevalent Western hegemonies.

Is Ali then taking a step behind Rushdie's postmodernism in an attempt to reopen the discussion about modernism's problematic essentialisms? Although some readers may prefer this view with regard to Ali's affiliation with Britain's political left and hence, possibly, the traditional neo-Marxian critique of postmodern irresponsibility, this does not, I would argue, render full credit to the conceptual achievements of Ali's novels. His fictional enactment of an Islamic modernity can be constructed as an alternative metanarrative to the Eurocentric one that is questioned by postmodernism, albeit a metanarrative that does credit to Lyotard's and other postmodernists' critique of such constructs by opening the view for a multiple, parallel existence of metanarratives in all their reflected constructiveness. Thus, Ali moves beyond postmodernist positions to a new assertiveness in ethical, cultural, political, and social matters without falling prey to any essentialist fallacy, rejecting fundamentalist positions while showing their Islamic adherents viable alternatives outside what they perceive as succumbing to Western imperial hegemonies.

CONCLUSION

What characterizes both Ali's and Rushdie's approaches, and what could also be claimed for O'Connor, is their belief in the power of literature as a social and cultural force. Tariq Ali is perhaps the most vivid example, insofar as his own biography can be seen as a development from political activist to novelist. The importance attributed to literature in these negotiations with fundamentalism may have part of its rationale in the nature of fundamentalism itself, as Bruce observes:

> [T]he particularly bitter battles that we now see about foundational texts and traditions seem particular to literate cultures and to cultures where, however vaguely articulated, some notion of a hermeneutic principle is abroad.[35]

It is precisely this hermeneutics of history, of culture, that writers such as Rushdie or Ali, in their various ways, reclaim for meeting the fundamentalists on their own ground. Thus, Rushdie writes,

> Let me be clear: I am not trying to say that *The Satanic Verses* is "only a novel" and thus need not be taken seriously, even disputed with the utmost passion. I do not believe that novels are trivial matters. The ones I care most about are those which attempt radical reformulations of language, form and ideas, those that attempt to do what the word novel seems to insist upon: to see the world anew . . . Central to the purposes of *The Satanic Verses* is the process of reclaiming language from one's opponents.[36]

If fundamentalism can be perceived as symbiotically bound to modernism, O'Connor's, Rushdie's, and Ali's writings can conversely be read as parasitic on fundamentalism's prior devotion to literary hermeneutics. Only because fundamentalists lay such great store by textual constructions in their ways of world making can they both constitute a source of inspiration for O'Connor's fiction and at the same time become so vulnerable to Rushdie's and Ali's fictional interpellations on their own hermeneutic, historical, cultural, and social turf.

What distinguishes Ali's as much as O'Connor's from Rushdie's negotiations with fundamentalism is the fact that they venture answers to the questions they raise where Rushdie's serious playfulness is arrested in ever-reformulated questioning. What distances Ali's from O'Connor's answering is the contingent, self-reflexive way of Ali's answers. Both Rushdie's questions and Ali's answers, finally, lack O'Connor's sympathetic approach, Rushdie's hybridities pulling the rug from under the fundamentalists, and Ali satirically excluding them from his possible utopias. As not all fundamentalists are bomb-blasting maniacs, however, O'Connor's empathetic inclusiveness could still have potential to enrich the discussion. Both Rushdie and Ali might, I would argue, reread her with great profit.

NOTES

1. Karen Armstrong, *The Battle for God: Fundamentalism in Judaism, Christianity and Islam* (London: Harper Collins, 2000), 177.
2. Quoted in Will Herberg, *Protestant—Catholic—Jew* (Garden City, NY: Doubleday Anchor, 1960), 84.
3. Jon Lance Bacon, *Flannery O'Connor and Cold War Culture* (New York: Cambridge University Press, 1993), quoted in Ralph C. Wood, "Flannery O'Connor's Strange Alliance with Southern Fundamentalists," in *Flannery O'Connor and the Christian Mystery*, ed. John J. Murphy, Linda Hunter Adams, Richard H. Cracroft, and Susan Howe (Provo, UT: Brigham Young University, 1997), 76.
4. Herberg, *Protestant—Catholic—Jew*, 81.
5. Robert H. Brinkmeyer, "A Closer Walk with Thee: Flannery O'Connor and Southern Fundamentalists," *Southern Literary Journal* 18, no. 2 (1986), 3–13, 4.
6. Ibid., 8.
7. Ibid., 9.
8. See critics' voices quoted by Gloria L. Cronin, "Fundamentalist Views and Feminist Dilemmas: Elizabeth Dewberry Vaughn's *Many Things Have Happened Since He Died* and *Break the Heart of Me*," in *Traditions, Voices, and Dreams: The American Novel since the 1960s*, ed. Melvin J. Friedman

and Ben Siegel (Newark: University of Delaware Press, London: Associated University Presses, 1995), 255–256.

9. (New York: Doubleday, 1990) (New York: N.A. Talese, 1994).

10. Cronin, "Fundamentalist Views," 263.

11. See Steve Bruce, *Fundamentalism* (Cambridge: Polity Press, 2000), esp. 70–81.

12. See the statistical survey at http://www.religioustolerance.org/abo_viol.htm (accessed on January 20, 2006).

13. Bruce, *Fundamentalism*, 71.

14. Armstrong, *Battle for God*, x–xi.

15. Almond, Appleby, Sivan, 17 (original in italics, not reproduced here).

16. Armstrong, *Battle for God*, xi.

17. Quoted in Bobby S. Sayyid, *A Fundamental Fear: Eurocentrism and the Emergence of Islamism* (London, New York: Zed Books, 1997), 96.

18. Bruce, *Fundamentalism*, 39.

19. Sayyid, *Fundamental Fear*, 89.

20. Salman Rushdie, *Shame: A Novel* (New York: Henry Holt, 1983), 266. Subsequently cited parenthetically in the text.

21. Cf. Mark Wormald, "The Uses of Impurity: Fiction and Fundamentalism in Salman Rushdie and Jeanette Winterson," in *An Introduction to Contemporary Fiction: International Writing in English since 1970*, ed. Rod Mengham (Cambridge: Blackwell, 1999), 182–202, 188 and Amin Maalouf, *In the Name of Identity* (1996; London: Penguin, 2000).

22. Salman Rushdie, *The Moor's Last Sigh* (London: Jonathan Cape, 1995), 104. Bombay mix is a tasty, spicy mixture of nuts and other stuff.

23. Maalouf, *In the Name of Identity*.

24. The novel's title is taken from the legend that verses 53:19–23 of the Qur'an originally referred to three pre-Islamic deities. For further explanation see Hartmut Bobzin, *Der Koran: Eine Einführung* (München: C.H. Beck, 1999), 60–61, 77.

25. Salman Rushdie, "In Good Faith," *Imaginary Homelands* (London: Granta, 1991; repr. 1992), 394.

26. David Lowenthal, *The Past Is a Foreign Country* (Cambridge: Cambridge University Press, 1985; repr. 1997).

27. Salman Rushdie, *Imaginary Homelands*, 422–423.

28. Tariq Ali, *The Clash of Fundamentalisms* (London: Verso, 2002). Subsequently cited parenthetically in the text.

29. "The [ultrasecular; 246] J[ammu] & K[ashmir] Liberation Front meanwhile has published a map showing its favoured boundaries for an independent Kashmir, made up of territory currently occupied by India, Pakistan and China. Hashim Qureshi, one of the leaders of the organisation, told me that they did not want all the paraphernalia of a modern state. They weren't interested in having an army. They would be happy for their frontiers to be guaranteed by China, India and Pakistan, so that Kashmir, the cause of three wars, could become a secular, multicultural

paradise, open to citizens of both India and Pakistan. At the moment, it is a noble but utopian hope." Ali, *Clash of Fundamentalisms*, 251.

30. *Shadows of the Pomegranate Tree* (London: Verso, 1991); *The Book of Saladin* (London: Verso, 1998); *The Stone Woman* (London: Verso, 2000); *A Sultan in Palermo* (London: Verso, 2005). Subsequently cited parenthetically in the text.

31. Cf. Mario Apostolov, *The Christian Muslim Frontier: A Zone of Contact, Conflict, or Cooperation*, Routledge Curzon Advances in Middle East and Islamic Studies (London: Routledge Curzon, 2003).

32. Ali, *Shadows*, 4: Cisneros knows no Arabic.

33. Sayyid, *Fundamental Fear*, 105.

34. See Klaus Stierstorfer, "Wobbly Grounds: Postmodernism's Precarious Footholds in Novels by Malcolm Bradbury, David Parker, Salman Rushdie, Graham Swift," in *Beyond Postmodernism*, ed. Klaus Stierstorfer (Berlin, NY: W. de Gruyter, 2003), 213–234.

35. Bruce, *Fundamentalism*, 13.

36. Rushdie, *Imaginary Homelands*, 393, 402.

CHAPTER 9

LITERATURE AS THE "SCHISMATIC OTHER OF THE SACRED TEXT"[1] OR ITSELF SACRED? THE *BLACK ALBUM* BY HANIF KUREISHI

HELGA RAMSEY-KURZ

In his post-fatwa essay "Is Nothing Sacred?" Salman Rushdie reports that though he was trained as a child to revere books, to the point of kissing them if they accidentally fell to the floor, he would have said as an adult that nothing is sacred, that everything should be open to question.[2] For "to respect the sacred is to be paralyzed by it."[3] As Rushdie admits, the turmoil following the publication of *The Satanic Verses* in 1988 caused him to reconsider his liberal views about books[4] and to reflect on the feasibility of protecting literature against anti-intellectual vandalism by setting it up as sacred. The ventures remained but a brief flirtation with secular fundamentalism, finding expression in the first part of the aforementioned essay, in which Rushdie also declares the novel, of all literary genres, superior to every other art form of "the post-modern age."[5] For Rushdie, the novel possesses a unique capacity to make visible the "exceptionality" or "unlikeness" of the author, of her (or his) ability *not* to stand "in any regimented line."[6] As a document of human originality, he argues, it urges a reconsideration of the idea of the absolute freedom of the imagination and, more importantly, of the legitimacy of declaring this idea inviolable and holy. Against Roland Barthes's famous declaration that "once an action is recounted, for intransitive ends, and no longer in order to act directly upon reality . . . , the author enters his own death,"[7] Rushdie holds the author of any text to be alive and well. In "the secret act of reading," Rushdie contends, reader and writer merge, through the medium of the text, and become "a collective being" that "both writes as it reads and reads as it writes, and creates, jointly, that unique work, 'their' novel."[8]

According to Rushdie, the "secret identity" of writer and reader is not only the "greatest and most subversive gift"[9] of the novel form but also that which renders it the "schismatic Other" of the sacred and, by definition, author*less* text. The holy scriptures of Judaism, Christianity, and Islam, on the other hand, in possessing no earthly author, resist dialogue and thereby effectively place their own languages above all others, and themselves above all other books. However, in transfixing (and institutionalizing) their holy scriptures, religions also totemize them. Recalling a lecture by Arthur Koestler on language as the prime cause of aggression, Rushdie observes, "And once people [have] erected totems, they . . . go to war to defend them."[10] Any sacralization of literature, then, would be dangerous too, even if it were on the grounds that, in contrast to the "authorless" book, the novel "does not seek to establish a privileged language, but . . . insists upon the freedom to portray and analyze the struggle between the different contestants for such privileges."[11] Of all literary genres, Rushdie grants the novel particular political importance as a means of asserting the principles of liberal capitalism, democracy, and freedom against the challenges of an emergent theocratic, foundationalist model of Islam. He also concedes that literature is "the one place in any society where, within the secrecy of our own heads, we can hear *voices talking about everything in every possible way*" (author's italics).[12] Still, for Rushdie, these reasons do not suffice as a justification for imaginative writing to be ascribed the same sacredness as prophetic literature. Only too aware of the dangers of such totemization, he insists that all one can and should do for secular literature is "to remember that it is necessary."[13]

Throughout his emphatic defense of the absolute freedom of the imagination (or more precisely, of literary imagination and its cardinal product, fiction), Rushdie exhibits not only his indebtedness to Western literature[14] but also his "Westernized" relationship to Islam. This relationship seems to be informed by an acute awareness of the vulnerability of postmodern literary discourse in a cultural climate in which the notions of certainty and absolute truth have been under vehement attack on the one hand, yet found equally vehement defendants on the other. The resultant tensions are captured in the portrayal of late twentieth-century multicultural Britain that Hanif Kureishi offers in his novel *The Black Album*. In this text, the themes of literature and authorship, of the freedom of the imagination, and of the legitimacy of fiction raised in Rushdie's essay are treated fictionally against the historical background of the notorious banning of *The Satanic Verses*. Also like Rushdie's essay, albeit without the same euphemistic indirectness, Kureishi's novel constructs a binary opposition between Western postmodern culture (and specifically Western literature) and its espousal of uncertainty on the one hand and Islamic fundamentalism and its assertions of certainty on the other. The similarity between Rushdie's and Kureishi's texts is not surprising. After all, like Rushdie's concern in "Is Nothing Sacred?" Kureishi's in *The Black Album* is to reassess the sociocultural role of literature in a climate in which different cultures are fighting a holy war over the totems through which they define themselves. Unlike Rushdie, however, Kureishi does not assume an overtly anti-Islamist stance from the outset. His "flirtation" with the idea of declaring secular literature sacred is evidently tempered not only by a reluctance to venture a head-on assault on those conventions of totemization that prompted the Islamist attacks on Western civilization to which he refers in his novel but also by an unwillingness to reject these conventions wholesale.

Accordingly, the central character of Kureishi's novel, Shahid Hasan, a British-born son of well-to-do tourist agents from Pakistan and an eager student of literature, is shown to exist and painfully oscillate between Western and Eastern, secular and religious, postmodern and Islamist worldviews. How the tensions ensuing from this oppositional constellation pertain to the protagonist's endeavors to position himself as what he most wants to be—namely, a writer—is impossible to understand without consideration of the different notions of scripture and textual authority held in Judaeo–Christian and Islamic cultures, respectively, and of the role the scribal traditions of these cultures play in the formation of fundamentalist discourses. Originally religious, these traditions have undergone rather dissimilar developments in the "West" and the "East." "Just as Christianity is the religion of and about Jesus," Frederick Denny notes, "Islam is the religion of the Qu'ran."[15] Just as Christianity is the religion of and about an individual, one could paraphrase Denny's observation—Islam is the religion of a book, dictated by God to Muhammad. As is important for non-Muslims to bear in mind, the prophet's biography is not a concern of the Qur'an. While Christianity, for instance, ascribes a very particular status to the life story of the *Son* of God, the Islam attributes far more significance to the event and the manner of the revelation and transmission of the *Word* of God. While the former includes in its reflections the evolution of events and their beginning, progress, and conclusion within a certain context, the latter focuses on the formulation of general rules and their enduring applicability to everyday life. Where Christian cultures may thus have generated a sense of the sacredness of narrative, Islamic cultures may be said to have developed a more acute sense of the sacredness of linguistic expression. Speculative as this assumption may appear at first glance, it is corroborated by several of the structural dissimilarities between the Bible and the Qur'an: thus the Bible consists not only of poetry but also of stories told from different perspectives with major as well as minor characters who enact certain plots in certain settings. As McConnell suggests:

> The Bible spans the gap between narrative and prophecy . . . It begins, *Bereshit,* "in the beginning," which may be the most wholly satisfactory opening any story can have . . . And from that absolutely narrative opening it moves, through the most complex of structures, toward the mighty and stunning assertion that is almost the last sentence of the book of Revelation: "If any man take away from the words of the book of this prophecy, God shall take away his part out of the book of life."[16]

More than that, the Bible effectively transmutes from an epic (the Old Testament) into biography (the New Testament), from folk sociology into existential self-discovery,[17] in the process adopting the features of a plurality of narrative genres.

By contrast, the Qur'an is "a book to which narrative is merely an incidental concern."[18] In fact, the narrative elements seem almost systematically confined to ancillary Muslim literature such as *hadith,* classical commentaries, antiquarian histories, and collections of so-called prophetic legends. Logically, the genre to which the Qur'an appears most obviously related is poetry. Indeed, the conspicuousness of this affinity has given rise to extended and not infrequently heated controversies over Muhammad's indebtedness to pre-Islamic poets.[19] Still, it seems legitimate enough to note that, whether erroneously or not, the self-consciously oral character of the Qur'anic text, its direct appellations to the reader and its resultant immediacy, its composition of rhythmical (albeit unrhymed) verses, and, above all, its special reflexivity on its own language as a uniquely fashioned sacred expression do prompt associations with poetry rather than with narrative. Actually *being* Allah's dialogue with the believer (rather than *representing* the dialogue of its main characters with *some* of God's believers, as the Bible does), the Qur'an is a representation of oral utterances and of language in general and, by implication, a reflection on signification, whereas the Bible appeals primarily to an awareness of what "the Word" or "the Scripture" designates and records, the signified.[20] Hence in Islam, the linguistic medium itself, Arabic, is sacralized to such a degree that translations of the Qur'an into other languages forfeit any status as scripture.[21] Unlike Christians, Muslims, whatever their nationality and primary language, are therefore obliged to learn, read, and write the language in which the Holy Book was originally set down. This has assured the dominance of Arabic as well as the spread of the Arabic script throughout the Muslim world and given rise to one of the finest calligraphic traditions in the world. By the same token by which Muslims believe the special language of the Qur'an to be inimitable in purity and beauty,[22] they ascribe special value both to the skillful recital and to the truthful transcription of the Qur'an. Apart from creating a rich and predominantly textual exegetical tradition (sustained inter alia by the practices of memorizing and reading the Qur'an aloud, as well as by extensive linguistic and paleographic studies), this respect for recital and transcription has engendered not only an appreciation but also an acceptance of the written and the spoken sign difficult for a Christian outsider to comprehend.

After all, Christian exegesis originated from the allegorical interpretation of classical Greek philosophical and poetical texts. For 1,500 years its main ambition was to ascertain the *spiritual* meaning of the scriptures, the *transhistorical* divine truth hidden in the recorded history of salvation. Only with the Reformation did a shift toward an exploration of the literal meaning of the scriptures occur. Only with Luther did the letter come to be apprehended not only as speaking historically of the work of Christ but also as representing the salvation event itself. Arguably, it is directly to Luther's assertion of the unequivocal "clarity" of the letter that the late nineteenth-century American millenarian movement and its dogmatic avowal of the inerrancy of the scriptures can be traced back. Unlike in Islam, though, the emphatic valorization of scripture, and with it, of the literal meaning of the Bible during the Reformation, was restricted neither to a single language nor to a single writing system. One reason for this is that the Bible has never been conceived of as the utterance of a single author, but rather as an anthology of separate texts noted down by different scribes, as a compilation of "little books."[23] As a result, Christianity was able to develop into one of the few "translating faiths,"[24] founded on scriptures whose intrinsic intertextuality precluded its adherents from assigning special religious value to a particular medium. The relative indifference of Christians to writing and their unwillingness to perceive it as a God-given skill encouraged the gradual proliferation and eventual secularization of literate practices in the West,[25] a development which in the Islamic world commenced much later and never took place to the same extent.[26] For Sidahmed and Ehteshami, the enduring sacralized status of writing in Muslim cultures explains the problematic nature of the label "Islamic fundamentalism," which, in their view, is a tautology. Specifically with regard to Muslims' unanimity on the authenticity and primacy of the Qur'an they suggest that "if one is to judge by their attitude towards scripture, all Muslims may be classified as 'fundamentalists.'"[27] By inference, one could likewise argue that, if one were to judge by their notoriously willful exegetical practices, Islamic fundamentalists cannot be classified as "devout Muslims." Indeed, in the light of their tendency to bypass (or ignore altogether) recognized Islamic exegetical authorities and to blatantly forge their own readings of the Qur'an to fit their political ends, the application of the originally Christian concept of fundamentalism to the Islamic field proves highly problematic.

The meaning of the term becomes even more bewildering when it is used to designate positions assumed at the interface of Christian and Muslim cultures, as is the case in Kureishi's novel *The Black Album,* which evokes a sense of the religious origins of Western literature while exposing the stark profanity of the fundamentalist Islamic discourse ascendant in late twentieth-century Britain. Ironically, in the process, the sacredness of secular literature comes to be charted as a reservoir poorly valued, used, and defended by the agents of Western culture, while evidently recognized, feared, and even fought over by its South East Asian critics. Accepting Wendy O'Shea-Meddour's reading of *The Black Album,* one could no doubt argue that the former's loss of faith in and the latter's weary suspicions of the cultural significance of literature are each associated with a different form of fundamentalism: with secular fundamentalism turned cynical on the one hand and with an ascendant religious (Islamic) fundamentalism on the other.[28] Yet the close coexistence of both positions causes their hybridization, as epitomized by Shahid. To fully understand the implications of his intimacy with both Western and Islamic scribal and exegetical traditions, the most obvious aspects of their incompatibility, outlined above, will be taken into account in the following analysis.

Upon beginning a cultural studies course at a London polytechnic, the central character of *The Black Album* finds himself wedged between the fashionably libertine attitude of his "official" teacher and lover-to-be, Deedee Osgood, and the views of his self-appointed mentor and fellow-lodger, Riaz al Hussain, student of "the law" and leader of a group of young Muslims with fundamentalist leanings. Compared with his two tutors and his streetwise elder brother, Chili, Shahid appears to be a naive and confused connoisseur of literature at the outset. Though sensitized by his extensive reading to the signifying capacity of visual details[29] and accustomed to probing them for their less-obvious meanings, his immersion in the world of letters has transplanted him into a state of consciousness in which he feels out of tune and touch with his physical environment. The characters, places, and events he takes in read like texts following a logic impossible for him to decode correctly at first. In his confusion, Shahid, for instance, presumes that the "derelict young men" he sees hanging around in the streets clutching beer cans "like hand grenades"[30] or lying in doorways immobilized and "with fluids seeping from them, as if they'd been pissed on by dogs" (3) are students like him. He naively believes that the proliferation of thrift and charity shops in London is a sign of the town's particular munificence (4). He finds Riaz sitting at a desk overflowing with books, papers, files, and letters and gladly interprets the scene as evidence of "scholarship, study and the thirst for knowledge" (14), unaware that his new acquaintance's notion of "wisdom" is utterly irreconcilable with his own ideas of learning. Having wandered aimlessly through a vast, dark, housing estate, he sits down under a muddy streetlight and starts writing to "keep at bay the excesses of reality" (16), while someone steals the clothes he has left unattended in a launderette. Not only does Shahid literally seem to be crossing a space "illuminated by a push button light sweetly timed to switch off before you reached your destination, however swiftly you moved" (1), as in the novel's opening scene, metaphorically, his capacity to decipher the signals he receives is impaired by insufficient illumination.

The gentle irony with which Shahid's misconceptions tend to be disclosed still allows for his bookishness to remain a thoroughly endearing feature. In fact, Kureishi takes considerable trouble to assert this impression against all odds and, more importantly, to sustain it throughout the novel. For all his blundering and the damage he allegedly causes by it, Shahid stands out among all the other characters for his relative innocence and harmlessness. His tacit retreats into texts that he has either produced himself or that he has consumed as a reader indicate that what he seeks is not so much an escape from reality as a truth that allows for a creative and peaceful mode of human coexistence. This does not mean, however, that Shahid's function in *The Black Album* is to represent some form of idealistic inexperience or inexperienced idealism. He is not the fool that Chad, a keen member of the posse Riaz has assembled around himself, makes him out to be as he challenges Shahid's unembarrassed confession of his love of literature with the scornful words, "How old are you—eight? Aren't there millions of serious things to be done?" (20). "Out there . . . ," Chad goes on to remind him, "it's genocide. Rape. Oppression. Murder. The history of this world is—slaughter. And you reading stories like some grandma" (21). Still, Shahid continues to believe that reading must be undertaken "seriously" and with "dedication." His musings about the purging effects of literature or about the college library as a sanctuary to which he can escape from the "bustling diversity of the city" insistently re-create the impression of an almost religious veneration of the written word, a seriousness too thoroughgoing to be explained away as an endearing eccentricity or a quaint neoromantic fad.

Shahid's unique passion for literature must be attributed to the special cultural position he inhabits. Shahid has grown up in what appears to be a successfully Westernized household. Yet for all the obvious material benefits of assimilation he and his family enjoy, he cannot easily forget his uncle Asif warning them not to betray their cultural origins: "It's easy for people, especially if they're young, . . . to forget that we've barely arrived over in England," he recalls Asif saying. "We think we're settled down, but we're like brides who've just crossed the threshold. We have to watch ourselves, otherwise we will wake up one day to find we have made a calamitous marriage" (54). His uncle's bitterness makes perfect sense to Shahid. He attributes it to the corrosive effects "of living in a country which couldn't accommodate intelligence, initiative, imagination, and in which most endeavour bogged down into hopelessness" (54). The anti-intellectualism of his fellow countrymen, which Asif so deplores, is manifest also in Shahid's father, who insistently derides his younger son's artistic pursuits; in Shahid's mother, who opposes his literary ambitions even more fiercely than her husband; and in his brother, Chili, who after learning that Shahid has submitted a short story documenting his experiences of racism for publication warns him that he will "break [his] bloody fingers" (75) should he ever try to do so again. Still, his family's disregard for any form of imaginative self-expression proves only mildly disturbing compared with the venomous rejection of Western art and literature voiced in the Muslim brotherhood into which Shahid is swiftly accepted at the beginning of the novel. There he finds himself confronted with furious negations of the social significance of literature. Literature is entertainment, he is told, and entertainment is sacrilege.

It is precisely this view against which Kureishi has his protagonist rebel. From the outset, Kureishi does not allow the reader to doubt for a minute that Shahid's devotion to writing is fuelled by anything other than a sincere faith in the indispensability of literature. Whenever Shahid declares his convictions about literature's truth-value and his faith in its enlightening and cathartic capacity, he does so in absolute earnest. His statements on writing and other art forms are devoid of ambiguity, flippancy, or inse-curity. The calmness and clarity with which they are delivered point at the imperturbability of Shahid's beliefs and the seriousness with which he advocates them. Nevertheless there is also a certain amount of urgency that pertains to his defenses of literature, as if his mission were to persuade others to adopt his creed, formulations of which he offers in the form of simple maxims and rhetorical questions. "Novels are like a picture of life" (21), he declares, for instance, or "[Books] disturb us . . . . They make us think" (183–84). " . . . See by clear light . . . . Isn't that what art helps us to do?" he demands of Chad. "Life would be a desert otherwise" (79). He reiterates his entreaty at a meeting held to discuss the fatwa imposed on Salman Rushdie. Again he appeals to his audience with a rhetorical question as if he were still not prepared to accept that there is no one among his "brothers" who shares his convictions. "Surely literature helps us reflect on our nature?" (183), he probes his audience before he goes on to proclaim: "A free imagination . . . ranges over many natures. A free imagination, looking into itself, illuminates others" (183).

It is in such assertions that *The Black Album* echoes most clearly the plea of Kureishi's friend and mentor Salman Rushdie for a thoroughgo-ing reappraisal of human imagination. For Shahid, imagination, as expressed through literary texts, *is* sacred, so much so that he feels obliged to draw people's attention to it. "Sometimes I see certain people," he admits at one point in the novel, "and I want to grab them and say, read this story by Maupassant or Faulkner, this mustn't be ignored, a man made it . . . !" (21). Shahid is troubled and driven by the same ques-tions that Rushdie admits to posing in his essay "Is Nothing Sacred?" in the first place to test his own willingness "to set aside as holy the idea of the absolute freedom of the imagination and alongside it [his] own notions of the World, the Text and the Good":[31] "Does this add up to what the apologists of religion have started calling 'secular fundamental-ism?' And if so, must [one] accept that this 'secular fundamentalism' is as likely to lead to excesses, abuses and oppressions as the canons of reli-gious faith?"[32] The answer Rushdie supplies is that it is entirely a matter of rhetoric whether the advocacy of such a secular ideal like the absolute freedom of the imagination sets free as destructively fanatical forces as religious zeal has proven capable of generating. As the remaining part of this chapter will show, this is also the conclusion at which Kureishi's pro-tagonist ultimately arrives.

For all his brave attempts at communicating his belief in the sacredness of literature, Shahid is not a rhetorician. Throughout *The Black Album* his quiet communion with the texts he reads or has written himself remains the pursuit most natural to him. In contrast to both Riaz and Deedee, who seem to have little difficulty in exhibiting their public personae and attracting attention with impromptu speeches, Shahid likes to withdraw, at least mentally, into one of the books he carries with him wherever he goes; into the silence of the college library; or to his room, where he has set up for himself a "shrine" of "many Matisses . . . along with Liotard's portrait of Mary Gunning, Peter Blake's *Venice Beach* meeting of himself, Hockney and Howard Hodgkin, several Picassos, Millais's strange *Isabella,* a photograph of Allen Ginsberg, William Burroughs and Jean Genet, Jane Birkin lying on a bed" (19). In such environments he tends to become oblivious to the outside world, to "fall . . . into a dreamlike state" (72) and work "with discipline and concentration" (166), enjoying the tranquillity he needs for contemplation. The calm that overcomes him in the process compares to what he feels on a visit to the mosque. In the cool rooms of the sacred building where "race and class barriers [have] been suspended," the atmosphere is "uncompetitive, peaceful, meditative" (132). There Shahid's most mature notion of literature can finally take shape:

> His friends told stories, in religious form, about the origin of everything, about how God wanted them to live, about what would happen when they died, and why, while alive, they were persecuted. They were old and useful stories, except today they could be easily mocked and undermined by more demonstrable tales, which perhaps made those who held ancient ones even more determined. The problem was, when he was with his friends their story compelled him. But when he walked out, like someone leaving a cinema, he found the world to be more subtle and inexplicable. He knew, too, that stories were made up by men and women; they could not be true or false, for they were exercises in that most magnificent but unreliable capacity, the imagination, which William Blake called 'the divine body in every man'. Yet his friends would admit no splinter of imagination into their body of belief, for that would poison all, rendering their conviction human, aesthetic, fallible. (133)

The tone of this passage itself is "uncompetitive, peaceful, meditative." Devoid of exclamations, emphases, and questions, it lacks the urgency and defensiveness of Shahid's passionate appeals to his "brothers." For once not rendered in direct speech, Shahid's ideas about literature can take on a different direction and pace. They can meander and expand slowly and remain general, without specific direction. Not addressed to an "unbeliever" vis-à-vis, his musings are able to generate more generous images even of those committed to a notion of narrative diametrically opposed to his own. More than that, they allow for the notion to take shape that religious stories are just as useful and compelling as secular narratives. In this context, the word "friends" remains free of the ironical undertones that accompany the designation "brother" used so freely among Riaz's adherents, without any ironic undertones even when referring to Shahid's friends. Used without irony, the passage moves beyond the open disapproval marking so many other descriptions of Muslims in *The Black Album* and even manages to convey a sense of benevolent sadness and regret.

No such feelings are evoked by Kureishi's portrayal of Riaz, who approaches Shahid and urges him to join his group, intrigued by his young neighbor's earnest commitment to his studies and to his plan of becoming a writer. Shahid's determination strikes a chord in Riaz and prompts him to elect Shahid for the task of typing out his own writings, a small book of poems, "songs of memory, adolescence and twilight" inspired by Allah and meant by their author to "change the world a little too" (68). The scene in which the man with the "weak bookwormy eyes" (2) and a curiously hybridized accent appoints Shahid his scribe and hands over his manuscript to him is comically anticlimactic. Kureishi's ironical exposure of Riaz's patronizing airs on the one hand and of Shahid's perplexity and intimidation on the other effectively distorts Riaz's endeavor to stage the event as an initiation ceremony of sorts. At the same time it makes clear once more that Riaz's "literary airs" are of an entirely different quality than Shahid's. Even if it is true that, as Riaz claims, he too knows the state of obsession into which Shahid feels transported in the act of composition, there is no doubt that his writing is motivated by expectations totally alien to Shahid. As is not difficult for the reader to grasp, Riaz's work is propelled not by the naive, yet genuine, enthusiasm compelling Shahid to write but by an almost paranoid suspicion, if not hatred, of all things Western and a need to assert his Islamic identity against their influence. Hence, also Riaz's protest against the essentially postmodern idea held by Shahid that there is no single standpoint for any writer to claim his own, that, in fact, there is no standpoint at all. The idea is disconcerting for Riaz because it implies that there can be no serious conflict of attitudes, nor any need to defend one's own position, let alone a need to discuss such matters as authorial merit or authorial responsibility. It would also mean that no text could be disqualified as blasphemous nor any writer punished for what he or she says in his or her work. In Barthes's terms, the author would be dead long before anyone can sentence him (or her) to death.

Riaz, however, likes to be able to either sacralize or demonize the author as an actual person and stages himself accordingly, unashamedly claiming for himself the aura commonly attached to successful authorship and making clever use of the authority equally commonly attached to writing. Yet in the course of *The Black Album,* the celebrity status Riaz's posse willingly concedes its leader is exploded. To this end Kureishi has his unassuming protagonist make the uncomfortable discovery that Riaz's thin book of poetry titled *The Martyr's Imagination* is not really what he himself would want to have written. Riaz's single-mindedness, while mistaken for a sign of superiority by others, eventually causes Shahid to pity him. All Riaz ultimately represents is a curious combination of sentimentality and worldly pragmatism—according to Sidahmed and Ehteshami, not at all an untypical feature for contemporary Islamist exegetes and rhetoricians to assume.[33] In the end, Riaz does turn out to be the "informed amateur" as he describes himself, albeit only ironically, at the very beginning of the novel. Typically enough, while Shahid seeks, and finds, enlightenment on his visits to the mosque, "which always calmed him" (148), Riaz organizes for his group to undertake a sort of pilgrimage to a house in North London, "the House of Miracle" (172), where a local couple has allegedly discovered God's signature inscribed in the cross-section of an aubergine. In having the gifted propagandist shamelessly exploit the general excitement about the rapidly withering vegetable, Kureishi effortlessly reduces the allegedly God-inspired poet to a most prosaic opportunist.

The revelation of Riaz's worldly ambitions in chapter 14 warrants a reconsideration of the scene in which Riaz outs himself as a poet seven chapters earlier:

> "I didn't know you—" Shahid began turning the pages. He could see that Riaz liked adjectives but figured the verbs would be in there somewhere.
> "Oh, yes," Chad said. "Riaz a poet."
> Riaz smiled modestly. "It's God's work."
> "Yes," Riaz beamed. "*I am entirely to blame.*" (68, my emphasis)

Later in the novel, Riaz elaborates the idea of authorship he formulates in the above dialogue. "I am telling you," he explains, "that it is not ourselves in general, not the people, but the mind of the author that we are being informed of [by literature]. That is all. One man" (183). To him, he declares, the truths about the importance of faith and concern for others are deeper than "the ravings of one individual imagination" (184). This corresponds perfectly with Riaz's blanket condemnation of Rushdie, the author whose name no character in the novel dares, bothers, or wants to pronounce. Throughout *The Black Album,* Rushdie is referred to only as "the author" or "he" who has accomplished an accurate portrayal of Bombay in *Midnight's Children,* "[b]ut this time has gone too far" (9), or indirectly as one of "these corrupt, disrespectful natures, wallowing in their own juices, [who] must be caged as if they were dangerous carnivores" (183). Likewise, *The Satanic Verses* is mentioned only euphemistically as "this other filthy matter" (181), "the topic" (181), "the issue" (182), or "the book" (184). The omission marks a first attempt at killing *off* the author, one that foreshadows the symbolic execution of Rushdie at the public burning of *The Satanic Verses* toward the end of the novel.

On another level, Kureishi's strategic suppression of Rushdie's identity, naturally, only enhances it, thereby undermining the authority ironically attributed to Riaz and valorizing those features that distinguish Shahid from his "mentor" or "brother." The difference between the two characters is not clarified but only complicated by Shahid's relationship to his flamboyant teacher, Deedee Osgood. Not unlike Riaz's role in Kureishi's novel, Osgood's appears unambiguous at first glance. Together with her husband, Andrew Brownlow, she *embodies* a form of middle-class liberalism that stands in direct opposition to the resentful self-righteousness cultivated by "Brother Riaz." The fastidious and gentle manner of this man and the "lack of physical presence" Shahid notes in him help to throw into relief Deedee's conspicuous femininity, her at times almost exasperating carelessness, and her unruly extravagance. Typically, the motto she has pinned on the wall of her office is "All limitations are prisons" (25). Yet, her own attempts at escaping the limitations that imprison her prove tragically pointless. It is a sad indication of how little freedom she grants her own imagination that she chooses to devote her life to doing "a lot of nothing" and making "stabs at pleasure" (55). Willingly, or rather without a will of her own, she follows the call "Let's have a good time tonight!" with which a DJ in the novel summons his fans every evening. In the maze into which Shahid is lured by her sensuousness, by the drugs she offers him, and also by her modish intellectualism, she forms an oddly reliable point of reference insistently confirming the strange sense of bankruptcy of whose corrupting power Riaz keeps warning Shahid.

Under closer examination, the opposition between Riaz and Deedee dissolves. Deedee's notion of literature proves just as much in conflict with Shahid's as does Riaz's. For all her intellectualizing, Deedee has lost all faith in the power of books. Cast as a figure wandering around with "books, newspapers and student essays *tumbling . . . from her arms*" (28, emphasis added), she appears to be perfectly at home in the climate of cultural degeneracy that Shahid notices everywhere: in the dilapidated buildings of the college about to be privatized, in its ineffective library from which so many books have been stolen, in the dingy bookshops he frequents, even in the wallpaper in his room, which meaningfully droops off the wall "like ancient scrolls" (1). Unlike Shahid, Deedee no longer knows how to escape "the dismal tiredness of the place, the decay, . . . the absence of optimism everywhere" (122), let alone how to escape it with the help of literature. Knowing, like Riaz, that most of her students are at college not to be educated but only to be kept off the dole, she sees little reason why she should force them to study complex books rather than films and popular music. While her scornful pragmatism earns her the same popularity and notoriety among her students that Riaz enjoys among his compatriots for his acrimonious fanaticism, it still prompts Shahid to wonder whether it is not really learning that she offers in her classes but "only diversion dressed up in the latest words" (26) and to accuse her of having succumbed to the excessive cynicism characteristic of clever white people (110).[34]

The views of writing held by Riaz and Deedee finally clash only to be exploded and collapsed into each other as Kureishi's novel culminates in the public burning of *The Satanic Verses*. Nowhere else in the text does the absence of the condemned author become more palpable than at this point. Neither Deedee nor Riaz acknowledge his existence in the speeches they deliver on the occasion. For different reasons,[35] both remain silent about the human subject whose work is being vilified and violated. It is thus that both become implicated in what, to most onlookers, is "merely" a symbolic killing of the author. Even the reader is briefly led to believe that the event is but a badly choreographed, almost tragicomic instance of idiotic vandalism, in which Riaz and Deedee enact equally ineffectual parts. However, while the episode of the book burning closes with a gust of wind dispersing the ashes and some half-burned bits of *The Satanic Verses,* the novel continues beyond this image of destruction to reassert the gravity of the occasion and the significance of the burning as a symbolic act of obliteration. Not without reason is Shahid, from whose point of view the entire novel is narrated, placed at a distinctive distance from the scene of "execution." After all, he is the only character still convinced of the sacredness of literature and hence capable of being shaken as much by the actual destruction wrought as by what it symbolizes. Symptomatically, Shahid does not reply when a bystander who has noticed his displeasure at the demonstrative incineration of Rushdie's novel charges him with the words, "What you worried about? It only a book." All his attention is consumed by the burning text; he notices a shiver flare through its chapters, just before its scorched pages whirl across the assembled crowd (225). The image of "the flaming bouquet of the book" (225) marks a turning point at which Shahid, as if consciously taking the place of the absent author, at last recognizes the need to assert the text's authority, which has been negated or at least questioned by all other characters in the novel. Unlike both Riaz and Deedee, Shahid finally comprehends that this authority can be attained neither by fighting uncertainty nor by surrendering to it.

This dawns on Shahid at an earlier stage in the novel, when he contemplates the chaos caused by a bombing of Victoria Station and reflects that there is only one thing left that is absolutely clear: namely, that no one knows anything. To give expression to this "not-knowing" in writing, the novel finally establishes, must be the purpose of imaginative writing. The indirection of Shahid's nightly wanderings and, on another level, of Kureishi's narrative and its ending, may be read accordingly as the only adequate creative response to the brutally unoriginal, sound-bite affirmations continually spouted by fanatical ideologues of all camps. I therefore propose comprehending Shahid's explicit endorsement of Deedee's pledge that they will stay together "[u]ntil it stops being fun" (276) not as the return "to a place that is compatible with the now moderate, liberal and slightly postmodern Shahid," but as a conscious gesture of defiance. After the acts of violence he has witnessed others commit in defense of what they hold to be absolute truths, he does not make this promise frivolously. His emphatic subscription to an indefinite pursuit of fun is a serious disavowal of the definiteness he sets out to find at the beginning of the novel. In the end, Shahid does not remain wedged between two beliefs or two forms of fundamentalism. Rather, he emerges as the only believer among unbelievers.[36] He retains what Deedee has never acquired and what Riaz possesses at best in rather crippled form: a belief that one must acknowledge the value of books, feel and seek the sacred atmosphere of libraries, beware the signs of their dereliction and vandalization, and maintain an appreciation of the author as a vulnerable human being capable of unique feats of expression. Shahid has also preserved for himself what Riaz has never been able to cultivate and what Deedee adheres to only with great difficulty: an appreciation of the intrinsic value of fiction and the conviction that the freedom of human imagination is sacred.

Shahid's unbroken sense of sacredness does not only allow him to accept his place in a culture on the verge of losing faith in itself, but ultimately also frees him of the urge to mediate between the two worlds to which he belongs. It is true, that, as Chrissi Harris notes, neither mimicry, assimilation, nor rebellion bring relief to Shahid's fluctuating condition. However, whether this also means that Shahid's story closes on an entirely pessimistic note, ultimately presenting its protagonist as "lost somewhere in between; condemned to an identity of chaotic disarray"[37] is more than doubtful. Shahid in the end does not only realize the futility and profanity of purely rhetorical gestures of consecration and, for this reason, abandon advocating the sacredness of literature. Although he has been silenced by the indifference of others to what he once believed to be his mission, he still continues to remember that literature is necessary—necessary as a discursive space accommodating formulations of precisely that which prophetic writing must endeavor to dissuade, deny, or even demonize: the utterly human sensations of doubt and disbelief. In describing, exploring, and accounting for these sensations, secular literature gives expression to the fallibility of human constructions of truth and the limitations of human understanding. It admits to the smallness of (wo)man, which religious writing invariably subordinates to its cardinal purpose, the celebration of the greatness of God.[38] Writing that pays tribute to the obvious weaknesses of (wo)mankind may appear blasphemous to those required by their faith to respect the absolute inimitability of holy scriptures and to reject any overtly secular application of the written word. Still, given the dazzling proliferation of public discourses generating "totalized explanations"[39] and promoting them as God-inspired truths, there is hope that even such devout believers will begin to feel the need to revise their perception of secular literature and see it as a domain complementing, rather than competing with, religious writing. By not only appealing to an awareness of human imperfection but also by trying to reconcile its readers to their own shortcomings, imaginative literature after all opens up a way for humans to interact across religious and cultural barriers without pretending that some are closer to divine truth than others. Far more constructively, it encourages the humble acceptance of one's own limitations as the best reason for turning to an Other for instruction, advice, and perhaps even enlightenment.

NOTES

1. Salman Rushdie, "Is Nothing Sacred?", in *Imaginary Homelands: Essays and Criticism 1981-1991* (London: Granta Books, 1991), 424.
2. Ibid., 415: "In our house, whenever anyone dropped a book or let fall a chapati or a 'slice', which was our word for a triangle of buttered leavened bread, the fallen object was required not only to be picked up but also kissed, by way of apology for the act of clumsy disrespect. I was as careless and butter-fingered as any child and, accordingly, during my childhood years, I kissed a large number of 'slices' and also my fair share of books."
3. Ibid., 416: "The idea of the sacred is quite simply one of the most conservative notions in any culture," Rushdie explains further, "because it seeks to turn other ideas—Uncertainty, Progress, Change—into crimes."

4. For a particularly thorough critical account of the reactions triggered by Ayatollah Khomeini's pronunciation of the fatwa see Wendy Steiner, "Fetish or Fatwa?" in *The Scandal of Pleasure: Art in an Age of Fundamentalism* (Chicago: University of Chicago Press, 1995), 94–127.

5. Rushdie, "Is Nothing Sacred?" 424.

6. Ibid., 426.

7. Roland Barthes, "The Death of the Author," in *Image Music Text,* trans. Stephen Heath (London: Fontana, 1977).

8. Rushdie, "Is Nothing Sacred?" 426.

9. Ibid.

10. Ibid., 419.

11. Ibid., 420.

12. Ibid., 429.

13. Ibid.

14. Indeed, the pronounced exclusiveness with which Rushdie draws on Western writers (i.e., William H. Gass, Karl Marx, Herbert Read, Arthur Koestler, Carlos Fuentes, Laurence Sterne, Leo Tolstoy, Jean-Francois Lyotard, Herman Melville, Italo Calvino, James Joyce, Samuel Beckett, Nikolay Gogol, Mikhail Bulgakov, Saul Bellow, Richard Rorty, Don Cupitt, Plato, Michel Foucault, and Edmund Burke) and on Western mass, popular, and folk culture (such as Luis Bunuel, Ingmar Bergman, Federico Fellini, Enid Blyton, Super-, Bat-, Spider-, and Aquaman, cricket and Rolls-Royce cars, and the Holy Grail) can even be argued to be meant as a signal of his own distance or even alienation from "Eastern" civilization.

15. Frederick M. Denny, *An Introduction to Islam* (London: Macmillan, 1994), 345.

16. Frank McConnell, "Introduction," 4. Or, as Herbert N. Schneidau puts it, " . . . narrative is of the essence, if one may use the term, of the Bible, it is not merely a vehicle or adjunct or epiphenomenon." See "Biblical Narrative and Modern Consciousness," in *The Bible and the Narrative Tradition,* ed. Frank McConnell (New York: Oxford University Press, 1986), 132.

17. McConnell, "Introduction," 7.

18. Ibid., 3.

19. So did, for instance, the suggestion put forward by Crone and Cook that Islam's holiest scripture is actually nothing more than a compilation of variant traditions. This thesis was felt by many to offend the doctrine of the Qur'an's originality and inimitability. As has been argued in defense of this doctrine, any affinity of Muhammad's prophecies to pre-Islamic poetry is negated by the Qur'an itself, which contains the passage, "It [the prophecy] is not the word of the poet; little it is ye believe! Nor is it the word of a soothsayer: little admonition it is ye believe. (This is) a message sent down from the Lord of the worlds" (Q 69:40–43). Cf. Patricia Crone and Michael Cook, *Hagarism: The Making of the Islamic World* (Cambridge: Cambridge University Press, 1977), esp. 16–20.

20. One of the things it records and on which it thus also reflects is, of course, the act of recording itself and the consequences of this act, as Hans W. Frei illustrates in his article "The 'Literal Reading' of Biblical Narrative in the Christian Tradition: Does It Stretch or Will It Break?" in *The Bible and the Narrative Tradition*, 36–77.

21. This might even explain why there is no such thing as an Islamic semiotics.

22. *Ijaz* is the Arabic term for this doctrine. Indeed, any attempt to copy the style of the Qur'an is considered sacrilege, which, obviously, has exercised considerable influence on Islamic poetry.

23. In fact, this is the meaning of the Greek word *biblia*.

24. This is an idea implicitly suggested also by McConnell, "Introduction," 9.

25. This development has been outlined particularly well by Ivan Illich and Barry Sanders in their book *The Alphabetization of the Popular Mind* (London: Marion Boyars Publishers, 1988). Cf. also Albertine Gaur, *Literacy and the Politics of Writing* (Bristol: Intellect Books, 2000), 133.

26. On this cultural difference see also Srivinas Avaramudan, "'Being God's Postman is no Fun, Yaar': Salman Rushdie's *The Satanic Verses*," in *Reading Rushdie: Perspectives on the Fiction of Salman Rushdie*, ed. M. D. Fletcher, Cross/Cultures: Readings on Post/Colonial Literatures in English 16 (Amsterdam: Rodopi, 1994), 188.

27. Abdel Salam Sidahmed and Anoushiravan Ehteshami, "Introduction," *Islamic Fundamentalism*, ed. Abdel Salam Sidahmed and Anoushiravan Ehteshami (Boulder, CO: Westview Press, 1996), 2.

28. Cf. Wendy O'Shea-Meddour's essay in this volume, which draws on the opposition of secular and religious fundamentalism put forward by Salman Rushdie in "Is Nothing Sacred?" and offers a more direct response to the criticism voiced against *The Black Album* for its schematic characterizations, its all too blatantly symmetrical structure, and its representation of Islam.

29. What is meant here is a sensitization in the sense of Marshall McLuhan's idea of literalization, especially as an "interiorization of the technology of the phonetic alphabet," effecting a separation of sight from the other senses and thus a specialization of human vision. See *The Gutenberg Galaxy: The Making of Typographic Man* (Toronto: University of Toronto Press, 1962), 18.

30. Hanif Kureishi, *The Black Album* (London: Faber and Faber, 1995), 3. Henceforth cited parenthetically in the text.

31. Rushdie, "Is Nothing Sacred?" 418.

32. Ibid.

33. Sidahmed and Ehteshami, "Introduction," 11–12.

34. For another, much more damning interpretation of the character of Deedee see Bart Moore-Gilbert, who proposes reading her as "the 'benevolent' white woman who intervenes to save the brown man from his fellows." "This," Moore-Gilbert argues, "rearranges the terms of the colonial trope without disturbing the racialized power relations which underpin it."

Hanif Kureishi, Contemporary World Writers (Manchester: Manchester University Press, 2001), 142.

35. Arguably, this difference also accounts for the possibility to read Kureishi's omission, or suppression, of Rushdie's name in radically different ways. Moore-Gilbert, for instance, ignoring Rushdie's own reference to Michel Foucault's observation that the practice of identifying authors by their name is actually indicative of a society's need "*to find somebody to blame,*" Rushdie, ("Is Nothing Sacred?" 422), finds it curious that a novel on the evils of censorship "should itself be so circumspect about the fact that it is addressing the Rushdie affair." *Hanif Kureishi,* 148.

36. Rushdie would probably use the word "lover" here, rather than "believer," given his definition of the "True Believer" as someone who will always seek to convert whoever does not feel as (s)he does. By contrast, he argues, the devotion of the lover is not militant, which is exactly the point of Shahid's devotion to literature. Rushdie, "Is Nothing Sacred?" 415–16.

37. Chrissi Harris, "Insiders/Outsiders: Finding One's Self in the Cultural Borderlands," *Literature and Ethnicity in Cultural Borderlands,* ed. Jesus Benito and Anna Maria Manzanas, Rodopi Perspectives on Modern Literature 28 (Amsterdam: Rodopi, 2002), 183.

38. Or, as Salman Rushdie puts it, religion "helps us understand why life so often makes us feel small, by telling us what we are *smaller than.*" Rushdie, "Is Nothing Sacred?" 421.

39. Ibid., 422.

CHAPTER 10

NEVER BETTER THAN LATE: THE *LEFT BEHIND* SERIES AND THE INCONGRUITIES OF FUNDAMENTALIST IDEALISMS

KEVIN L. COPE

> When at first I took my pen in hand,
> Thus for to write, I did not understand
> That I at all should make a little book
> In such a mode; nay, I had undertook
> To make another, which, when almost done,
> Before I was aware, I this begun.
>
> —John Bunyan,
> "The Author's Apology" for *Pilgrim's Progress*

Incongruity is a fundamental condition of fundamentalism. For a religious tradition that fears the distortion of its sacred texts by centuries of erring interpreters and that aspires to return to the unsullied, "primitive" society that allegedly preceded the present corrupt times, being out of place is a normal state of affairs. John Bunyan's *Pilgrim's Progress,* one of the world's most widely read would-be fundamentalist texts, presents both characters and theologies that never manage to fit together with anything, including themselves. The more that Bunyan tries to explain what the English Puritans of his time regarded as the pure, true, and original version of Christianity, the more he is drawn into allegory, symbolism, and the metaphorical extension of "literal" meaning. The more Bunyan indulges his taste for "types," "shadows," and "dark figures," the more he veers from anything that could be understood as "literal" or "pure." As the quotation opening this chapter suggests, fundamentalists regard religious writing itself as an exercise in incongruity. Authors may believe that they are taking up the pen only to discover that they are really engaged in automatic writing guided by the "author of nature." Reverent writers start out to compose a new work but soon find themselves reiterating the eternal word; Bunyan writes a fresh chapter only to learn that "when almost done / Before I was aware, this [other book] I [had] begun." Literal-minded fundamentalist authors always end up doing something other than expected. They are always operating in other times or spaces and are always somewhat out of place.

The fervent sense of inevitable incongruity that enlivens fundamentalist discourse has most recently announced itself in an appropriately literal way in the almost miraculously popular *Left Behind* series, the title of which puts the issue of incongruity—of being left behind in the wrong place at the wrong time—in the middle of the foreground. The "authors" of the series—only one of whom actually *writes* the *Left Behind* novels—seem always to have been in the right place for people writing about the wrongness of the times. Having begun their series in the long and anxious lead-up to "Y2K," amid an assortment of millenarian anxieties, authors Tim LaHaye and Jerry Jenkins have progressed from rejection slips to sales reaching 60 million copies of their books, along with truckloads of paraphernalia, CDs, DVDs, explanatory books, and e-tail products.[1] Sales by Tyndale House, the publisher of the *Left Behind* series whose stated goal is to "minister to the spiritual needs of the people, primarily through literature consistent with biblical principles," have jumped to $160,000,000 owing to *Left Behind* revenues.[2] Although the *Left Behind* series is expected to conclude with the release of the fourteenth volume in 2006, "writer" Jenkins has already spun off a new trilogy with the anticipation-raising title *Soon*. Jenkins and LaHaye together have packaged the latest books in the *Left Behind* series as freestanding "prequels," stories about what transpired before the events in the series-opener *Left Behind*. A new sequence, *Babylon Rising*, has recently emerged. Spanish-language translations, aimed at the growing numbers of Latino evangelicals, have begun rolling off Tyndale's all-American presses. LaHaye and Jenkins have lived out a lucrative commercial incongruity: for them, being "left behind" has involved staying far ahead, including far ahead of the cadre of writers who appeal to smaller sectors of the "Christian fiction" market.

The *Left Behind* series has proved to be something of an embarrassment for mainstream academic literary criticism. Critical-theoretical movements stressing social history, popular movements, and noncanonical texts, which have dominated academic criticism for the last two decades, have been unable to respond to the largest literary phenomenon of Western publishing history (short of the Bible itself). Distaste for the themes, methods, and goals of evangelical, fundamentalist, Baptist, and Pentecostalist writers has made it difficult for otherwise level-headed scholars to assess what is very likely the most influential body of work in late twentieth- and early twenty-first-century prose. *Left Behind* appears on the edge of a big blind spot in academic vision. Two books from major university presses and a few scattered essays have dealt with the topic, but seldom from literary, critical, or otherwise appreciative viewpoints.[3] Both book-length studies take an anthropological approach, examining the attitudes, opinions, culture, and identity issues at play in evangelical reading communities. The journal essays either follow the anthropological approach or take a bibliographical turn, examining the place of *Left Behind* in publishing history. This scholarly "blind spot" is made all the wider by a reluctance to address the aesthetic or theological ideas of the LaHaye-Jenkins series. Once critics assume that the *Left Behind* phenomenon arises from the lack of socioeconomic privilege among its readers, they quickly lose sight of the place of this strange series in the long history of Protestant speculative writing (and in the somewhat awkward history of iconoclastic art). Cultural-historical approaches to the *Left Behind* series end up taking these "novels" both out of history and out of culture by treating them as case studies for contemporary sociological and literary theory but forgetting that they have a role in the history of popular dissenting religious thought and in the development of religious fiction. The charges of incompetence that are often brought against the *Left Behind* authors—that their prose is stilted, their characters one-dimensional, and their narrative hasty and patchworked—arise in part from an insistence that contemporary fiction should conform to mainstream critical norms rather than to the indigenous literary conventions within religious traditions.

This chapter will consider the *Left Behind* series with regard to its often inadvertent attempts to solve various aesthetic problems: problems arising from the collision, in the high-pressure environment of quickly written novels,[4] of novelistic conventions that have been developing since the time of Daniel Defoe with post-Reformation theology that has been fermenting since the time of Martin Luther and with recent media genres (cinema, television, Internet, radio, and gospel music) toward which fundamentalist Christians have a mixed mind. Whether or not one endorses their opinions, LaHaye and Jenkins have accomplished a major artistic feat simply by coordinating, in nervous prose and tense narratives, a large matrix of contradictory traditions in a new, composite, often awkward, occasionally daring mode that I shall call "fundamentalist baroque." LaHaye and Jenkins may or may not possess adequate cultural-historical knowledge to found an artistic movement, but they nevertheless evidence a prodigious capacity to assimilate the most diverse materials. Their hypertextual capacities—their ability to stack and superimpose snippets of cultural and historical information into a quickly glimpsed package—mark them as members of our cybernetically minded era and establish them as experts in multilayered approaches to fiction writing. Like the historical baroque, this collage approach uses quick and dazzling manipulations of perspective and viewpoint to combine striking dramatic scenes with complex arrays of information and thereby to produce a relentless sense of process.

Unwilling polymaths, LaHaye and Jenkins have produced, in the *Left Behind* series, a gigantic canon of material, one too large to be treated in any kind of detail in a brief chapter. This chapter will concentrate on the first three volumes—*Left Behind, Tribulation Force,* and *Nicolae*—in which the principal theological and aesthetic problems of "apocalyptic fiction" are confronted and in which the foundational events of the series—the "rapture" of Christians prior to the Apocalypse, the formation of a premillennial Christian response team, and the rise of the Antichrist—transpire.

CHALLENGES OF CONTEMPORARY CALVINIST NARRATIVE

In his *Defense of Poesy,* Sir Philip Sidney affirmed the Aristotelian and Horatian opinion that literature ought to "teach and delight." The impatient readers of our time are not always delighted by teaching. The first challenge confronting *Left Behind* readers accustomed to postmodern cheekiness or to post-Romantic complexity is its intense, straightforward didacticism. *Left Behind* takes as its starting point an interpretation of the Christian scripture that is so literal that it might be considered "more than literal" or even "pictographic." Fundamentalists take for granted that the Bible conveys clear and distinct ideas keyed to the dictionary sense of words. LaHaye and Jenkins, however, go a bit further: they affirm that the events mentioned in obscure passages in prophetic books such as Revelation, Daniel, Corinthians, and Thessalonians have literal and tangible components *both* in historical, biblical times *and* in the present, *as well as* in the apocalyptic worlds to come. The scriptures are *multiply* literal. References to the "Jews," for example, refer to the subjects of

Herod and Caiaphas, to the inhabitants of modern Israel, to the future beneficiaries of the Messiah, and to the (converted) citizens of the future heavenly kingdom. For the *Left Behind* authors, this multiplicity of reference never complicates the literal meaning of scripture, but rather "amplifies" it or leads to a "dynamic" understanding. Such multiplexed literalism allows the *Left Behind* authors to move between past, present, and speculative references without veering from their fundamentalist commitment to the exact meaning of holy writ. Almost any possible meaning can be declared "exact" in one of the foregoing senses.[5]

This twisting and braiding of literalisms is one source for the central thematic concerns of the *Left Behind* series. Drawing on the work of the nineteenth-century biblical explicator John Nelson Darby and on Cyrus I. Scofield's annotated Bible, the *Left Behind* authors focus on the notion of the "rapture," a preapocalyptic event vaguely described in 1 Thess. 4:16–17 and in Matt. 24–25 in which true and faithful Christians will be taken to heaven—literally, through the clouds to a "meeting in the air"—to enjoy the fruits of paradise while other, less-select Christians and heathens would endure the "tribulation," a period of misery and persecution during the reign of the Antichrist in which "tribulation saints" may either prove or lose their latter-day faith.[6] For LaHaye and Jenkins, the sparse supply of references to the rapture either in the Bible or in the first nineteen centuries of biblical commentary is all the more reason to write about the topic.[7] The miscellany of topics covered in the Old and New Testaments disappears while the single topic of the rapture produces reams of apocalyptic "Christian" fiction as well as exegesis and commentary, much of it based in the Internet.[8]

The story in *Left Behind* and its sequels is less a traditional narrative than an adventurous explication of theological details: a fast-paced gallop through the action-filled world of the four horsemen of the Apocalypse. A small band of high-profile but easygoing characters—the airline and later Air Force One pilot Rayford Steele; the award-winning cub reporter Cameron "Buck" Williams; Steele's Stanford-educated daughter (and later Buck's wife) Chloe; pastor and Tim LaHaye look-alike Bruce Barnes; and Rayford Steele's second wife Amanda Steele—find themselves thrown together in a last-ditch effort to save souls during the rise of the Antichrist. Antichrist emerges in the form of the suave young Romanian politician, Nicolae Carpathia, whose personal charm, charismatic power, and supernatural connections vault him through a series of offices, from Romanian president to United Nations secretary-general to eventual head of the "Global Community," a diabolical inversion of the former US President George H. W. Bush's "New World Order" and a fulfillment of both biblical prophecies and fundamentalist anxieties about a Babylon-based world government.[9] Between the "tribulation force" (Rayford Steele and his companions) and the Antichrist's world government floats a raft of lesser characters—Chaim Rosenzweig, a secular Jewish scientist and idealist whose secret formulae have made the Israeli deserts fertile and who dreams of a perfect but secular world; Steve Plank, Buck Williams's former editor and a dupe of the Global Community propaganda machine; Hattie Durham, Rayford Steele's former stewardess and onetime mistress to Carpathia; and Verna Zee, lesbian supervisor to rogue reporter Cameron Williams—who might be reclaimed in the "soul harvest" or who might capitulate to the devil. The *Left Behind* tales spin along as these uniquely talented but seemingly modest characters find themselves in the vanguard of a cosmological battle between good and evil, God and Satan. They take advantage of their privileged positions to advance various goals, whether the encouragement of Christianity or the currying of favor with the near-omnipotent Antichrist, Carpathia. The action gets underway in the opening novel, *Left Behind,* when the rapture occurs in a colloquial yet unexpected way. Worldwide, large numbers of people suddenly disappear, including passengers and crew aboard airliners, drivers of cars rumbling down the highway, and surgeons in their operating theaters. The world plunges into temporary chaos as the lead characters try to figure out what might be happening and what to do.

"Taking action" is a uniquely problematic concept in the *Left Behind* series. From Luther, Calvin, and Zwingli, American fundamentalism has inherited a strange mixture of predestinarianism and eschatology. The Reformation idea that God foresees the ultimate fate of souls blends with American confidence in progress to produce the hybrid suggestion that individual persons ought to observe and consent to, rather than entrepreneurially advancing or modifying, God's plan. It is more important to think or feel properly about what God is allowing to happen than to embark on independent projects. Time and again we hear comments such as "Amazing. . . . But even more amazing, it was all predicted in the Bible," in which a reverential, awestruck attitude accompanies indirect, acquiescent "action."[10] These ejaculations are amplified by affirmations of the familiar Protestant opinion that justification occurs through faith rather than works (*LB,* 4 and *passim*). The kind of action that critics since Aristotle have associated with narrative development proves ineffective or even impossible in a universe where the fates of all beings are already known to God. The compromise that *Left Behind* works out is a kind of passive action in which things happen *to* and *around* characters rather than as a result of characters' deeds.

The suggestion of the irrelevance of action extends beyond action to the actors themselves. A good number of the possible players in this cosmological drama are simply *not there,* having already vanished in the rapture. Whole classes of sin-free persons, including all infants and children, have been whisked away to heaven (*LB,* 37). The relation between presence and action in these stories is an inverse one; those who have been most effective at choosing their paths in life have gone to heaven— including "some truly wonderful people" (*LB,* 62) and "the new pope" who "had stirred up controversy in the church with a new doctrine that seemed to coincide more with the 'heresy' of Martin Luther than with the historic orthodoxy"[11]—while those who have done the worst job remain in the world to face the tribulation. The events in the *Left Behind* series constitute a narrative representation of a nonnarrative event in which the best characters exit while the worst characters remain on stage, there to figure out how to develop a story with a happy ending. The concluding page of the first chapter of the series makes this point with a kind of passive brutality. The utterly impersonal narrator coldly reports that the lead character Rayford Steele, along with all the other more-or-less nameless persons aboard Steele's aircraft, "had been left behind" (*LB,* 19), a phrase that echoes eerily throughout the series. The characters thus slide both behind and ahead of their tale. They are "left behind" with regard to the rapture and not quite able to catch up with their own accelerating story, not able to keep pace with the apocalyptic narrative unfolding around them.

Despite the bleakness of LaHaye and Jenkins's apocalyptic outlook, the "happiness" in the aforementioned "happy ending" is more than a worldly illusion. The characters can have little impact on the outcome of the story—time and again, readers are reminded that all has been "foretold" and that "Christ's followers" could only "simply bear up against him [the Antichrist]" (*TF,* 364–65)—but they must nevertheless undergo a "vast period of trial" (*TF,* 212), meaning that a vast narrative space needs filling by actions and events. Many of these interim actions turn out to be non- or at least somewhat abstracted events. LaHaye and Jenkins devote an unexpected amount of space to "psychological correctness": to the repairing of dysfunctional parent–child relationships (*LB,* 103–04); to wondering whether age differences in male–female relationships matter when only seven years remain before the end of time (*TF,* 191); to remarking "how Christ could change a person" (*TF,* 92); to getting believers into a general state of excited readiness (*LB,* 189). Evangelicalism may question the efficacy of works in comparison to grace or faith, yet psychological self-repair often takes center stage in these otherwise highly objective novels.

Perhaps the most frequently sounded motif in the *Left Behind* series is that of "phoniness" or being "phony." Historically, the word phony has carried the sense of "counterfeit" or "fake."[12] For LaHaye and Jenkins, it carries stronger psychological as well as cosmological connotations. Phoniness seems to originate in original sin, in the temptation to create religions in one's own image. It extends to indulgent self-delusions in which one convinces oneself of one's sanctity in daily Christian life and of one's safety vis-à-vis the Last Judgment. Rayford Steele had been "living a phony life, a shell of a man"; even Barnes, pastor of the ad hoc "New Hope Church," "had been a phony" who "had set up [his] own brand of Christianity that may have made for a life of freedom but had cost [him his] soul" (*LB,* 419, 298). Phoniness as a psychological attribute works well in a novel that stresses ineffective action, for phoniness is only discovered when it *fails* as a coping strategy. Phoniness is only known inwardly, in the minds of characters whose actions belie their motivations. The *Left Behind* novels rely on an inverse method of character development in which phony or otherwise complex characters are gradually weeded out so that apocalyptic narratives may run their course without complications from troubled persons who have not been "changed" by LaHaye and Jenkins's psychotherapeutic version of preapocalyptic events.

The action in the *Left Behind* series often occurs through deferred agency. Characters act out what was planned or foretold by some other, more authoritative person or power. Steele—who, despite being an action hero, spends most of his time sitting quietly in his cockpit aboard the Antichrist's airplane, passively listening to diabolical plans—goes so far as to pray for dramatic recasting. "Lord," he prays, "Is there no other role for me? Could I not be used in some sort of active opposition or judgment against the evil one?"[13] Through such calls for redirection or indirection, LaHaye and Jenkins solve a centuries-old problem of Protestant art: how to represent spontaneous action in a world whose fate is determined by God. The two authors have no story line of their own; their tale is borrowed from holy writ. Their characters, however, can act, and act extravagantly, by talking about and reacting to their roles or by making psychologically exploratory observations. Their publishers openly boast about their authors' derivative ways. The colophon pages of their volumes boast of their dependence on John Grisham, Tom Clancy, and other thriller writers. They openly borrow *topoi* from popular science fiction writers (e.g., the prophetic videotape in which the former pastor of New Hope Church explains the course of eschatological history derives from the holographic projection of the futurist Harry Seldon in Isaac Asimov's *Foundation Trilogy*). Whatever is useful and worthy of borrowing becomes part of revealed future history; in any case, whatever is out there to borrow is ultimately God's intellectual property.

COGNITION AND THE COMMONPLACE: THE DRAMA OF MIDDLE-CLASS LIFE

Spectator journalists Richard Addison and Joseph Steele tell us that John Milton's *Paradise Lost* qualifies as an epic owing to the magnitude of its action. The fall of man and the tainting of the universe by sin, death, trouble, and pain are suitably big subjects. While Addison and Steele require that epic characters have an appropriately high social standing *before* a saga begins, LaHaye and Jenkins rely on high genres to elevate ordinary characters on a post hoc basis. *Left Behind* is punctuated with "momentary catachreses": rhetorical or conceptual constructions in which fragments of popular culture are yoked together with fragments of fundamentalist eschatology to produce, for a fleeting moment, an insight, witticism, or truth. LaHaye and Jenkins's method is comparable to the "metaphysical imagery" seen in the works of seventeenth-century poets such as John Donne or Richard Crashaw, in which attributes of an object are disconnected from their source and then hooked up into new images or ideas (e.g., Donne's famous image, in his poem "The Flea," of the gullet of a flea, in which the blood of two bitten lovers commingles). LaHaye and Jenkins are challenged to explain why one small group of upper-middle-class characters should become the flash point in a vast battle between good and evil. They try to solve the problem of credibility by forcing occasional, catachretical links between the pedestrian and the cosmological.

There are many moments of "metaphysical wit" in the *Left Behind* books. In one moment of metaphysical metallurgy, Amanda White, soon-to-be Rayford Steele's second wife, recalls the name of his raptured first wife, "Irene Steele," because it "sounded like iron and steel" (*TF*, 312). For a fleeting moment, a phonic coincidence suggests the convergence of sturdy earthly minerals with resolute belief. The technique distracts readers from seeking further explanations; here, for example, it elides the question of Amanda's not altogether altruistic role as a widow in search of a husband or of Rayford's dilemma as to which of his multiple wives he might meet in heaven. The speed with which such catachretical moments fly by allows pop-culture ideas to pass as disciplined analysis. Early on in *Left Behind,* readers are presented with images of a happy domestic life in which sex plays only a secondary role. We see flannel pajamas, kitsch interiors filled with "country knickknacks" and "frilly" "needlepoint," and family photographs stressing genealogical rather than amorous connections (*LB*, 73–75). Flashes of prophetic insight, here suggesting that the lead character's raptured wife expressed her anticipation of the end times through middle-class domestic decor, create momentary connections between the routine and the religious. Genealogy, a favorite hobby among Americans who have not quite forgotten the old world but who have not bothered with scientific historical research, is a frequent focal point for "metaphysical moments." *Tribulation Force* considers the possibility that the first 144,000 converts following the rapture would include 12,000 each from the twelve tribes of Israel and that those missing Jews would "be gathered from all over the world" (*TF,* 366), as if the world were full of persons marked with genealogical tags. The experience of the modest person may thus be yoked at any moment with some or other unknown metaphysical experience.

Despite its reputation for anti-intellectualism, LaHaye and Jenkins's fundamentalism includes cognitive componentry. Believers must be ready to notice esoteric intellectual linkages at any moment. One of the biggest threats in their series is that of brainwashing, the elimination of the ability to think clearly. Antichrist Carpathia uses brainwashing and memory-erasure technique (*TF,* 50). Colead character Buck Williams resists brainwashing through self-directed cognitive therapy, in which he concentrates on thoughts of marital love (*TF,* 129). The rabbinical scholar Tsion Ben-Judah makes much ado about certifying Pastor Barnes's biblical commentaries as adequately scholarly. "Metaphysical moments," such as those mentioned above, frequently occur in scholarly contexts, as when Rabbi Tsion peruses Pastor Bruce's commentaries. Such encounters follow the example of the metaphysical poets in their quickness and ephemerality, seldom lasting more than a few paragraphs. After all, "end-time" events happen quickly. Snappy wit is more eligible than prolix narrative for turning eschatological conceits.

THE SPIRITUAL BAROQUE

Sir Philip Sidney, along with many others, faced the problem of becoming a "Protestant knight errant": a practitioner of chivalry, as developed by continental Catholic cultures, who lives on an anti-Papist island. Similarly manageable contradictions exist today at the bibliographical level. Many Protestant households possess opulent "family Bibles" enhanced by lavish reproductions of art by painters who were in the employ of the Vatican. Sidney solved his ecumenical problem by secularizing and simplifying the gestures and manners of Catholic sonneteers. Style, mode, and genre eclipsed theology. Today's Christian fundamentalism faces an analogous problem: it is highly "word" and image oriented yet is hostile to literature owing both to moralistic concerns and to anxieties about the second commandment (per Exodus), which forbids making images of God or God's works. LaHaye and Jenkins, who are in flagrant violation of this commandment, avoid this issue, but as a practical matter they must decide what to represent and how to represent it. The problem is meliorated by the fact that *Left Behind* takes place in the future and is presented as a conjecture about apocalyptic scenarios. One can hardly make a "graven image" of something that does not yet exist. On the other hand, the story is written in the present tense and with an excruciating concern for what characters are thinking about Apocalypse-related information.

The *Left Behind* saga is a highly various work using many techniques, but its dominant mode could be described as the fundamentalist baroque. In the historical, primarily Catholic baroque, extravagant ornamentation draws attention to and elaborates upon the drama implicit in assorted classical and religious themes. Drapery, exaggerated postures, strange lighting, and bizarre perspectives intensify representations of otherwise familiar themes. In fundamentalist baroque, specific Catholic and classical references are removed while mannerisms such as dramatic posturing or the selection of bizarre themes are emphasized. Those who stereotype fundamentalist groups as know-nothings will be surprised to learn that the fundamentalist baroque is essentially cognitive. Conventional, representational imagery is rejected in favor of elaborate intellectual conceits requiring both cerebration and connoisseurship. The most striking instances of hyperintellectualized imagery occur in the opening scenes of *Left Behind*, when the sudden disappearance of raptured Christians creates peculiar situations. With a melancholy visual humor not seen since Crashaw imagined Herod's slaughtered innocents nursing their way to heaven by swimming through the Milky Way,[14] LaHaye and Jenkins imagine pregnant women delivering only placenta (because the innocent child has been raptured away), grooms disappearing from weddings, bodies vanishing from caskets, and even pallbearers stumbling under the weight of a casket when the rapture thins their numbers (*LB*, 46–48). LaHaye and Jenkins develop an art of scientific process not unlike the laboratory paintings of Joseph Wright of Darby when they try to portray an ongoing reproductive drama in which all mothers-to-be must submit to amniocentesis (*N*, 370).

Startling as they might be, such conceits demand more conceptualization than visualization. One must know fundamentalist theories about the rapture-Resurrection to grasp the dark wit of the aforementioned funeral scenes. LaHaye and Jenkins likewise elicit twisted, surreal images from mechanical aspects of the rapture. Borrowing from cinematic appreciations of dark, menacing machinery such as the *Alien* or the *Terminator* film series, they offer horridly beautiful scenes of the mechanical arising from the conceptual hardware of "pre-tribulation dispensationism." In a mixed popular-homiletical language combining the dry hardness of Arnold Schwarzenegger's dialogue in *Total Recall* with the erudite pluck of Reformation theologians, LaHaye and Jenkins work out images that call to mind Winckelmann's account of *Laocoön,* with its writhing serpents and confused onlookers. In one scene, an urban cab driver contemplates the twisted cacophony of men, machines, steel, and tools resulting from a rapture-induced traffic jam in a parking structure:

> They peered at a six-story garage with cars seemingly jammed into each other at all angles in a gridlock so tight and convoluted that cranes worked to lift them out through the open sides of the structure.
>
> "They were all in there after a late ballgame that night," she [a cab driver] said. "The police say it was bad anyway, long lines of cars trying to get out, people taking turns merging and lots of 'em not taking turns at all. So some people who got tired of waiting just tried to edge in and make other people let 'em in, you know."
>
> "Yeah."
>
> "And then, poof, they say more than a third of the cars ain't got drivers, just like that. If they had room, they kept going till they hit other cars or the wall. If they didn't have room, they just pushed up against the car in front of 'em. The ones that were left couldn't go one way or the other. It was such a mess that people just left their cars and climbed over other cars and went looking for help. They started at dawn moving the cars on the ground levels with tow trucks, then they got them cranes in there by noon, and they been at it ever since."
>
> Rayford and Chloe sat and watched, shaking their heads. Cranes normally used for hoisting beams up to new buildings were wrapping cables around cars, tugging, yanking, dragging them past each other and through openings in the concrete to clear the garage. It appeared it would take several more days. (*LB,* 234–35)

The roughness, crudeness, and coarseness of this imagery in no way disqualifies it for the tag "baroque"; rather, such passages escort art-historical conventions drawn from diverse traditions, including the Catholic and continental baroque, into the hard, dry, underclass, and clamorous world of modern fundamentalism. In place of the marble of Catholic baroque ornamentation we get the crunching steel of the modern production line; in place of the Protestant "work ethic" on that production line, we get an unstable end-product alternately suited for the scrap yard of history or the gated community of heaven.

What is most difficult for nonfundamentalists to grasp is that such imagery is, in its own way, funny. Baroque sculptors routinely found a dark wit in mortuary monuments depicting the strangely comic possibilities of the Resurrection. One thinks of the surprised-looking dukes and earls being ripped naked out of their sepulchers in city-center cathedrals, possibly while happy geriatrics in an adjacent *Dom Café* heave into heaven amid their *Kaffee-und-Kuchen*. Seriocomic juxtaposition is key to another *Laocoön*-reminiscent scene in which gas-guzzling SUVs rampage over a rolling earth while divine justice is meted out to an unrepentant bystander during an apocalyptic earthquake:

> He carefully drove around and through destruction and mayhem. The earth continued to shift and roll, but he kept going. Through his blown-out window he saw people running, heard them screaming, saw their gaping wounds and their blood. They tried to hide under rocks that had been disgorged from the earth. They used upright chunks of asphalt and sidewalk to protect them, but just as quickly they were crushed. A middle-aged man, shirtless and shoeless and bleeding, looked heavenward through broken glasses and opened his arms wide. He screamed to the sky, "God, kill me! Kill me!" And as Buck slowly bounced past in the Range Rover, the man was swallowed into the earth. (*N*, 408–09)

Clashing expectations and clashing genre conventions were essential ingredients in the historical baroque. The fantastic elaborations that accompanied highly serious episodes, whether the Last Judgment or the Assumption of the Virgin or the binding of Satan, could alternately elicit awe, amazement, confusion, skepticism, laughter, or chagrin. In the foregoing example of the fundamentalist baroque, furious action appropriate to a sci-fi film coincides with the cheeky urbanity of automobile advertisements and with a seriocomic representation of an atheist being dragged down to eternity under asphalt. An oversupply of conflicting aesthetic states ranging from laughter to horror leaves readers unsure whether to laugh or cry—but nevertheless continuously and variously stimulated.

Despite its action-film pace, the *Left Behind* series is highly dependent on "compositions": set scenes, tableaux, and other posed arrangements. Like baroque statuary, Jenkins and LaHaye's books ask readers to take a paused moment to contemplate still photographs of volatile processes. Calvinist theology may seem impersonal, but *Left Behind* abounds in emotionally charged scenes, especially crying jags:

> Rayford felt so small, so inadequate before God, that he could not seem to get low enough. He crouched, he squatted, he tucked his chin to his chest, and yet he still felt proud, exposed. Bruce had been praying aloud, but he suddenly stopped, and Rayford heard him weeping quietly. A lump

formed in his own throat. He missed his family, but he was deeply grateful for Chloe, for his salvation, for these friends.

Rayford knelt there in front of his chair, his hands covering his face, praying silently. Whatever God wanted was what he wanted, even if it made no sense from a human standpoint. The overwhelming sense of unworthiness seemed to crush him, and he slipped to the floor and lay prostrate on the carpet. A fleeting thought of how ridiculous he must look assailed him, but he quickly pushed it aside. No one was watching, no one cared. And anyone who thought the sophisticated airplane pilot had taken leave of his senses would have been right.

Rayford stretched his long frame flat on the floor, the backs of his hands on the gritty carpet, his face buried in his palms. Occasionally one of the others would pray aloud briefly, and Rayford realized that all of them were now facedown [sic] on the floor.

Rayford lost track of time, knowing only vaguely that minutes passed with no one saying anything. He had never felt so vividly the presence of God. So this was the feeling of dwelling on holy ground. . . . He was not sure how long he lay there, praying, listening. After a while he heard Bruce get up and take his seat, humming a hymn. Soon they all sang quietly and returned to their chairs. All were teary-eyed. (*TF*, 240–41)

Such passages are written from and about postures of repose. By *Left Behind* standards, this passage rambles on at great length given its paucity of action. Its characters "move" between various forms of declination, whether sitting, reclining, squatting, or prostrating. The postures represented are always extraordinary, awkward, demanding, or uncomfortable. Explorations of improbable balance and positioning that would be the envy of any yogi or baroque sculptor, they yoke together in contorted catachresis the conflict of intense psychological action and predestinarian immobility. Weeping, crying, prostrating, and finally conversion scenes abound throughout the series, often serving to counterpoint the high-speed action of the more adventurous scenes. Contemporary, media-savvy fundamentalism as practiced by "televangelists" and their Internet successors makes abundant use of such scenes. Sermons, hymns, psalms, and prayers are routinely punctuated with postured fits of paralyzed weeping, scenes suitable for framing on television or computer screens. In *Left Behind*, one emotive conversion even takes places in the straitened confines of a men's restroom (*LB*, 446). LaHaye and Jenkins take the genre of the ready-for-framing weeping spell to its highest level, positioning the crying scene at the still center of the turbulent apocalyptic universe and linking it up to the kind of detached, witty speculations that occur more often in John Donne than in John Calvin.

FAITH TRUMPS WORKS, BUT INFORMATION TRUMPS BOTH

The prominence of passively experienced emotional paroxysms in *Left Behind* points up a problem that has bedeviled English-language fundamentalism since the seventeenth century. "Empiricism," a philosophical movement with roots among Puritan-influenced British "virtuosi" such as John Locke, as well as among the secularized dissenters who filled out the early Royal Society, linked revelation to "experience." This link explains the emphasis among today's fundamentalists on inner spiritual experience despite their countervailing concern for God's objective plans. In post-Romantic times, an emphasis on personal experience is easily associated with education and with the gathering of information—with "the growth of the poet's mind." Thus, despite commitments to the inevitability of God's plan, to the direct and literal interpretation of the scripture, and to the unhesitating consent to God's will, the *Left Behind* books place information (and its management) in a position of paramount importance.

The apparent contradiction between a devotionalist commitment to God and the gathering of corroborative information is handled in a way consonant with fundamentalist baroque aesthetics. LaHaye and Jenkins concentrate less on information per se than on *images* and *scenes* of information absorption. Rabbi Tsion Ben-Judah, for example, appears throughout the story as an emblem of information competence. Always pictured in some quasi-academic context—surrounded by books, reading from a manuscript, surfing the Internet—he doubles as a character and a sign, as a living image of biblical scholarship replete with all the stereotypes pertaining to a wizened rabbinical scholar (LaHaye and Jenkins feel compelled to explain his ability to move about more nimbly than might befit the standard *old* rabbi by pointing out that he is only forty-six years old). Characters are always reading, often in recumbent or passive postures. They most often read in bed, even when with their spouses (*LB*, 191). In addition to providing fundamentalist baroque visual novelty, these semidormant reading scenes function as a form of elementary hermeneutical and research instruction, explaining to naive readers what kind of tools they might need—guides, indices, concordances, dictionaries—to realize the Lutheran ideal of the priesthood of all believers.[15]

For practitioners of the fundamentalist baroque, reading and information processing is as much about performance as it is about learning or education per se. Part of pictorial space, information counts as a virtual object. In a manner reminiscent of the lead character in John Bunyan's *Pilgrim's Progress,* Rayford arms himself for his first encounter with Carpathia with Psalm 91 (*TF,* 293). Pastor Barnes uses Revelation as a foundation text for recommending an emergency food stockpile (*LB,* 311). The approach of the *Left Behind* series to textual interpretation may be described as *more than literal:* the fundamentalist aversion to scriptural interpretation is maintained, but literal meanings always trigger supplemental actions that move texts out of books and into meaning-supplementing additional actions. Hence the notion that the famine mentioned in Revelation should be understood not only as an Apocalypse-era shortage of food but also as a call to begin stockpiling rations.

The need to amplify "literal" meanings is debated throughout this saga. Despite his fundamentalist literalism, Pastor Barnes, the ad hoc leader of New Hope Church, produces, in his brief career, over 5,000 pages of biblical commentary (*N,* 31). Characters routinely receive dream visions that extend, amplify, and interpret scripture—not, perhaps, with regard to the content of a biblical text, but rather with regard to how a character should relate its literal meaning to present or to apocalyptic times. LaHaye and Jenkins repeatedly admonish readers that scripture reveals more than "mere symbolism" (*TF,* 65), but equally often they show themselves willing to extend meanings into historical space, as when they gladly declare that a "week" of tribulation is in fact seven years long (*TF,* 374). The utter transparency of the "symbolism" that does occur within *Left Behind*—the fact that Antichrist Carpathia is thirty-three years old and could otherwise be easily identified as the Antichrist even by an undergraduate lacking an Internet-plagiarized paper; the naming of the ever-interpreting rabbi after Zion; the multiply-apostolic moniker of the Pope "Peter Matthews"; the founding of the New Age religion "Enigma Babylon"—is surely a fault for those who seek subtlety in modern narratives. For avid readers of this series, however, simple-minded translucency eases the transition between the often-inscrutable passages in Revelation, Daniel, and other timeless prophetic books and the obvious facts of immediate, historical experience.

Ease and *immediacy* are important twin concepts in the cybernetic world of modern fundamentalist fiction. From an outside perspective, the *Left Behind* characters are more or less simple people whose God-given talents help them to navigate a bewildering maze of signs, types, and other meaning-laden statements, images, and texts. Their task is greatly eased by an astounding array of electronic media, data-processing equipment, and communication devices. Powerful personal data devices intercede between the invisible, highly semantic world of Revelation and the immediate experience of ordinary folks. In a kind of secondary or technical literalism, the Antichrist's global regime both requires and is opposed by a gigantic network of information-processing devices that allow for instant worldwide communication or for immediate recovery of dispersed information. The hero Rayford Steele's late wife was tuned in to Christian radio at all times; indeed, her radio continued to receive it after her rapture (*LB*, 66–67); telephones, the most obvious devices for compressing vast distances into moments of instantaneous communication, are everywhere (*LB*, 150); to keep pace with apocalyptic events, Pastor Barnes has "taken it upon" himself "to keep CNN on all the time" (*TF*, 23); Pastor Barnes's raptured predecessor leaves behind a videotape outlining the course of future history (*LB*, 155); prayer requests are assisted by Internet searches (264); Rabbi Tsion rejoices in his library of powerful Bible-research software (*N*, 306) while junior journalist and cohero Buck Williams deploys an assemblage of FAX machines, modems, couriers, and computer peripherals (*N*, 358); "a computer with virtually no limitations" and a suite of laptops are available regardless of cost (*N*, 45–46); dignitaries' airplanes come equipped with surveillance microphones accessible only to the pilot (*N*, 48); Apocalypse-proof underground shelters are assembled in characters' spare time. The production and acquisition of such equipment would seem to require both superhuman funding and superhuman science, but in the *Left Behind* series it colloquializes a story that is fundamentally supernatural. The possession of such equipment makes it possible for ordinary human beings to engage in a vast, cosmological conflict fought across a gigantic theater of war that would normally require flying Miltonic angels, superhuman logistical support, prodigious teleporting skills.[16] The underground shelter in or through which much of this equipment is used, stored, or transported stands on (or rather sinks to) the brink of invisibility. A few feet underground, it is within reach of human tools and yet not fully of this world.

This technological colloquialization of the supernatural is at its best in one of the most bizarre incidents in the *Left Behind* epic. Early on in the tale, two "witnesses" named Eli and Moishe appear at the Wailing Wall (the west wall of the Temple Mount) where, in accord with prophecy, they begin to prophesy, cajole, exhort, chastise, and otherwise harangue increasingly large crowds, even hosting Christian rallies in Teddy Kollek stadium. Eli and Moishe exhibit supernatural powers, including the ability to address, simultaneously and telepathically, any and all comers in their native languages. When Rabbi Tsion decides to affirm that Jesus is the Messiah and to convert to Christianity, one of the eerie prophets, Eli, telephones him to congratulate him, having gotten his telephone number from a television broadcast (*TF*, 398). The dialogue in this conversation sounds more like a sidewalk cell-phone chat than the mysterious auguries typical of these uncanny prophets. These incidents could easily be criticized as lapses from even minimally coherent character development, yet lapses can be informative. Through such stunning interruptions of the supernatural with the technical and colloquial, LaHaye and Jenkins keep pushing and poking and otherwise intruding their supernatural story into ordinary experience. Antichrist Carpathia, who also can telepathically brainwash his followers and who has enough magical charisma to take over the whole world in but a few weeks, is routinely stymied by technical details, whether air traffic control delays or office equipment troubles. This "interruptive" technique falls within the purview of the fundamentalist baroque, for it somewhat whimsically represents ordinary mortals in the most extraordinary and contorted situations that can still pass as *minimally believable*—and minimally believable in a world where belief, and only belief, matters.

"THE LITTLE GUY": SMALLNESS AND AT LEAST A LITTLE BIT OF HUMOR

Minimally believable incidents such as Eli and Moishe's cell phone call are appropriate to American fundamentalism, where the so-called little guy, the ordinary person stuck in a frustrating job or struggling with a small business who feels at a disadvantage with respect to "big brother" or "the new world order" or "the company" or some other juggernaut, is a key player. Phrasing such as "the little guy doesn't have a chance against the system" is common enough in the lower-middle-class communities that comprise most of the *Left Behind* readership.[17] The little guy may be seen as the secular counterpart to the ordinary fundamentalist worshiper who receives, through the inner light or the holy ghost or fervid prayer, a special revelation to which the skeptical world pays little heed. LaHaye and Jenkins play with and upon this kind of pejorative self-stereotyping. They render their hip, savvy, and clever characters as if they were ordinary, confused, and frightened folks living in small-tract homes in outer suburbia. This mirage of mediocrity extends to stylistic matters. Most of the lead characters affect a degree of verbal innocence that is inconsistent with their station in life but that makes them more accessible to and sympathetic for a less empowered readership.

Whether or not the language and characterizations in *Left Behind* result from clever strategies or from accident and incompetence, it is nevertheless still the case that smallness, littleness, and crampedness all play an important part in "the big picture" of this saga. For one, most of the incidents take place within small environments, whether office interiors or airliner cabins or waiting rooms or restaurants or rooms within family homes. The series has a reputation for its panoramic action scenes, but a quantitative analysis would show that almost everything of note happens in a small space. One of the longest scenes of the story—and a turning point for the series as a whole—is Buck's initial descent into the tiny survival bunker, a twenty-four-foot-square area laden with everything needed to survive the end of the world (*N*, 297–99). Traditional harrowing-of-hell scenes tend to stress the immensity of the underworld—one thinks of Dante's colossal inferno—but LaHaye and Jenkins limit the subterranean probe to a place that is at best surprising in its "lack of claustrophobia" (*N*, 289). A sense of aggressive smallness also characterizes personal and family relationships. Buck is startled at "how connected our little family has become" (*N*, 87); although from a distant land, Rabbi Tsion ends up as the pastor of New Hope Church (*N*, 242); modest Hattie Durham, Rayford Steele's former stewardess, might give birth to the child of the Antichrist, with Buck and Chloe serving as surrogate parents (*N*, 383–84). Part of the fundamentalist baroque aesthetics of the *Left Behind* books is a persistent attempt to pack as much startling, jarring, or even conflicting material into as many small spaces or small family networks as is minimally believable but maximally exciting.

Excitement and modesty mingle in LaHaye and Jenkins's post-Calvinist aesthetics. Early in *Nicolae,* Chloe, now Buck's wife, gets involved in a high-speed chase that terminates in an accident:

> "Well, I guess what I thought was an exit wasn't really an exit. I never hit the brake, but I did take my foot off the gas. The Range Rover was in the air for a few seconds. I felt like I was floating for a hundred feet or so. There's some sort of dropoff next to me, and I landed on the tops of some trees and turned sideways. The next thing I knew, I woke up and was alone here."
>
> "Where?" Buck was exasperated, but he certainly couldn't blame Chloe for not being more specific.
>
> "Nobody saw me, Buck," she said dreamily. "Something must have turned my lights off. I'm stuck in the front seat, kind of hanging here by the seat belt." (*N*, 97–98)

Chloe's wreck occurs in the context of a wide-ranging chase, yet the event itself seems placeless. Her car floats in the air for a good while; she experiences little other than a dreamless sleep. Chloe ends up in a sort of survival capsule, hanging somewhat ridiculously from a harness, unaware of her physical location, waiting for something to happen but not covering any distance. A character at the center of a great religious drama remains in a womblike capsule suspended who-knows-where by the double umbilical cords of a seat belt and a cell phone.

In the nervous world of American fundamentalism, blood-stirring scenes end up creating more wry humor than terror. Readers of the *Left Behind* series know that the characters all operate under a special Providence. No matter how great the threat, the major characters will certainly survive to perform their role in God's plan. Sympathizing readers of this series experience a lesser version of the kind of aesthetic disinterestedness that aestheticians from Shaftesbury and Kant to Bergson and Husserl have associated with laughter. Knowing that God will always protect the main characters, readers are free to marvel, smile, and even laugh at the wondrous ways in which God protects his people. There is something slightly amusing, for example, about an oversized SUV such as is usually associated with plain-Jane "soccer moms" becoming a factor in God's plans. However apocalyptic its tone, *Left Behind* has more in common with comedy and romance, where characters are sure to come to a good end, than with those sober genres where characters are in jeopardy. The smallness of the persons, environments, and situations in LaHaye and Jenkins's middle-class Apocalypse only increases the sense that the novel might be more funny than frantic.

It is only slightly surprising that the *Left Behind* books abound with humor of a "small" kind: humor based on the offbeat situations in which ordinary people find themselves during apocalyptic times or humor based on interpersonal interactions among the oddballs who meet up when the world is falling apart. When the rapture occurs, for example, one confused woman finds her husband's empty clothes and shrieks "I'm afraid he's gone off naked. He's a religious person, and he'll be terribly embarrassed" (*LB*, 22). Sex and the body, sources of anxiety in puritanical congregations, give rise to potentially witty situations as readers learn that beauty salons continue to operate during the tribulation (*LB*, 381). Ethnic humor draws a laugh when a penurious rabbi wangles a free cab ride (*TF*, 298). Affectionate nicknaming among close friends and family members gets a send up when Hattie wonders whether "you could call him Antichrist, or A. C. for short" (*N*, 180). Much of the humor in the *Left Behind* series is rather cerebral, albeit cerebral in a way that celebrates the encounter of modest, tightly knit cohorts with big, corporate, or cosmological forces. Buck checks into a hotel in the holy land in the guise of a representative for International Harvester, a joke that plays upon Buck's own identity uncertainties as he becomes an unlikely crusader working against rather than for international corporations such as this farm machinery giant. This joke also requires a quick reference to the language of the favorite Bible translation among fundamentalists, the 1611 King James Version, with all its talk about the harvests of heaven, the harvest of souls, and simply the "Harvest," in its capitalized form.[18] Language and its perceived corruption is an important concern of literal-minded fundamentalist literary theorists. Hostile humor is often directed at examples of psychobabble, newspeak, or jargon that might threaten the linguistic purity of the scriptures. LaHaye and Jenkins satirically snarl at "men and women 'faith guides' (no one was called a reverend or a pastor or a priest anymore)" (*N*, 358). Characters humorously philosophize about "the idea of buyers securing a thirty-year mortgage" (*TF*, 406) when only seven years remained until the "glorious appearing" that would signal Jesus' return.

A CONCLUSION ABOUT (ENDLESS) FICTIONS OF CONCLUSION

Like Pastor Barnes's impromptu Bible commentaries, the *Left Behind* series tallies up to over 5,000 pages. Yet readers of all sorts—professional literary critics, fundamentalist churchgoers, correspondents to the review areas on Amazon.com—routinely comment that it is a quick read, that it seems to move along so fast that it concludes before it is fully enjoyed. The series itself is quickly "left behind" in a blur of episodes, impressions, and bizarre conceptual jests. Through a series of fundamentalist baroque vignettes, the series tries to reconcile an invisible world built on colossal theological concepts with the tangible, minimal world in which most of its readers reside. The *Left Behind* series is "never better than late": presenting future events as if they had happened only a few minutes ago, it bypasses demands for historical accuracy, biblical fidelity, or even adherence to its own theology by continually suggesting that its readers have only just now missed something wondrous but that they still have a last-minute chance to see in retrospect the future events that might not quite happen in their lives. The *Left Behind* series is truly *neo*-baroque. It continually suggests that there are new and even more prodigious events forthcoming, as evidenced by what readers just saw—or missed—only minutes ago. To its series of baroque scenes and fundamentalist-mannerist compositions it adds a nervous mix of anticipation and retrospection, converting the fear of being left behind—by culture, by society, by God himself—into a nonstop anticipation of things to come, of future gallery showings of well-composed apocalyptical scenes.

NOTES

1. On the expansion of Christian-publishing product lines into nonprint media and paraphernalia, see Joanne M. Swenson, "From Dogma to Aesthetica: Evangelical Exchatology Gets a Makeover," *Cross Currents* 53 (2004): 566–78, especially 567. Swenson coins the term "irridescent

urgency" to describe the colorful and yet hard-edged packaging that intensifies the air of emergency surrounding these products.

2. Tyndale Press evidences a certain genius for the combination of commercial and spiritual purposes in snappy, aphoristic language. On its website, http://www.tyndale.com, one may read that its "corporate purpose" is to "honor God, excel in business, sustain controlled economic growth, operate profitably, [and] help employees grow" (accessed on December 1, 2005). The condensation of big ideas into compact language bears on the promotion of the *Left Behind* series, which is characterized in such cinematic terms as "the world hurtles through the countdown to the Rapture," see http://www.tyndale.com/products/details.asp?isbn=1-4143-0896-5 (accessed on December 1, 2005).

3. See Glenn W. Shuck, *Marks of the Beast: The "Left Behind" Novels and the Struggle for Evangelical Identity* (New York: New York University Press, 2005) and Amy Johnson Frykholm, *Rapture Culture: Left Behind in Evangelical America* (New York: Oxford University Press, 2004).

4. Since the appearance of the first novel, *Left Behind*, in 1995, LaHaye and Jenkins have released an average of one and one-half novels per year in the series, in addition to their many other productions.

5. The "more than literal" quality of the *Left Behind* books applies likewise to readers' understanding of their place in soteriological history. Paul C. Gutjahr reports that many readers regard these novels as quasi-sacred texts that played a key role in their own salvation, that give unusually forceful and convincing descriptions of "intense physical" events such as earthquakes that scripture describes cryptically, and that are easily confused with or blurred over into the Bible, "No Longer Left Behind: Amazon.com, Reader-Response, and the Changing Fortune of the Christian Novel in America," *Book History* 5 (2002): 225.

6. For a summary of the Darbyite movement and the emergence of the Scofield Bible, see Frykholm, *Rapture Culture,* 15–18.

7. The scarcity of rapture-related material prior to the nineteenth century is a sore point among tribulationists. The Internet hosts a considerable body of theological speculation on this lacuna (or on the possibility that the rapture was indeed discussed among earlier religious writers, albeit in slightly different nomenclature). For example, see "A Brief History of the Rapture" at the site for the "Pre-Trib Research Center," http://www.pre-trib.org/article-view.php?id=250 (accessed on December 2, 2005) and "Morgan Edwards and the Pre-Trib Rapture" at the "Last Trumpet" website of the rival "Post-Trib Research Center," http://www.geocities.com/last-trumpet_2000/timeline/morgan.html (accessed on December 2, 2005). Although these two groups are locked in often bitter controversy—pre-tribulationism, supported by LaHaye and Jenkins, argues that the rapture will occur before the tribulation; post-tribulationism argues that the rapture will occur either during or after the tribulation; and a third, less popular position, mid-tribulationism, holds that the rapture will occur during the seven-year tribulation—they share a concern to demonstrate that the

rapture is not a modern invention but was proclaimed in biblical times, as part of what is now the Bible.

8. LaHaye, for example, operates his own website, which originates in his Southern California "ministry" (www.timLaHaye.com) and which opens with an online animated sequence showing a shaft of light striking the earth and drawing nimbus-like souls up to heaven. LaHaye's principal disciple, Thomas Ice, described by the Associated Press as a one-man think tank, operates a website abounding in documents, essays, chat rooms, and other controversial writings (www.pre-trib.org). LaHaye's competitors likewise operate related efforts at popular, interactive, and allegedly literal biblical exegesis. A prominent example is the "The Last Trumpet" (www.lasttrumpet.com) which articulates the "post-tribulationist" position. Jerry Jenkins also maintains his own site with a rather more commercial "look" (www.jerryjenkins.com) in which generic Christian ideas, book-order options, and biographical reflections intertwine with ease.

9. The status of the candidate Antichrist Nicolae Carpathia is an interesting one and is indeed worthy of an essay in its own right. LaHaye and Jenkins are committed to the idea that the full "inhabiting" of the Antichrist by the devil will only occur at the midpoint of the tribulation, when the Antichrist will be assassinated but then raised from the dead in a mock-Resurrection effected by Satan himself. LaHaye and Jenkins experience considerable difficulty in keeping the character of Carpathia consistent owing to this uncertainty about his natural or supernatural status, a problem that resists resolution within the literalist discourse of fundamentalist exegetes. Sometimes Carpathia seems to use a kind of supernatural hypnosis to perform such evil wonders as erasing the memories of his lackeys; at other times, he seems remarkably cramped in his style, as when he is unable to speed up flight times or accomplish other, seemingly more routine tasks without very mundane help.

10. Tim LaHaye and Jerry B. Jenkins, *Left Behind: A Novel of the Earth's Last Days* (Wheaton: Tyndale House Publishers, 1995), 385. Henceforth cited intratextually as "LB."

11. Tim LaHaye and Jerry B. Jenkins, *Tribulation Force: The Continuing Drama of Those Left Behind* (Wheaton: Tyndale House Publishers, 1996). Henceforth cited intratextually as "TF."

12. See *Oxford English Dictionary (Online Edition),* entry for "phoney."

13. Tim LaHaye and Jerry B. Jenkins, *Nicolae: The Rise of Antichrist* (Wheaton: Tyndale House Publishers, 1997), 132. Henceforth cited intratextually as "N."

14. In "To the Infant Martyrs."

15. The practical implementation of this Protestant ideal is a flash point in contemporary fundamentalist factionalism. For but one example, see the somewhat polemical internet page devoted to this topic by Grace Valley Christian Center: http://www.gracevalley.org/articles/Priesthood.html.

16. The abundance of advanced or electronic equipment in the *Left Behind* series has been noted by Melani McAlister, "Prophecy, Politics, and the

Popular: The *Left Behind* Series and Christian Fundamentalism's New World Order," *South Atlantic Quarterly* 102 (2003): 783. McAlister notes that the characters' technological competence helps to counter the stereotype of fundamentalists as ignorant and backward. What she does not explain is that this strategy succeeds specifically because technology makes extraordinary actions and events more believable and thereby more amenable to an audience preoccupied with belief.

17. "Most" should not be confused with "all" of the readership. On the diversity of *Left Behind* readers, see Frykholm, *Rapture Culture,* 67–68. Market studies by Tyndale House have made the surprising discovery that "the average buyer of the books is a Southern, white, married female, age 25–54" (see McAlister, 784), suggesting that the most common audience member is at home with family and somewhat out of the limelight.

18. One of the most curious phenomena of contemporary American fundamentalism, including that of the *Left Behind* series, is its nostalgic attachment to the King James Bible, which was produced to steer the English Church in a more Catholic direction and to take some of the momentum out of Puritan and other fundamentalist ambitions.

BIBLIOGRAPHY

Adam, A. K. M. *What Is Postmodern Biblical Criticism?* Minneapolis: Fortress Press, 1995.

Ali, Monica. *Brick Lane.* London, New York: Doubleday, 2003.

Ali, Tariq. *The Book of Saladin.* London, New York: Verso, 1998.

———. *The Clash of Fundamentalisms: Crusades, Jihads and Modernity.* London, New York: Verso, 2002.

———. *Shadows of the Pomegranate Tree.* London, New York: Verso, 1991.

———. *The Stone Woman.* London, New York: Verso, 2000.

———. *A Sultan in Palermo.* London, New York: Verso, 2005.

Antoun, Richard T. *Understanding Fundamentalism: Christian, Islamic, and Jewish Movements.* Walnut Creek, CA: Alta Mira, 2001.

Apostolov, Mario. *The Christian Muslim Frontier: A Zone of Contact, Conflict, or Cooperation.* RoutledgeCurzon Advances in Middle East and Islamic Studies. London: RoutledgeCurzon, 2003.

Armstrong, Karen. *The Battle For God: Fundamentalism in Judaism, Christianity and Islam.* London: Harper Collins, 2000.

Avaramudan, Svirinas. "'Being God's Postman Is No Fun, Yaar': Salman Rushdie's *The Satanic Verses.*" *Reading Rushdie: Perspectives on the Fiction of Salman Rushdie.* Ed. M. D. Fletcher. Cross/Cultures: Readings on Post/Colonial Literatures in English 16. Amsterdam: Rodopi, 1994. 187–208.

Bacon, Jon Lance. *Flannery O'Connor and Cold War Culture.* New York: Cambridge University Press, 1993.

Bar-Efrat, Shimon. *Narrative Art in the Bible.* Journal for the Study of the Old Testament Supplement Series, Bible and Literature Series 17. Sheffield: Almond Press, 1989.

Barsamian, David. *The Checkbook and the Cruise Missile: Conversations with Arundhati Roy.* Cambridge, MA: South End Press, 2004.

Barthes, Roland. "The Death of the Author." *Image Music Text.* Trans. Stephen Heath. London: Fontana, 1977. 142–48.

Behlau, Ulrike, and Bernhard Reitz, eds. *Jewish Women's Writing of the 1990s and Beyond in Great Britain and the United States.* Mainz University Studies in English 5. Trier: WVT, 2004.

Bobzin, Hartmut. *Der Koran: Eine Einführung.* München: C. H. Beck, 1999.

Boer, Roland. *Novel Histories: The Fiction of Biblical Criticism.* Playing the Texts 2. Sheffield: Sheffield Academic Press, 1997.

Brasher, Brenda E., ed. *Encyclopedia of Fundamentalism.* New York, London: Routledge, 2001.

Breckenridge, Carol, and Peter van der Veer, eds. "The Burden of English." *Orientalism and the Postcolonial Predicament: Perspectives on South Asia.* Philadelphia: University of Pennsylvania Press, 1993. 143–57.

"A Brief History of the Rapture." Pre-Trib Research Center. http://www.pre-trib.org/article-view.php?id=250.

Brinkmeyer, Robert H. "A Closer Walk with Thee: Flannery O'Connor and Southern Fundamentalists." *Southern Literary Journal* 18.2 (1986): 3–13.

Brockmeier, Jens, and Donal Carbaugh, eds. *Narrative and Identity: Studies in Autobiography, Self and Culture.* Studies in Narrative 1. Amsterdam, Philadelphia: John Benjamins, 2001.

Bruce, Steve. *Fundamentalism.* Cambridge: Polity Press, 2000.

Bukiet, Melvin Jules. *Strange Fire: A Novel.* New York: Norton, 2001.

Burns, John F. "Another Rushdie Novel, Another Bitter Epilogue." *New York Times* (December 2, 1995).

Caplan, Lionel, ed. *Studies in Religious Fundamentalism.* London: Macmillan, 1987.

Cheyette, Bryan. "Madness Now and to Come." *TLS* (October 14–20, 1988): 1154.

Corbridge, Stuart, and John Harriss. *Reinventing India: Liberalization, Hindu Nationalism and Popular Democracy.* Malden, MA: Blackwell Publishers, 2000.

Crone, Patricia, and Michael Cook. *Hagarism: The Making of the Islamic World.* Cambridge: Cambridge University Press, 1977.

Cronin, Gloria L. "Fundamentalist Views and Feminist Dilemmas: Elizabeth Dewberry Vaughn's *Many Things Have Happened Since He Died* and *Break the Heart of Me.*" Melvin J. Friedman, and Ben Siegel, eds. *Traditions, Voices, and Dreams: The American Novel since the 1960s.* Newark: University of Delaware Press, London: Associated University Presses, 1995.

Davis, Herbert, ed. *The Prose Works of Jonathan Swift.* Oxford: Blackwell, 1957.

Demant, Peter. *Jewish Fundamentalism in Israel: Implications for the Mideast Conflict.* Jerusalem: IPCRI, 1994.

Denny, Frederick M. *An Introduction to Islam.* London: Macmillan, 1994.

Deonadan, Ray. "The Source of the Rage." http://www.podium.on.ca/kureishi.html (browsed February 24, 2002). The article originally appeared in *India Currents Magazine* (February, 1996).

Derrida, Jacques. *Of Grammatology.* Trans. Gayatri Chakravorty Spivak. Baltimore, London: Johns Hopkins University Press, 1976.

Djavann, Chahdortt. *Bas les voiles!* Paris: Gallimard, 2003.

The Doctrine of a Future State . . . in a Second Letter to a Free-Thinker. London: J. Pemberton, 1721.

Dumont, Louis. *Homo Hierarchicus: The Caste System and Its Implications.* Delhi: Vikas, 1970.

Durix, Carole, and Jean-Pierre. *Reading Arundhati Roy's The God of Small Things.* Dijon: Collection U21, 2002.

Durruty, Suzy. "Dédoublement identitaire et ennemis intérieurs dans *Loving Kindness* de Anne Roiphe." *Annales du Centre de Recherches sur L'Amerique Anglophone* 21 (1996): 43–48, 196.

Eagleton, Terry. "Pedants and Partisans." *The Guardian* (February 22, 2003).

Ehrenpreis, Irvin. *Swift: The Man, His Works, and the Age.* 3 vols. Cambridge, MA: Harvard University Press, 1983.

Encyclopaedia Judaica. Jerusalem: Keter, 1970–1971.

Foucault, Michel. *Surveiller et Punir: La Naissance de la Prison.* Paris: Gallimard, 1975.

Foxman, Abraham H. "To the Editor of *The Nation Online*" (February 6, 2004); quoted from http://www.adl.org/media_watch/magazines/20040206-TheNationOnline.htm (retrieved July 29, 2004).

Frei, Hans W. "The 'Literal Reading' of Biblical Narrative in the Christian Tradition: Does It Stretch or Will It Break?" *The Bible and the Narrative Tradition.* Ed. Frank McConnell. New York: Oxford University Press, 1986. 36–77.

Friedman, Menachem. "Jewish Zealots: Conservative versus Innovative." *Jewish Fundamentalism in Comparative Perspective.* Ed. Silberstein. New York: New York University Press, 1993. 148–63.

Frykholm, Amy Johnson. *Rapture Culture: Left Behind in Evangelical America.* New York: Oxford University Press, 2004.

Furman, Andrew. *Israel through the Jewish–American Imagination: A Survey of Jewish–American Literature on Israel, 1928–1995.* Albany: State University of New York Press, 1997.

Gardiner, Anne Barbeau. "'Be ye as the Horse!'—Swift, Spinoza, and the Society of Virtuous Atheists." *SP* XCVII (Spring 2000), 229–53.

[Gastrell, Francis]. *The Principles of Deism Truly Represented.* London: W. and J. Innys, 1722 (1708).

Gätje, Helmut. *Koran und Koranexegese.* Die Bibliothek des Morgenlandes. Zürich: Artemis, 1971.

Gaur, Albertine. *Literacy and the Politics of Writing.* Bristol: Intellect Books, 2000.

Gilbert, Sandra M., and Susan Gubar. *The Madwoman in the Attic.* New Haven: Yale University Press, 1984 (1979).

Glazer, Miriyam. "Male and Female, King and Queen: The Theological Imagination of Anne Roiphe's *Lovingkindness.*" *Studies in American Jewish Literature* 10 (1991): 81–92.

Goldsmith, Meredith. "Thinking through the Body in Hasidic Culture: Reconciling Gender, Sexuality, and Jewishness in the Fiction of Pearl Abraham." Ulrike Behlau and Bernhard Reitz, eds. *Jewish Women's Writing.* 247–54.

Grace Valley Christian Center. http://www.gracevalley.org/articles/Priesthood.html.

Griffin, Roger. "Fascism." *Encyclopedia of Fundamentalism.* Ed. Brasher. 171–78.

Gunesekera, Romesh. *Heaven's Edge.* London: Bloomsbury, 2002.

———. *Reef.* London: Granta/Penguin, 1994.

Gunn, David M., and Danna Nolan Fewell. *Narrative in the Hebrew Bible.* Oxford Bible Series. Oxford: Oxford University Press, 1993.

Gutjahr, Paul C. "No Longer Left Behind: Amazon.com, Reader-Response, and the Changing Fortune of the Christian Novel in America." *Book History* 5 (2002): 209–36.

Haarman, Harald. *Universalgeschichte der Schrift.* 2nd ed. Frankfurt/Main: Campus, 1991.

Hall, Stuart. "Cultural Identity and Diaspora." *Colonial Discourse and Post-Colonial Theory: A Reader.* Patrick Williams and Laura Chrisman, eds. New York: Harvester Wheatsheaf, 1993. 393–403.

Harris, Chrissi. "Insiders/Outsiders: Finding One's Self in the Cultural Borderlands." *Literature and Ethnicity in Cultural Borderlands.* Jesus Benito and Anna Maria Manzanas, eds. Rodopi Perspectives on Modern Literature 28. Amsterdam: Rodopi, 2002. 175–87.

Herberg, Will. *Protestant—Catholic—Jew.* Garden City, NY: Doubleday Anchor, 1960.

Hirst, David. "Pursuing the Millennium: Jewish Fundamentalism in Israel." *The Nation* (February 2, 2004); quoted from http://www.thenation.com/doc.mhtml%3Fi=20040216&s=hirst (retrieved July 29, 2004).

———. *The Gun and the Olive Branch: The Roots of Violence in the Middle East.* London: Faber and Faber, 2003 (1977).

http://www.dalits.org

http://www.rediff.com/news/2001/nov/05spec.htm

http://www.rediff.com/news/nov/29roy.htm

http://www.religioustolerance.org/abo_viol.htm

Huff, Peter A. "Haredim." *Encyclopedia of Fundamentalism.* Ed. Brasher. 207.

Hunter, James Davison. "Fundamentalism: An Introduction to a General Theory." *Jewish Fundamentalism in Comparative Perspective.* Ed. Silberstein. 27–41.

Huntington, Samuel P. *The Clash of Civilizations and the Remaking of World Order.* London: Simon and Schuster, 2002 (1996).

Ice, Thomas. http://www.pre-trib.org

Illich, Ivan, and Barry Sanders. *The Alphabetization of the Popular Mind.* London: Marion Boyars Publishers, 1988.

Jameson, Fredric. "Third World Literature in the Era of Multinational Capitalism." *Social Text* 15 (Fall 1986): 65–88.

Jamieson, Teddy. "Miracle Worker." *The List* (April 4–17, 1997): 91.

[Josephus, Flavius]. *Josephus.* Trans. Henry St. J. 9 vols. Vol. 3, *The Jewish War, Books IV–VII.* The Loeb Classical Library. London: Heinemann and Cambridge, MA: Harvard University Press, 1957 (1928).

Kabbani, Rana. *Europe's Myths of the Orient: Devise and Rule.* London: Pandora Press, 1988.

Kaplan, Jeffrey. "Mahdi." *Encyclopedia of Fundamentalism.* Ed. Brasher. 291–92.

Kirschenbaum, Aaron. "Fundamentalism: A Jewish Traditional Perspective." *Jewish Fundamentalism in Comparative Perspective.* Ed. Silberstein. 183–91.

Kirschenbaum, Blossom S. "Tova Reich (1942)." *Contemporary Jewish–American Novelists: A Biocritical Sourcebook.* Eds. Joel Shatzky and Michael Taub. Westport, CT: Greenwood Press, 1997: 305–13.

Kunzru, Hari. *The Impressionist.* London: Penguin Books, 2003 (2002).

Kureishi, Hanif. "Faith, Love and Fundamentalism." *The Guardian* (November 5, 2001) http://books.guardian.co.uk/departments/generalfiction/story/0,6000,586724.

———. "Loose Tongues and Liberty." *The Guardian* (June 7, 2003).

———. *The Black Album.* http://www.powells.com/biblio/66-0571177522-1 (accessed August 17, 2006).

———. *The Black Album*. London: Faber and Faber, 1995.

———. *The Buddha of Suburbia*. London: Faber and Faber, 1990.

———. *The Word and the Bomb*. London: Faber and Faber, 2005.

Kurten, Marina. "Negotiating Identities: Expressions of 'Culture' in British Migrant Literature." *Atlantic Literary Review* 3.2 (2002): 47–55.

LaHaye, Tim. http://www.timlahaye.com (accessed August 17, 2006).

LaHaye, Tim, and Jerry B. Jenkins. *Left Behind: A Novel of the Earth's Last Days*. Wheaton: Tyndale House Publishers, 1995.

———. *Nicolae: The Rise of Antichrist*. Wheaton: Tyndale House Publishers, 1997.

———. *Tribulation Force: The Continuing Drama of Those Left Behind*. Wheaton: Tyndale House Publishers, 1996.

Law, William. *Remarks upon a Late Book*. London: Will and John Innys, 1724.

Looten, Camille. *La Pensée religieuse de Swift et ses antinomies*. Lille, Paris: Desclée, 1935.

Louvish, Simon. http://www.simonlouvish.com (accessed August 17, 2006).

———. *The Days of Miracles and Wonders: An Epic of the New World Disorder*. Emerging Voices. New York: Interlink, 1999 (1997).

Lowenthal, David. *The Past Is a Foreign Country*. Cambridge: Cambridge University Press, 1997 (1985).

Lustick, Ian S. *For the Land and the Lord: Jewish Fundamentalism in Israel*. New York: Council on Foreign Relations, 1988.

Maalouf, Armin. *In the Name of Identity*. London: Penguin, 2000 (1996).

Martin, Henri-Jean. *The History and Power of Writing*. Chicago: Chicago University Press, 1994.

Marty, Martin E., ed. *The Fundamentalism Project*. 5 vols. Chicago: University of Chicago Press, 1991–1995.

McAlister, Melani. "Prophecy, Politics, and the Popular: The *Left Behind* Series and Christian Fundamentalism's New World Order." *South Atlantic Quarterly* 102 (2003): 773–98.

McConnell, Frank, ed. *The Bible and the Narrative Tradition*. New York: Oxford University Press, 1986.

McLuhan, Marshall. *The Gutenberg Galaxy: The Making of Typographic Man*. Toronto: University of Toronto Press, 1962.

Mendelsohn, Oliver, and Marika Vicziany. *The Untouchables*. Cambridge: Cambridge University Press, 1998.

Mistry, Rohinton. *A Fine Balance*. London: Faber and Faber, 1996 (1995).

———. *Family Matters*. London: Faber and Faber, 2003 (2002).

Modood, Tariq. *Not Easy Being British: Colour, Culture and Citizenship*. London: Runnymede Trust, 1992.

Moore-Gilbert, Bart. "Hanif Kureishi and the 'Fringe' Tradition." *English Literatures in International Contexts*. Heinz Antor and Klaus Stierstorfer, eds. Anglistische Forschungen 283. Heidelberg: Carl Winter Universitätsverlag, 2000. 105–17.

———. *Hanif Kureishi*. Contemporary World Writers. Manchester: Manchester University Press, 2001.

"Morgan Edwards and the Pre-Trib Rapture." Post-Trib Research Center. http://www.geocities.com/lasttrumpet_2000/timeline/morgan.html

Mukherjee, Bharati. *Desirable Daughters.* New Delhi: Rupa, 2002.

———. *Jasmine.* London: Virago, 1989.

Mullaney, Julie. *Arundhati Roy's* The God of Small Things: *A Reader's Guide.* New York: Continuum, 2002.

Nasreen, Taslima. *Lajja.* Trans. C.B. Sultan. Paris: Stock, 1994 (1993).

Needham, Anuradha Dingwaney. "'A New Way of Being British': Hanif Kureishi's Necessary Defense of Mixtures and Heterogeneity." *Using the Master's Tool: Resistance and the Literature of the African and South-Asian Diasporas.* Houndmills: Macmillan, 2000. 111–28.

New, David S. *Holy War: The Rise of Militant Christian, Jewish and Islamic Fundamentalism.* Jefferson, NC: McFarland, 2002.

Observations upon Lord Orrery's Remarks on the Life and Writings of Dr Jonathan Swift. London, W. Reeve and A. Linde, 1754.

Oliva, Juan Ignacio. "Literary Identity and Social Criticism in Hanif Kureishi's *The Black Album.*" *On Writing (and) Race in Contemporary Britain.* Fernando Galvan and Mercedes Bengoechea, eds. Alcala de Henares: Universidad de Alcala, 1999. 147–52.

Ondaatje, Michael. *Anil's Ghost.* London: Bloomsbury, 2000.

Passmann, Dirk F., and Heinz J. Vienken, eds. *The Library and Reading of Jonathan Swift. Part I: Swift's Library in Four Volumes.* Frankfurt: Lang, 2003.

Pesso-Miquel, Catherine. "'Queen Cigars' and 'Peppermint Children': Foreign Arrivals in *The God of Small Things.*" *Reading Arundhati Roy's* The God of Small Things. Dijon, 2002: 23–40.

Peters, Susanne. "Excluding the Other from Within: Protective Effects of Cooking in Memories of the Past in Romesh Gunesekera's Novel *Reef.*" Monika Gomille and Klaus Stierstorfer, eds. *Xenophobic Memories*: Otherness in Postcolonial Constructions of the Past Heidelberg: Winter 231–42.

Piscatori, James. "Islamic Fundamentalism in the Wake of the Six Day War: Religious Self-Assertion in Political Conflict." *Jewish Fundamentalism in Comparative Perspective.* Ed. Silberstein. 79–93.

Ranasinha, Ruvani. *Hanif Kureishi.* Devon: Northcote House Publishers, 2002.

Raphael, Marc Lee. *Judaism in America.* New York: Columbia University Press, 2004.

Reich, Tova. *Master of the Return.* Library of Modern Jewish Literature. Syracuse, NY: Syracuse University Press, 1999 (1988).

———. *The Jewish War: A Novel.* Library of Modern Jewish Literature. Syracuse, NY: Syracuse University Press, 1997 (1995).

Rétat, Pierre. *Le Dictionnaire de Bayle et la lutte philosophique au XVIIIe siècle.* Paris: Audin, 1971.

Ricoeur, Paul. "Toward a Hermeneutic of the Idea of Revelation." *Essays on Biblical Interpretation.* Philadelphia: Fortress, 1980. 73–118.

Robbins, Vernon K., and Gordon D. Newby. "A Prolegomenon to the Relation of the Qur'an and the Bible." *Bible and Qur'an: Essays in Scriptural Intertextuality.* Ed. John C. Reeves. Society of Biblical Literature: Symposium Series 24. Atlanta: Society of Biblical Literature, 2003. 23–42.

Roberts, Alexander, and James Donaldson, eds. *Ante-Nicene Fathers.* 10 vols. Peabody, MA: Hendrickson, 1995; repr. of 1886 ed.

Robertson, David. *The Old Testament and the Literary Critic.* Philadelphia: Fortress Press, 1977.

Roiphe, Anne. *Lovingkindness.* New York: Warner Books, 1997 (1987).

Rosenfeld, Alvin H. "The Progress of the American Jewish Novel." *Response* 7 (1973): 115–30.

Roth, Philip. *The Counterlife.* New York: Vintage International, 1996 (1986).

Roy, Arundhati. *The God of Small Things.* London: Flamingo, 1997.

——. *War Talk.* Cambridge, MA: South End Press, 2003.

Rushdie, Salman. *Imaginary Homelands.* London: Granta, 1991.

——. *Midnight's Children.* London: Cape, 1981.

——. *Shame: A Novel.* New York: Henry Holt, 1983.

——. *The Ground Beneath Her Feet.* New York: Henry Holt, 1999.

——. *The Moor's Last Sigh.* London: Cape, 1995.

——. *The Satanic Verses.* London: Viking, 1989 (1988).

Sardar, Ziauddin, and Merryl Wyn Davies. *Distorted Imagination: Lessons from the Rushdie Affair.* Grey Seal: London, 1990.

Sayyid, Bobby S. *A Fundamental Fear: Eurocentrism and the Emergence of Islamism.* London, New York: Zed Books, 1997.

Schaff, Philip, ed. *Nicene and Post-Nicene Fathers.* 1st ser., 14 vols. Peabody, MA: Hendrickson, 1995; repr. of Oxford 1886 ed.

Scholem, Gershom. *On the Kabbalah and Its Symbolism.* Trans. Ralph Manheim. New York: Schocken Books, 1965.

Several Letters. London: Richard Sare, 1705.

Shahak, Israel, and Norton Mezvinsky. *Jewish Fundamentalism in Israel.* Pluto Middle Eastern Studies. London: Pluto, 1999.

Shohat, Ella. "Columbus, Palestine and Arab-Jews: Toward a Relational Approach to Community Identity." *Cultural Readings of Imperialism: Edward Said and the Gravity of History.* Eds. Keith Ansell-Pearson, Benita Parry, and Judith Squires. London: Lawrence and Wishart, 1997. 88–105.

Shuck, Glenn W. *Marks of the Beast: The Left Behind Novels and the Struggle for Evangelical Identity.* New York: New York University Press, 2005.

Sidahmed, Abdel Salam, and Anoushiravan Ehteshami, eds. *Islamic Fundamentalism.* Boulder, Co: Westview Press, 1996.

Silberstein, Laurence J., ed. *Jewish Fundamentalism in Comparative Perspective: Religion, Ideology, and the Crisis of Modernity.* New Perspectives on Jewish Studies. New York: New York University Press, 1993.

Simpson, Evelyn M., and George R. Potter, eds. *The Sermons of John Donne.* 10 vols. Berkeley, Los Angeles: University of California Press, 1958.

Spaeth, Anthony. "Rushdie Offends Again." *Time* (September 11, 1995): 53.

Spivak, Gayatri Chakravorty. "In Praise of *Sammy and Rosie Get Laid.*" *Critical Quarterly* 31.2 (1989): 80–89.

Stähler, Axel. "Mothers in Israel? Female Jewish Identities and *Eretz Yisrael* in the Works of Jewish Women Writers of the Anglo-American Diaspora: Anne

Roiphe, Tova Reich and Linda Grant." *Jewish Women's Writing.* Eds. Ulrike
  Behlau and Bernhard Reitz, 201–15.

Stein, Mark. "Posed Ethnicity and the Postethnic: Hanif Kureishi's Novels."
  English Literatures in International Contexts. Eds. Heinz Antor and Klaus
  Stierstorfer. Anglistische Forschungen 283. Heidelberg: Carl Winter
  Universitätsverlag, 2000. 119–39.

Steiner, Wendy. "Fetish or Fatwa?" *The Scandal of Pleasure: Art in an Age of
  Fundamentalism.* Chicago: University of Chicago Press, 1995. 94–127.

Stierstorfer, Klaus. "Wobbly Grounds: Postmodernism's Precarious Footholds in
  Novels by Malcolm Bradbury, David Parker, Salman Rushdie, Graham Swift."
  Beyond Postmodernism. Ed. Klaus Stierstorfer. Berlin, New York: W. de Gruyter,
  2003. 213–34.

Suresh, Vidya Bhavani. *What is Kathakali?* Chennai: Skanda Publications, 2003.

Swenson, Joanne M. "From Dogma to Aesthetica: Evangelical Eschatology Gets
  a Makeover." *Cross Currents* 53 (2004): 566–78.

Swift, Deane. *An Essay upon the Life, Writings and Character of Dr Jonathan Swift.*
  New York, London: Garland, 1974; repr. of London: Charles Bathurst, 1755.

Swift, Jonathan. *Gulliver's Travels.* Ed. Christopher Fox. Boston, New York:
  Bedford Books of St. Martin's Press, 1995.

Templeton, Douglas A. *The New Testament as True Fiction: Literature, Literary
  Criticism, Aesthetics.* Playing the Texts 3. Sheffield: Sheffield Academic Press,
  1999.

Thormann, Janet. "The Ethical Subject of *The God of Small Things*" *Journal for
  the Psychoanalysis of Culture & Society* 8.2 (Fall 2003): 299–307.

Tindal, Matthew. *The Rights of the Christian Church Asserted,* 4th ed. London:
  [Richard Sare], 1709.

Webber, Jonathan. "Rethinking Fundamentalism: The Readjustment of Jewish
  Society in the Modern World." *Studies in Religious Fundamentalism.* Ed. Lionel
  Caplan. London: Macmillan, 1987. 95–121.

Weinberg, Leonard. *Religious Fundamentalism and Political Extremism.* London:
  Cass, 2004.

White, Hayden. *Metahistory: The Historical Imagination in Nineteenth Century
  Europe.* Baltimore, London: Johns Hopkins University Press, 1973.

———. *Tropics of Discourse: Essays in Cultural Criticism.* Baltimore, London:
  Johns Hopkins University Press, 1978.

White, W. Hale, and Amelia Hutchinson Stirling, eds. *Spinoza's Ethic,
  Demonstrated in Geometrical Order.* 4th ed. London: Humphrey Milford and
  Oxford University Press, 1937.

Wolf, A., ed. *The Oldest Biography of Spinoza.* London: Allen and Unwin, [1927].

Wood, Ralph C. "Flannery O'Connor's Strange Alliance with Southern
  Fundamentalists." John J. Murphy, Linda Hunter Adams, Richard H. Cracroft,
  and Susan Howe, eds. *Flannery O'Connor and the Christian Mystery.* Provo,
  UTH: Brigham Young University, 1997. 76.

The Works of Lancelot Andrewes. 11 vols. New York: AMS Press, 1967; repr. of
  Oxford 1841 ed.

Wormald, Mark. "The Uses of Impurity: Fiction and Fundamentalism in Salman Rushdie and Jeanette Winterson." *An Introduction to Contemporary Fiction: International Writing in English since 1970.* Ed. Rod Mengham. Cambridge: Polity, 1999.

Young, Robert. *White Mythologies: Writing, History and the West.* London, New York: Routledge, 1990.

Zirker, Herbert. "Horse Sense and Sensibility: Some Issues Concerning Utopian Understanding in *Gulliver's Travels.*" *Swift Studies* 12 (1997): 85–98.

LIST OF CONTRIBUTORS

GORDON CAMPBELL is a professor of Renaissance Studies at the University of Leicester, where he teaches in the English department and writes mostly about Milton but also about European cultural history (especially art and architecture). He is also the university's international relations adviser and has a particular interest in the Islamic world.

KEVIN L. COPE is a professor of English and comparative literature at Louisiana State University. He is the author of *Criteria of Certainty* (Lexington, KY: UP of Kentucky, 1990), *John Locke Revisited* (New York: Twayne, 1999), and the forthcoming *In and After the Beginning: Inaugural Moments and Literary Institutions in the Long Eighteenth Century.* Professor Cope has edited several volumes of essays, including, most recently, *Imagining the Sciences: Expressions of New Knowledge in the "Long" Eighteenth Century* (New York: AMS Press, 2003); he is the editor of the journal *1650–1850* as well as the co-editor of *ECCB: The Eighteenth Century Current Bibliography.* While enrolled in several editorial boards, he has also served as president of the South-Central Society for Eighteenth-Century Studies and as president of the Delta Chapter of the Alexander von Humboldt Association of America.

ANNE BARBEAU GARDINER is a professor in the English department at John Jay College, City University of New York. She has published two books on John Dryden—*The Intellectual Design of John Dryden's Heroic Plays* (New Haven, CT: Yale University Press, 1970) and *Ancient Faith and Modern Freedom in John Dryden's* The Hind and the Panther (Washington, DC: Catholic University of America Press, 1998)—and numerous essays on Milton, Swift, and English Catholics of the late seventeenth century.

WENDY O'SHEA-MEDDOUR is a British Academy Postdoctoral Research Fellow at Oxford University. She is currently writing a book about the representation of Muslims in contemporary British literature and has recently published on the works of V.S. Naipaul, Hanif Kureishi, and Monica Ali. Her research interests include poststructuralism, feminism, and postcolonial theory.

CATHERINE PESSO-MIQUEL has been a Maître de Conférences in English Studies at the University of the Sorbonne in Paris, France, since 1995. She studied at the École Normale Supérieure and received her PhD at the University of the Sorbonne Nouvelle in Paris. Her research focuses on the contemporary novel in English, and more particularly on the works of Graham Swift and Paul Auster and on Indian literature in English. Her publications include *Toiles trouées et déserts lunaires dans* Moon Palace *de Paul Auster* (Paris: Presses Universitaires de la Sorbonne Nouvelle, 1996) and a study of Willa Cather's *Alexander's Bridge* (Paris: Editions du Temps, 2001). She is currently writing a book on Salman Rushdie, to be published in 2006.

SUSANNE PETERS received her PhD for a study on James Joyce from Giessen University and worked as an assistant professor at the University of Düsseldorf, where she completed a major study on written communication in plays. Since then she has held temporary professorships at the Universities of Leipzig, Düsseldorf, and Stuttgart and at International University Bremen. She has published widely on sense perception in literature, orality and literacy in plays, contemporary anglophone drama, and British and American fiction.

HELGA RAMSEY-KURZ has taught at the Universities of East Anglia, Graz, and Innsbruck and currently is an associate professor at the English department of the University of Innsbruck. She has written a book on female–female hostilities in the works of contemporary women writers and published articles on several postcolonial novelists. At present she is completing a book on representations of illiteracy in twentieth-century novels in English, funded by the Austrian Science Foundation through a Charlotte Bühler Habilitation Grant.

AXEL STÄHLER is presently project coordinator of the Fundamentalism-Project at the University of Münster and teaches in the North American Studies Program at the University of Bonn. He studied English, German, and art history at Bonn. Formerly a fellow of the Sonderforschungsbereich "Judentum–Christentum," he has published widely on anglophone Jewish writers, German-Jewish literature, and on European festival culture of the Renaissance and Early Baroque periods.

KLAUS STIERSTORFER is a professor of English at the University of Münster, Germany. He studied at the Universities of Regensburg and Oxford, received his DPhil at the University of Oxford, trained as a secondary school teacher, and became an associate professor at the University of Würzburg, from where he moved on to take up his professorships at Düsseldorf and, since 2004, at Münster. His publications include *John Oxenford (1812–1877) as Farceur and Critic of Comedy* (Frankfurt: Lang, 1996); (ed., introd., annot.), *London Assurance and Other Victorian Comedies.* Oxford World's Classics (Oxford: Oxford University Press, 2001); *Konstruktion literarischer Vergangenheit* (Heidelberg: C. Winter, 2001); and (ser. ed.) *Women Writing Home,* 6 vols. (London: Pickering and Chatto, 2006).

INDEX